THE OCEANSIDE HISTORY OF ALASKA

MIKE COPPOCK

Epicenter Press

Kenmore, WA

⋀⋀⋀ Epicenter Press

6524 NE 181st St., Suite 2, Kenmore, WA 98028

Epicenter Press is a regional press publishing nonfiction
books about the arts, history, environment, and diverse cultures
and lifestyles of Alaska and the Pacific Northwest.
For more information, visit www.EpicenterPress.com

Copyright © 2024 by Mike Coppock

All rights reserved. No part of this publication may be reproduced,
stored in a retrieval system, or transmitted in any form by any means, electronic,
mechanical, photocopying, recording, or otherwise, without
the prior written permission of the publisher. Permission is given for
brief excerpts to be published with book reviews in newspaper,
magazines, newsletters, catalogs, and online publications.

Library of Congress Control Number: 2023945714

ISBN: 978-1-68492-149-2 (Trade Paperback)
ISBN: 978-1-68492-150-8 (Ebook)

Cover and interior design by Scott Book & Melisssa Vail Coffman

FOR PAT LYNN,
Valdez Alaska mentor and friend

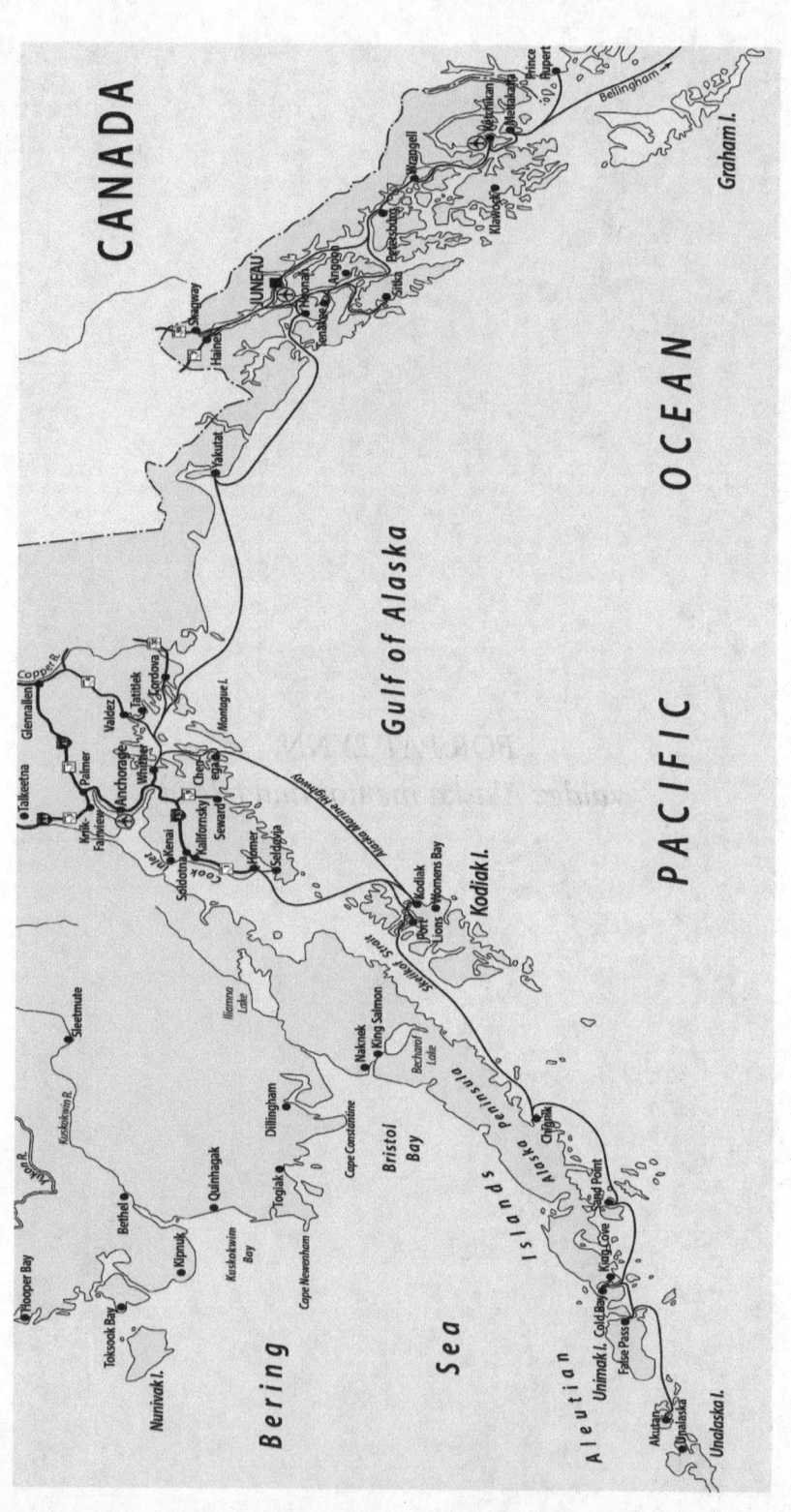

Introduction

I HAD JUST SEEN MY FIRST KODIAK bear and it had made me as giddy as a schoolboy when I entered the lodge where I was staying at in Port Lions.

Two couples were inside having returned from a day of fishing. They were watching a mist roll in over the bay draping the surrounding forest until the silhouette of the trees could barely be made out. Everyone was snacking and sipping wine. Soft classical music was on as everyone stared out. "Now this is the real Alaska," said the lodge's owner in a reflective tone.

Eight days later, and 300 miles to the west, I was standing on a beach at Sand Point in the Shumagin islands with a prospector named Tommy from Missouri. Tommy was in his 60s and grinning like a mad man as a gale bathed us both with a cold horizontal rain. In his pan were flakes of gold, "Now this is the real Alaska," the grizzled Tommy said with a laugh.

This book had given me a treasury of memories as I encountered the "real" Alaska over and over again.

I structured this book to explain the history of Alaska's seaports a visitor would encounter if one traveled on the Alaska Marine Highway. The blue ocean-going state ferries of the Alaska Marine Highway takes one in a great arch. They churn their way through the tranquil waters of the Tongass rain forest to the granite rocks and glaciers of the upper portion of the Inside Passage.

Turning west across the North Pacific, the ferries venture into the fjords and inlets of Alaska's Gulf coast. After Homer, one lone ferry, the Tustumena, heads out for the Westwards, a treeless emerald strand of isles and volcanoes peppered with the blue and green onion domes of Orthodox churches bathed in the warming waters of the Japanese current.

There are 36 ports in all and only 6 are connected to the North American road system. One of them, in fact, Homer, is virtually where the road system ends. The ferry system has dropped only one community in its history: Hyder at the end of the 71-mile-long Portland Canal marking the Alaska-British Columbia border.

Remarkably, there are very few connecting threads these ports share in common. Three of the communities are or were capitals of Alaska. Some are Native villages but of differing peoples and cultures; Hoonah is Tlingit, Tatitlek is Alutiiq, and False Pass is Aleut for example.

Kodiak, Seldovia, and Unalaska have maintained their Russian heritage while Petersburg and Sand Point are distinctively Scandinavian.

You would think all these ports would be the traditional rubber boot or fishermen communities and Petersburg, Pelican and King Cove certainly are.

Surprisingly, many are not.

Skagway, Juneau, Douglas, Tenakee Springs, and Valdez are children of the gold rush. Cordova and Seward began as railroad towns. Whittier and Cold Bay began as secret military bases. Akutan had the distinction of having been a secret Soviet base. A Soviet Officer's Club still stands at Cold Bay. Several like Homer, Haines and Gustavus began as farm towns.

For such small towns, their histories run deep. Valdez for example, site of Alaska's first hanging, had a gold rush, a railroad shooting war, Alaskan aviator Bob Reeve and Alaskan artist Sydney Laurence, the Good Friday Earthquake, the building of the Trans-Alaska Pipeline and the Exxon Valdez oil spill.

Everywhere I went, I encountered people eager to tell what their community has had to endure just to still exist in this primal land. I found myself hopping from one slip to another at Homer's boat harbor as people told me about Unga, Sand Point, and Sanak. Long serving Valdez mayor Bert Cottle took me in hand to meet individual small-time miners working in Prince William Sound.

Two resources I must mention are the Alaska Geographic Society and Merle Colby. There is no Alaska Geographic Society today. They disbanded as the 21st Century opened. Their name has been absorbed by the Alaska Natural History Association. Their books, edited by Penny Rennick, cover various locations in Alaska capturing each region's history and a moment in time. Most of these books are now out of print.

Merle Colby worked for the Federal Writer's Project during the Great Depression. He has the reader hopping tramp steamers and traveling on horseback and dog teams, visiting nearly every corner of Alaska in 1938. Colby's epic book ALASKA, is a must read for those with a hunger for Alaskan history.

Inside Passage South

The Southeast, as Alaskans call the Alaska Panhandle or the Inside Passage, is physically the size of Florida.

It is made up of islands and waterways and no roads, with isolated communities of various sizes carving out their own domain. Across the Southeast, people's lives, school activities and sports orbit around the sailing schedule of the Alaska Marine Highway System. That system operates both large ferries and small feeder ferries hauling everything from passengers to vehicles to freight to the larger ports such as Juneau and Ketchikan and to small, isolated hamlets like Tenakee Springs and Kake.

The Southeast is actually two regions.

The northern end of the Inside Passage is drier and is a land of glaciers and ice fields. Its history centers around gold prospecting and one dominate Native group, the Tlingits. Americans took the primary role in its development and the development of the northern section of the Inside Passage occurred many years after the U.S. purchase of Alaska.

The south end of the Inside Passage is far wetter and consists of an extensive system of islands, channels, and sea passages. The Alexander Archipelago is made up of 1100 islands, mostly consisting of the peaks of submerged mountains with deep and narrow channels of ocean water separating each.

This world is clothed by the world's largest remaining temperate rainforest, most of which lies within the nation's largest national forest, the Tongass, created by President Theodore Roosevelt in 1907 and expanded in 1909 during his last months in office. The Tongass National Forest consists of 17 million acres, much of it, old growth forest, and sees over a million visitors a year from all corners of the world.

The Tongass underscores that the primary difference between the northern end of the Inside Passage and the southern end of the Inside Passage is water, whether in the form of the sea or from the sky. The southern portion of the Southeast measures rainfall in feet per year, far exceeding what the northern end of the Inside Passage experiences.

Port Alexander on the southern tip of Baranof Island is one of the wettest locations in the world.

Instead of a singular dominate Native group as the northern end of the Inside Passage has, the south part of the Inside Passage is inhabited not only by the Tlingits, but the Haida and the Tsiamshians. All three Native groups were so attuned with the sea that early anthropologists thought they may be related to the Polynesians of the South Pacific. Not only did Americans enter this ethnic mix, but so did Russians and Norwegians. It is the south end of the Inside Passage that the Russians set up settlements and fought the Battle of Sitka, the consequences of that Russian victory being Alaska would not be absorbed into British holdings which later became Canada.

Before the arrival of the Europeans, plunder, revenge, and acquiring fresh slaves were the business of the day for native clans. Decorative war canoes, many over seventy feet long, carried a hundred warriors onto the shores of rival villages. Wearing wooden masks with animal designs, their bodies transformed by paints of black, reds, and white, warriors would emerge from the forest striking hard with skull crushing clubs.

The south end of the Inside Passage saw fierce clashes between native groups and both Russians and Americans: Sitka, Kake, Angoon, and Wrangell to name a few.

Like the northern section of the Inside Passage, the southern region had its fair share of gold mines, but mineral rich Prince of Wales Island also held copper, silver, uranium, and rare earths. Gold dominated the north end, but it was copper which dominated the south end. Some of the largest towns in Southeast Alaska such as Hadley, Coppermount, and Sulzer were born and died based on the going price of copper. Today ghost towns pepper the landscape.

Though mining and logging were key elements that made up the south end's economy, salmon is what built the south end of the Inside Passage.

The Russians tried fishing salmon commercially for San Francisco markets during the California Gold Rush, but it spoiled before arriving.

When canning replaced salteries as a means of preserving salmon, the rich fisheries of Southeast Alaska beckoned. Two canneries were built in 1878 at Klawock on Prince of Wales Island and at Sitka. During that short fishing season, 8,159 cases of 48 one-pound cans were produced selling wholesale for $50,000: a very impressive figure for the time. By 1889, Alaska had 37 canneries in operation, primarily in the southern region of the Inside Passage, earning $2.8 million annually. By the beginning of the 20th Century, salmon canneries were outpacing the value of gold production in Alaska.

The southern portion of the Inside Passage is a land of parks on an immense scale. There are three national monuments and 15 national wilderness areas. Out of the 955,747 acres making up the Admiralty Island National Monument, all but 18,000 acres are within the Kootznoowoo Wilderness Area. Admiralty has one of the highest concentration of bears in the world.

With fjords sculpted by glaciers and bracketed by vertical granite walls reaching upward from 2,000 to 3,000 feet on each side of the fjords, the 2.2-million-acre Misty Fjords National Monument is nearly all within a wilderness area. The much smaller Sitka National Park is the site of where Russians and Tlingits battled for Sitka along with historic totem poles and a totem workshop.

The State of Alaska has complimented the national park system here with 16 marine parks for kayaking and boating along with several state historical parks and recreational sites.

METLAKATLA

There was a time before the Europeans arrived that the Tsimshians of British Columbia could send a thousand war canoes into battle. They were a military power along the Pacific Northwest Coast, pressing the Tlingits ever farther north and even challenging them for control of the Stikine River, the gateway into the Interior. Massive Tsimshian longhouses dotted the coast everywhere, and the tribe prospered from the region's abundant natural resources.

Suddenly though, in the 1860s, eighty percent of the tribe died during a smallpox epidemic, breaking their power over the region.

Anglican missionary William Duncan was in his third year working among the Tsimshian when the epidemic struck. Duncan had learned to speak their language through the aide of Arthur Wellington Clah, a Tsimshian head man and employee of the Hudson's Bay Company at Fort Simpson. It had been Clah who had saved Duncan's life when Chief Paul Legaic tried to shoot him for ringing the church bell during a tribal ceremony. Legaic later converted and joined Duncan's church.

In 1862, Duncan led sixty Tsimshian converts from Lax Kw'alaams, the main Tsimshian village near Fort Simpson to establish a Christian utopian community near Prince Rupert. The new colony, called Metlakatla, "saltwater passage," soon grew to several hundred members. When smallpox reached the area, five hundred people died in Lax

Kw'alaams, yet Duncan's settlement had only five fatalities. The reverend had no trouble convincing the Natives that it was divine providence.

Because some of the Tsushima's were cannibalistic, Duncan did not perform the sacrament of communion, fearing it would seem like an acceptance of cannibalism. This, plus Duncan's demanding full control over the community he founded, led to his expulsion from the Church of England in 1881. He tried to continue working with his congregation as an independent native church, but Anglican officials had influence with Hudson's Bay Company and British Columbian authorities, who pressured Duncan to shut down. Undeterred, Duncan decided to move his colony to Alaska.

His scouts found a calm bay on the Pacific side of the Annette Island, with a gentle, sloping beach and a waterfall nearby. After obtaining permission from Chief Johnson of the Tongass Tlingits to settle at Taquan, the site's Tlingit name, he traveled to Washington, D.C., to obtain permission to establish a Native settlement on the island. Aiding him in influencing Congress was his good friend, famed inventor Thomas Edison.

With a green light from Congress, Duncan began preparations for his colony, dubbed New Metlakatla. The town site was laid out in a grid pattern, and Duncan made plans for a church, a school, a tannery, and a sawmill. Construction began in 1882; added to the original plan were a cannery and a power plant.

With most of the construction completed, Duncan led eight hundred Tsimshian followers on a mass canoe voyage from Metlakatla, B.C., to New Metlakatla in 1887. The "New" was dropped from the settlement's name the following year. Once his colony was firmly established on Alaskan soil, he sent a canoe party back to the original Metlakatla to burn down his old church.

Within a year, the congregation had opened a mine and had purchased a ship for trading furs along the coast, offering better prices to freelance trappers than Hudson's Bay Company.

Each family had its own home and a share in profits from the community's various enterprises.

Duncan officially set himself up as the community's spiritual leader, as well as business manager, justice of the peace, and law officer. In 1891, after another trip to Washington, Duncan won the status of Indian reservation for the entire 86,000-acre island. Annette Island was one of only six reservations in Alaska, and today is the state's only reservation.

When Duncan created his colony, most of the surrounding Tlingit villages on Annette Island were Presbyterian. Before long, the Presbyterians began to win converts among Duncan's Tsimshians. In 1892 Rev. Edward Marsden led the Presbyterian Tsimshians from Metlakatla to a new community called Port Gravina, which lasted until 1904.

Marsden also pushed for the Bureau of Indian Affairs to oust Duncan as leader of Metlakatla, claiming he had too much control; he even hinted at sexual misconduct by Duncan.

Metlakatla Tsimshians were also tiring of Duncan's authority. In 1912, despite strong protests from Duncan, some of the villagers persuaded the government to open a school in Metlakatla independent of Duncan's rule. After Duncan died of natural causes on August 30, 1918, at age eighty-six, Metlakatla continued to be a religious colony.

A fire in 1948 burned the double-steepled William Duncan Memorial Church, but it was rebuilt a few years later. Duncan's cottage was turned into a museum, with several of Thomas Edison's early inventions on display.

World War II brought tremendous change when the U.S. Army built a massive airfield seven miles from the town. The facility, completed in 1942, included long runways, hangars, watchtowers, gun emplacements, and housing for up to 10,000 troops. The airfield also served as a civilian airport for both Metlakatla and nearby Ketchikan and as a base of operations for the Coast Guard until 1976, when a new airport was built in Ketchikan.

It was also during World War II that Metlakatla became part of Alaska aviation history. Legendary Bush pilot Harold No Kill 'Em Gillam met his end in heroic fashion in 1943. Gillam had become famous for his piloting skills in the 1920s and 1930s. He was known for boldly flying through Alaska's worst fogs and blizzards, earning him the nickname "Thrill 'Em, Spill 'Em, but No Kill 'Em Gillam."

Due to his exploits, Alaskans soon spoke of three types of flying weather: clear skies were "Pan American weather," and inclement weather was "the usual"; the most severe fogs and storms were "Gillam weather."

In January 1943, Gillam was flying five passengers from Seattle to Anchorage in a Lockheed Electra, planning to make a nighttime stop in Metlakatla for refueling. He was near Annette Island when his left engine quit, and a sudden downdraft pushed the plane headlong into a mountain side. Alive, but bleeding from a deep cut on his head, Gillam made a fire, built snow shelters, and tended to the five injured passengers while they waited for a rescue party. One of the passengers died the next day. Although the victims were only a few miles from Annette Island, no rescuers were able to find them in the dense woods. On the sixth day, Gillam set off on his own down the mountain with a parachute to try to wave someone down. He would never return.

A month passed before the Coast Guard found the passengers' signal fire. After rushing the four survivors to the hospital, the rescuers discovered, wrapped in his parachute only a mile away, the body of No Kill 'Em Gillam. He had been attempting to locate help when he bled to death.

In 1948 the U.S. government signed a treaty with the Tsimshians promising them a road that would connect their ocean side town with the Inside Passage, allowing year-round ferry service with Ketchikan. It was not until fifty years later that the project began. From April to September for fourteen years, 360 military personnel worked on the Walson Point Road. The road was completed in 2012.

In 1971 the Tsimshians rejected the Alaska Natives Claims Settlement Act, making them the only indigenous North Americans in Alaska with sovereignty over their own land. Annette Island has its own court system, and it is the only place in Alaska without restrictions on the use of fish wheels by tribal members.

Metlakatla's economy changed over the decades. The town's cannery and two sawmills have closed, and the largest employer is now the Metlakatla Indian Community, which operates a fish hatchery on

Tamgas Creek as well as the Annette Island Packing Company, a cold-storage facility. Modern Metlakatla also has nine churches, one of the highest per capita concentrations of churches in Alaska.

Of the 1400 Tsimshians on Annette Island today, only thirty still speak the tribal language fluently. Over the years, the tribe's traditional arts also began to fade. The Tsimshians were once envied for their ceremonial blankets, which were woven into dramatic, bilaterally symmetrical patterns of brilliant colors. They were also expert carvers of totem poles, masks, and many other items.

Cultural concerns such as these induced artist Jack Hudson to return to Metlakatla in 1974, after a successful career in Seattle, to teach traditional Tsimshian wood-carving techniques to local high school students.

KETCHIKAN

KETCHIKAN RECEIVES SO MUCH RAINFALL, MORE than 155 inches annually, that visitors are told the town's name stems from how residents use to get their drinking water. Each home had an outdoor rain catcher before city water lines came into being. Water captured this way was then used in the home and thus catch-a-can, or Ketchikan.

However, the name Ketchikan is from a Tlingit word. The name derives from the Tlingit word Kitschk-Hin meaning the creek of the thundering wings of an eagle.

Archeological evidence indicates the region around Ketchikan has been inhabited for more than 10,000 years, but not by Tlingits. Artifacts show the Tlingits have only been around for a few hundred years and probably migrated to the coast from Canada's Mass River country.

The Tongass Tlingits along with the Cape Fox Tlingits have the oldest of the numerous Tlingit dialects.

Britain's Captain George Vancouver was the first European to map the area in 1793. He was surprised to find that the Tlingits at Fish Creek had liquor and flintlocks already in their possession. When Vancouver questioned the natives where they had gotten the items, the Tlingits said in trade from the Boston and King George men. Americans and the British were already competing with each other in this distant corner of North America just a decade after the American Revolution.

Vancouver named the island after the Viceroy of New Spain, Juan Vicente de Guemas Pachaco de Padilla Horcasistas y Aquayo, Conde de Evilla Gigedo. Time shortened the name to Revillagigedo Island. Vancouver split up from his main expedition sailing around the island with two small boats in order to explore the coves and bays. He was attacked by Tlingits using firearms. He and his party were nearly wiped out if it had not been for the firepower of the small cannons he had brought along.

Though there are a few ruins around Port Seward where the Russians had mined for coal, it was the Americans who impacted the region.

The U.S. Deputy Collector of Customs stationed in Wrangell noted in his records that a man named Snow had a base somewhere around Fish Creek for the smuggling of British goods into the District of Alaska. The same Snow started a summer saltery along Fish Creek in 1883.

During the winter of 1886-87, A. W. Berry bought 160 acres along Fish Creek from Charlie Paper-Nose Dickson whose clan owned the fishing rights to the stream. Irishman Mike Martin from County Cork persuaded investors in Portland, Oregon, to buy Berry's acreage for the establishment of a year-round salmon cannery.

The sale was made on April 17, 1887; recognized as the establishment of Ketchikan with Martin as the founding father.

Martin's cannery burned in August 1889. He then opened a saltery on the land, but it failed shortly afterwards. However, four gold claims had been filed when Martin opened the cannery including the Gravina Gold and Silver Mine across the bay where the airport is today. In 1888, four more claims were filed in Sitka for the area including a mine along "Cathkan" Creek. With miners needing supplies, Martin opened a general store becoming Ketchikan's first mayor.

The settlement was first called Fish Creek. When a post office opened in 1892, it took the name "Cathkan" Creek using Ketchikan for the settlement officially for the first time.

A miners' meeting at the Clark and Martin store in 1897 organized the Ketchikan Mining District. By now, the town was bracketed with small gold mines to the north and south. In all, twelve mines were in operation with such names as Sea Breeze, Boo Goo, and Yellow Dog.

A hotel was built for the miners. but when mining began slowing, the hotel's owner went to Boston to woo a cold storage plant to Ketchikan. The plant created a fishing boom. Oil firms built storage plants for the fishing fleet as accommodations and retail outlets opened for fish buyers and fishermen. Ketchikan soon had eight canneries packing a million cases of salmon annually.

The first woman moved to Ketchikan in 1898, a Mrs. N.G. House. Martin and his employees took it upon themselves to shovel the sidewalks clear of snow every winter. Wrangell was now beginning to lose people to Ketchikan as a lawyer, a shoemaker, two doctors, and two female postal workers relocated to Ketchikan.

The rainforest invited the lumber industry. There were already sawmills in the region beginning with the first built at Dolomi on Prince of Wales Island in 1898. The Dolomi mill was moved to Ketchikan reopening on St. Patrick's Day1903. The Ketchikan Spruce Mill supplied the area with board feet until the Federal Housing Authority ruled only kiln-dried wood could be used in housing construction. Eventually though, it became cheaper to import lumber from Canada than install the kilns. The mill closed in1973.

One of the world's largest pulp mills costing $55 million opened at nearby Ward Cove in 1953 and was in operation until 1997.

Fort Tongass located south on an isolated rock near Canadian waters was the original port of entry for U.S. Customs, but the fort had no harbor so U.S. Customs moved the port of entry to Mary Island.

Ketchikan civic booster Orlando "Six Shooter" Grant worked to have the customs house relocated to his community. Ships clearing customs at Ketchikan meant wharf fees, custom employees, piloting fees, office space rented, and the need for additional housing. To entice the move, Grant offered the federal government free land.

The ploy worked.

In March 1900, the Deputy Collector of Customs moved his office into Ketchikan and with him came all the fees Grant had anticipated. The move did not stop smuggling, especially liquor which was prohibited in the District of Alaska. Bottles were smuggled in labeled Wheat

Phosphates and Nervine. Nervine cocktails became the name for the local drink of choice.

The town evolved into a linear three-mile-long waterfront. The original streets and sidewalks were wooden trestles due to the steep slope of the coast. Today most of the waterfront business district and residential homes rest on pilings just above the sea.

Orlando Grant's efforts did not mean Ketchikan's future as the main town for the southern portion of the Alaska Panhandle was assured. Several new mining towns were popping up on nearby Prince of Wales Island. Plummeting copper prices in 1907 was the kiss of death for these communities.

Serious competition for prominence did come from Loring further west.

Nearly a hundred Chinese workers migrated to Loring in the summer months to work alongside Tlingits and Tsimshians either at the brilliantly painted red canneries or loading cargo ships tied up along its massive wharfs. Originally a salting station and a trading post for furs, the first cannery was built there in 1888. Other canneries soon followed transforming Loring into the largest fishing station in Southeast Alaska. One of Alaska's first post offices opened in Loring.

Loring was one of the few Alaskan communities Americans knew of in the 1800s. Albert Bierstadt's oil painting "Wreck of the Ancon, Loring, Alaska" painted in 1889 still hangs in the Boston Museum of Fine Arts.

What happened? Ketchikan securing the customs house and becoming the shipping point for Prince of Wales Island convinced many prominent Loring businessmen to move their operations to Ketchikan.

Tongass and Cape Fox Tlingits decided to build a more centralized village with a Presbyterian church and a Bureau of Indian Affairs school. Presbyterian missionary Samuel Saxman stationed at Loring, a Cape Fox elder, and a third man set out to find a new site only to be lost at sea. The town of Saxman is named in the missionary's honor. The two tribes moved to Saxman in 1894.

In 1899, railroad tycoon Edward Harriman led a scientific expedition to Alaska with such notaries as naturalists John Muir and John

Burroughs. On the way back to Seattle, the expedition learned from a gold prospector of an abandoned village with 24 immense totem poles. The abandoned village was Cape Fox Village. The Harriman Expedition looted the village taking the totem poles and distributing them to museums and colleges across the United States. Some of the totems such as the 26-foot Neix.adi from Chicago's Field Museum were returned in 2001. Others were in too bad shape or had been destroyed.

In 1938 CCC workers restored many of the old and abandoned totem poles from outlying villages. Some fifteen poles and a clan house were restored by 1942 using skilled elder Native craftsmen at Mud Bight. The state took over the land in 1959 renaming it Totem Bight State Park. It is the largest display of totem poles in the U.S.

Meanwhile Ketchikan began to boom.

A series of hotels were built in the 1920s. By the 1930s over 12 canneries were in operation serviced by a fishing fleet numbering close to a thousand. Ketchikan laid claim to being the Salmon Capital of the World.

As the fishing fleet grew, prostitutes swarmed into town centering their business activities around Fish Creek in rows of over 20 small houses. Fishermen moored their boats to the pilings under the structures climbing up ladders leading to trap doors. The sporting women of the red-light district were required to place screens over their windows so drunken fishermen would not try to break out their windows. To advertise, several women posed nude in front of windows standing behind lace curtains. The twelve two-story whorehouses along the creek bragged at being the "only place on earth where both fish and fishermen go upstream to spawn."

Ketchikan's first radio station, KGBU, got its start out of one of these houses of ill repute to inform its audience when rumrunners were arriving in town.

Some of these women became unofficial banks loaning fishermen funds to tide them over if there had been a bad season. One of the more famous Madams was Dolly Arthur who operated legally from 1919 to 1954. She died in 1975.

Social pressure and cleaning up the city's act in preparation for statehood forced the Fish Creek red light district to close during the Korean War in 1953, but not without one last blowout.

CLOSE OUT
In the interest of national defense, and the
moral, mental, and physical rehabilitation of
ourselves and dear Fellow Citizen -
3 Glorious Weeks
Exotic Bargains
On Creek Street
Hurry! Hurry! Hurry!
The day of rehabilitation Draws Near, and the
Bargains can't last Forever!
A Variety of Sizes in Five Popular Colors
Available. Come early . . . Avoid the Rush!
No exchanges . . . No charges . . . No Refunds.
Signed,
Norma, Anna, Goldie, Alta, Ollie, June, Nell, Helen, Jane, Rose.

Today Fish Creek remains a spawning creek for salmon. The houses of ill repute are now gift shops and cafes.

Due to the large fishing fleet, the United States Coast Guard expanded its personnel during World War II. Today, the Coast Guard is a major presence along the Ketchikan waterfront.

Ketchikan remained a major logging and milling center until the 1990s. Several factors played a role in the decline of logging in Southeast Alaska. Demand from overseas markets fell at the same time environmentalists pressed for stronger protections for the Tongass forest. In 2000, President Bill Clinton announced a policy of no more logging roads into the Tongass.

In 1978, President Jimmy Carter set aside some 2,294, 000 acres of the Tongass for Misty Fjords National Monument is just to the southeast of Ketchikan. Often called the Yosemite of the North, glacial action molded the 70-million-year-old light-colored granite into vertical drops of 2,000 to 3,000 feet along the narrow fjords.

Commercial fishing is still strong in Ketchikan. Norquest Seafoods alone produces 500,000 cases of canned salmon each year between July and September.

Ketchikan is becoming more dependent on tourism by way of the cruise ship lines and small-scale logging is done by native corporations. A cable car, the Cape Fox Hill Funicular, was built in 1990.

Ketchikan is the home for the Great Alaskan Lumberjack Show where modern loggers compete against each other. The locally produced comedy, *Fish Pirates Daughter*, has been playing continuously for 40 years.

In 2005, Ketchikan made national news as the location for the "bridge to nowhere," a $223 million bridge proposal within the 2005 Federal Highway Bill to connect Ketchikan with Gravina Island where the airport is located. Outcry against the proposal caused Gov. Sarah Palin to drop the project.

HOLLIS and PRINCE OF WALES ISLAND

HOLLIS MAY NOT SEEM MUCH AT FIRST GLANCE. The few homes with their outhouses a mile or more from the ferry dock is a far cry from a population of a thousand it had in 1900.

Gold and silver were found near Hollis at the beginning of the 20th Century. The town soon had a hotel, bank, and in 1901, a post office. The mines played out by 1915 and Hollis became a ghost town.

In 1953, the Ketchikan Pulp Company selected the site as a major logging camp after signing a long-term timber contract with the U.S. Forest Service. The area grew to a population of around 300. Then in 1962, the camp moved to Thorne Bay 52 miles to the north. Houses in Hollis were literally jacked up the year before and moved in preparation for the relocation.

With the island's main community, Craig, less than thirty miles away on the Pacific side of the island, the Alaska Marine Highway System selected Hollis as its port for offloading passengers and vehicles from Ketchikan. In 1980, the state offered land tracts and the town soon had permanent residents again engaged in logging, government services, and fishing.

For three decades, the town served as the only port of entry to Prince of Wales Island. Displeasure over ferry service to the island led the communities to join with Petersburg and Wrangell in 1996 to organize the

Inter-Island Ferry Authority (IFA) creating its own ferry system. Two ferries were ordered constructed with Hollis and Coffman Cove up the island's coast designated as ports. A shuttle service running passengers between the two ports was organized.

The Alaska Marine Highway System discontinued ferry service to Hollis in 2002. The IFA took over the route with the new *M/V Prince of Wales*. A few years later a second IFA vessel, *M/V Stikine*, began sailing from Coffman Cove to Mitkif Island as a connection to Petersburg.

Today Hollis has a library, community church, boat launch, and school. It remains the main entry point to Prince of Wales Island, called POW by locals. The island is the third largest in the United States after Hawaii and Kodiak. Running 135 miles long and 45 miles wide, the island is mountainous and heavily forested with a cool moist climate. Most of the island is within the Tongass National Forest with five designated wilderness areas.

Sitka deer and black bears are numerous while the rivers and streams support salmon and trout. The island is the sole home for the Prince of Wales Island flying squirrel.

Geological evidence hints that the island drifted northward to its present location from the Klamath Mountains region. An ice sheet covered POW until roughly 14,000 years ago. The land emerged with minerals such as gold, silver, copper, and uranium. Alaska's only uranium mine is located at Kendrick Bay.

The northern end of the island has a vast system of over 850 limestone caverns. The largest is El Capitan Cave reaching some 598 feet deep with the deepest vertical shaft found in the United States. These caverns have yielded prehistoric remains. Several caverns were co-inhabited by both black and brown bears, an unusual situation in nature.

Human remains dating back 10,300 years were found in On Your Knees Cave. In 1996. DNA sampling taken from the remains demonstrated a relationship between the On Your Knees Man and individuals in California, Mexico, Ecuador, Chile, and Argentina. Yet, there was no DNA linkage between the On Your Knees Man and local Tlingit and Haida populations.

Tlingit clans began landing on the island around 600 A.D. Haida clans settled the southern and central sections of Prince of Wales Island from the Queen Charlotte Islands in the 1700s.

Russia's Alexis Chirikov mapped the northern end of the island in 1741. Spanish explorer Don Juan Francisco Bodega y Quadra mapped the island in 1775. Britain's Captain James Cook explored the island in 1778. The French under Comte de La Persouse came in 1786. Captain George Vancouver named the island in 1793 during a second British expedition.

POW was a place of Tlingit and Haida fishing camps with small parties of Russians, Americans, and British trappers roaming the forests for furs. Sometimes the relationship between Tlingits and trappers was cordial and sometimes deadly. New York papers reported the killing of a trader by Tlingits in the 1890s.

George Hamilton established a fur trading post and saltery at the Tlingit summer fishing camp of Klawock in 1868. The village became the site of Alaska's first cannery in 1878. The Klawock cannery demonstrated the value of Southeast Alaska's salmon fisheries.

Mineral exploration began in the mid-1800s when deposits of gold, silver, copper, zinc, lead, and palladium were discovered. Uranium was mined in the 1950s and the 1970s. Marble quarried around Tuxekan in the early 1900s was used for the construction of state capital buildings in Juneau and Olympia, Washington.

Prince of Wales Island became a crazy quilt of communities based on mining, fishing, or traditional Tlingit and Haida villages. Some of Alaska's largest communities were located on POW such as Coppermount, Sulzer, and Hadley—all based on mining. Kasaan, Sukkwan, Howkan, Kaigani and Klinkwan were Haida villages while three Tlingit clans held the northern end and central sections of the island in villages like Klawock and Tuxekan.

Copper prices worldwide began falling as did gold production on the island. Within a few years most of the mining towns were abandoned.

Several Haida villages merged together forming Hydaburg in 1911. The next year the Hyderburg Indian Reservation was created for the Haida. In order to preserve Haida totems and artifacts, President

Woodrow Wilson created a national monument in 1916 encompassing 28 acres around the Old Kasaan town site. In the 1930s, the Civilian Conservation Corps both restored and built replicas of significant historical totems at Kasaan and Klawock.

Elizabeth Peratrovich, wife of Klawock Mayor Roy Peratrovich, led a campaign to stop Native discrimination in Juneau in the 1940s targeting "No Natives Allowed" signs. Her sponsored Anti-Discrimination Act was passed by the Alaska Territorial Legislature in 1945 after being defeated in 1943. It was the first racial anti-discrimination law in the United States.

Craig Mallar built a small saltery and cannery on Fish Egg Island along the Pacific side in 1907. In 1911, the town of Craig became briefly the second largest city in Alaska when his new cannery attracted many workers. His cannery that year processed an amazing 57,501 cases of salmon. The next year, a post office was opened. A five-room hospital with a doctor and nurse opened in 1919. Pink salmon runs were so strong in the 1930s that five more canneries were built. Commercial fishing slowed in the late 1960s. but Craig for the most part, was still a seasonal community until as late as 1972. when Ed Head opened a sawmill providing year around employment.

The Ketchikan Pulp Company was awarded a logging contract from the U.S. Forest Service in 1953 for logging operations on POW. Towns like Hollis, Thorne Bay, Coffman Cove, Naukati (a former mining camp), and Whale Pass came alive as logging camps. Thorne Bay evolved into the largest logging camp in the world. The surrounding forests were soon webbed with logging roads becoming the island's highway system of today.

Point Baker on the far northern end of Prince of Wales Island successfully sued the U.S. Forest Service in 1975 to prevent the logging of 400,000 acres of forest in the northern half of the island. Congress overruled this decision in 1976 and logging returned to the northern section, but only half of the original acreage was logged.

After the Alaska Native Claims Settlement Act in 1971, four Native corporations soon began their own logging operations in the 1980s.

Logging peaked in 1989 with 500 million board feet of which 240 million were taken from private tracts. When logging camps began closing, the State of Alaska stepped in offering tracts for sale to individuals. Logging camps transformed some of the camps into towns such as Thorne Bay, Coffman Cove, and Whale Pass.

Some of the newest towns in Alaska can be found on Prince of Wales Island.

Alaska's deadliest mass murder took place on POW in 1982. Mark Coulthuirst, his pregnant wife Irene, their four-year-old son and five-year-old daughter along with four teenage deckhands were shot and killed onboard the 58-foot purse seiner *Investor* which was then set on fire. The boat burned for 42 hours. A suspect was later tried twice for the killings but was never convicted. The murders remain unsolved.

In 1997 the pulp mill in Ketchikan closed bringing the era of large-scale logging and that of logging camps on Prince of Wales Island to a close.

WRANGELL

It is the Skitine River which created and shaped Wrangell.
The community has been known by five different names: Place of the Willows, Redoubt Saint Dionysius, Fort Stikine, Fort Wrangel, and finally Wrangell. Various peoples came here due to the mouth of the river. No other large river in Southeast Alaska penetrates the peaks and glaciers of the Coastal Range. The 400-mile-long Stikine is a natural thoroughfare from the ocean into the interior.

Wrangell is home to many of Alaska's oldest institutions: the oldest Protestant church (1879), the oldest Catholic parish (1879), what had been Alaska's oldest racially integrated school, and the state's oldest continuously published newspaper (1902). The forty some petroglyph drawings nearby date back 8,000 years.

Wrangell is also the last town where frontier legend Wyatt Earp served as marshal.

Tlingit Era - Place of the Willows

The Tlingits built a village 25 miles south of the present town. They planted willows around the village taken from the banks of the river to underscore their ownership. It was here during a siege by Sitka Tlingits that a Skitine chief allowed himself to be executed so both sides could prepare for the oncoming winter.

Tlingit oral tradition claims trade with the Interior came about after a young man of the tribe had an incestuous relationship with a woman of his own clan. The man was given clothing, dried food, a bow with arrows and then banished. The young man followed the Stikine into the Interior until he entered Dease territory of Northern British Columbia.

Welcomed by a village, he married the chief's daughter. After telling of the riches his clan obtained from the sea, canoes of furs were loaded and sent under his guidance to the Place of Willows. There he was welcomed as a rich merchant who had come to trade. He exchanged the furs for seal skins, seal meat, and fat. When the Skitine froze solid, the Tlingits ventured to the Dease village with more trade goods.

Thus, the trade route was born.

Before the arrival of the Europeans, a massive fleet of Tsimshian war canoes came to seize control of the Skitine and its valuable trade route. Not only were the Tsimshians defeated, but their Chief Shakes captured. Pleading for life, the captured chief offered his name to the Tlingit leader.

Thus, Chief Shakes of the Skitine Tlingits came into being with a house on a small island located in Wrangell's inner harbor.

Russian Era - Redoubt St. Dionysius

In 1821, Czar Alexander ordered all foreign vessels out of Alaskan waters.

Angry British protests over the decree led to concessions with the British Empire. In 1824, the boundary between Russia Alaska and British North America was officially set with the Hudson's Bay Company allowed usage of navigable rivers from the Alaskan coast into the Interior.

Two rivers met this description: the Taku south of present-day Juneau and the Stikine.

The British wanted control of the Stikine, but their negotiators had overlooked the importance of a minor clause placed in the treaty by Alaska Governor Ferdinand von Wrangel. Neither Russia nor Britain could approach a port belonging to the other without first obtaining permission.

Governor Wrangel sent Lt. Dionysius Zarembo in 1833 to build a military post. The Russian warship *Chichagof* landed 25 miles north of the Tlingit village. The Tlingits immediately saw the advantage of a Russian post. Instead of paddling 500 miles round trip to trade in Sitka, the Russians had come to them. Calling the fort Redoubt St. Dionysius, the Russians maintained a total of fifty troops at the post.

A few days later the British brig *Dryad* arrived with eight officers and 84 men under the command of American mountain man Peter Skene Ogden, the first white man to have explored the Great Salt Lake, now working for Hudson's Bay Company.

Zarembo rowed out to the brig asking to see Ogden's papers giving him permission to be here. The Hudson's Bay men were furious when told they had failed to obtain the treaty required permission. They had to wait in the harbor until granted by Governor von Wrangel in Sitka.

While waiting the brig was surrounded by Tlingit war canoes. Chief Shakes himself informed Ogden that the British were not welcomed. River trade was reserved for the Tlingits alone. Even the Russians did not go up the river.

After eight days, the decision and a company of Russian Marines arrived from Sitka. Ogden was denied permission. Upon returning to Fort Vancouver, Hudson's Bay Company filed a claim for damages against the Russian American Company in London.

Representatives of the British and Russian governments along with representatives from the two commercial trade companies met in Hamburg, Germany, in 1839 to work out their differences. Claims of damages made by Hudson's Bay were dropped. The Russian American Company agreed to lease the mainland of Southeast Alaska to Hudson's Bay, including Redoubt Saint Dionysius, for ten years with the payment in otter skins—two thousand a year—plus food from Hudson's Bay farms in Puget Sound and along the Columbia River.

British Era - Fort Skitine

On June 1, 1840, the Russians lowered their flag and sailed off for Sitka. Hudson's Bay placed William Glen Rae, son-in-law to company director John McLauglin, in command with McLaughin's son, John Junior, second in command. The post was renamed Fort Stikine.

The younger McLaughlin had a reputation for drinking when Rae left him in charge of Fort Stikine. Upon given command, McLaughlin set down orders trying to stop his eighteen men from obtaining sexual favors through liquor or force. The night of April 20, 1842, McLaughlin was assassinated.

Two days later Sir George Simpson arrived to find the fort in a drunken frenzy. Simpson had two Russian trappers, Urbain Hereeux and Pierre Kanaquassi, arrested for young McLaughlin's murder and shipped off to Sitka. The Russian American government felt it had no jurisdiction in the matter. The two men were then sent to Ottawa for trial, but the court there claimed it was the Russians who had jurisdiction. The court added that since Kanaquassi was part Indian, he would have to be tried in London. The entire matter of McLaughlin's murder was eventually dropped.

Smallpox outbreaks in 1836 and 1840 cut the number of Tlingits living at the British fort in half. The British did however come to terms with the Russians in 1843 to not sell liquor to the Tlingits.

Western Union Telegraph Company made the outpost a supply depot in their mad scheme of connecting North America with Europe by way of telegraph lines through Siberia.

From Fort Stikine, Western Union men marched upriver to Telegraph Creek. From there, the telegraph wire was to go due north into unknown wilderness. For a year, Fort Stikine buzzed with activity then in the summer of 1867, construction came to a halt. An Atlantic cable had been successfully laid connecting the East Coast with Europe. Western Union left as suddenly as it had arrived.

American Era - Fort Wrangel

Though the United States took possession of Alaska in 1867, it would take another year before U.S. troops took formal possession of Fort Stikine. The U.S. constructed a new fort at the cost of $26,000 giving it the name of Fort Wrangell.

Fort Wrangel became one of only three custom ports in Alaska. The U.S. Army decided to sell the fort in 1871. William King Lear bought the fort for $600. Lear turned the army barracks into a trading post. By 1874 Fort Wrangel had a population of only three white men and a few Tlingits as the Native population still struggled from earlier smallpox epidemics.

Two prospectors found gold near Dease Lake at the headwaters of the Stikine River. By late spring of 1873, the *Otter* arrived with the two prospectors along with others looking for gold. Captain Billy Moore, who later founded Skagway, and his two sons were among them. More than a hundred prospectors passed through Wrangell that summer for the Dease Lake region. More men arrived during the winter going into the Interior without waiting for spring thaw. Wrangell saw a building boom. Lear even opened a dance hall. In the spring of 1874, the *Otter* brought three hundred more prospectors, The *California* another two hundred and fifty.

When Moore and his sons returned from the Interior, they had close to a hundred thousand dollars in gold. Moore built the steamboat *Gertrude* and later added three other river boats, *Grappier, Minnie,* and *Western Slope* for the growing river trade. Moore's fleet were not the only riverboats plying the Stikine. Four other ships sailed out of Wrangell up into the Interior. One of them, the *Beaver,* wrecked on her first voyage.

Gambling houses offered liquor, dance hall women, faro, poker, and roulette wheels. Fiddle music filled the night air. Cook tents popped up offering hot meals and of all things milk, even though it came out of a can. Lear himself acted as a bank, offering easy credit for miners who had proven claims. They were soon "stewed, screwed, and blued" as an old mining camp saying went.

A local scandal erupted when a few British miners entered the house of a Tlingit woman, forcibly getting her intoxicated before raping her. They then set her house on fire, not allowing her to escape and seemed to get a hideous pleasure from her screams for help as she was burned alive.

Some three hundred Chinese came as laborers. Those Chinese who died were salted and buried in a separate cemetery on Deadman's Island. In 1900, they were dug up and removed to China.

Trade with Asia was not just in laborers. Wrangel became a hub for illegal opium smuggling. Law enforcement discovered the drug being sent out to other locations in North America by being hidden in barrels of salted salmon bellies after it arrived from China.

The U.S. Army returned in 1875 giving Lear $2,500 instead of the $50,000 he demanded. Two years later, the U.S. Army pulled out again not to return. This time to fight Chief Joseph and the Nez Perce in Montana.

Wrangell

American Protestant missionaries began arriving to save the Tlingits' soul. Sheldon Jackson set up a Presbyterian mission here in 1877 arranging for the school to be opened under the guidance of Mrs. Amanda McFarland. Religious zealot and newly Princeton graduate Hall Young came to the mission.

The Tlingits still lived in large communal long houses until the arrival of Presbyterian missionary Amanda McFarland in 1877. Despite a constant clash of wills with Chief Shakes, McFarland was able to convince the Stikines to give up communal living.

She opened a school for Native girls while Young and his wife constructed the First Presbyterian Church in 1879. The lit cross on its steeple served as a beacon for fishing vessels for decades. Not to be outdone, Fathers C.J. Seghers and J. Althoff established the first Catholic church in Alaska a few doors down in that same year, St. Rose of Lima Catholic Church.

The early missionaries did not have complete success. Though forbidden by the U.S. Constitution after the Civil War, some Tlingits practiced slavery until around 1900. There were reports well into the 1890s of Tlingits burning witches alive, and inter-tribal warfare came right up to the gates of Fort Wrangell. Such warfare even took the life of fame naturalist John Muir's Tlingit Christian guide.

When naturalist John Muir arrived in 1879, he found the town picturesque with a lawlessness that had a surprising appeal for him. With haphazard residential huts, drinking dens, and dance halls, Wrangell stretched out for a mile along a boggy shoreline.

Muir used Wrangell as his base as he explored and recorded Southeast Alaska's natural beauty. With Young and Muir's dog Stikine along, Muir explored Glacier Bay making it famous through his writings on Alaska.

In 1887, the Aberdeen Packing Company opened a cannery at Wrangell. The next year a sawmill providing packing crates.

The Klondike Gold Rush

When the Klondike strike was reported in 1897, the Canadian government decided to develop an all-Canadian route to the gold fields bypassing the disputed ports of Skagway and Haines. The Canadians planned a railroad. Captain Moore had surveyed for the Canadian government a route along the old Western Union Telegraph line in 1874. Canada sent seventeen shallow draft river steamers up the Stikine from Wrangell with laborers and supplies.

Once again Wrangell became a supply point for Stikine development.

It was not long before the route from Dease Lake to Teslin in the Yukon District proved impassable. Wrangell though had become one of the main routes to the Klondike.

Western outlaw Soapy Smith looked Wrangell over before going on to Skagway. Some 5,000 stampeders swarmed Wrangell, far too many for Smith to ignore. He left part of his gang in Wrangell and quickly took over the town's vice operations. Wrangell's reputation became wild and woolly as dance hall girls in Smith's employ danced nude on the bar tops of local saloons. During the winter, a whiskey dealer was put on trial for selling alcohol in the so-called dry District of Alaska.

He suddenly stood up, shooting a man in court who was testifying against him.

Wyatt Earp and his wife Josie found themselves stranded in Wrangell and out of funds on their way to the Klondike. Earp was offered the temporary position of Deputy U.S. Marshal. It was only for ten days until the real deputy marshal arrived.

Earp called Wrangell "Hell on Wheels" due to its wild, dangerous nature. He was called out only once to disarm a newcomer who had become drunk and was shooting up one of the local saloons. As Earp came walking in, the man shouted, "I know you! You're Wyatt Earp!" Earp had arrested him more than twenty years earlier in Dodge City. The two men had a drink together ending the evening cordially. As soon as the new deputy marshal arrived, the Earps boarded the first available ship for Juneau.

Local wits declared Wrangell was "too wild for Wyatt!"

The boom ended as routes to the Klondike through Skagway and Haines became more developed. The town shrank dramatically. The small numbers who stayed turned to fishing and logging.

Cannery firms placed fish traps at the mouth of nearly every stream in Southeast Alaska. Wrangell was no exception. The fish traps did severe damage to the salmon runs on the Stikine River. The fish traps around Wrangell though were habitually pirated; the catch sold back to the very canneries who owned the traps. If the traps had a watchman, the watchman was paid off.

Wrangell at the beginning of the 20th century could boast of several mercantile shops, saloons, butcher shops, barbershops, and a hotel. The *Wrangell Sentinel* newspaper started in 1902. Natives built the St. Phillip's Episcopal Church in 1902 under the direction of Rev. H.P. Courser. The Episcopal church operated the town's hospital until the city took over in the 1960s. Electricity came to Wrangell by 1904. A massive fire consumed downtown in 1906.

By the 1920s, downtown Wrangell boasted of having the Bear Totem Store. Operated by Walter Waters, it held a significant collection of Tlingit art and crafts as well as a priceless totem pole collection. Waters was a fur buyer who traveled the many islands of Southeast Alaska trading in pelts. He gradually acquired Tlingit art as well. His Bear Totem Store became world renowned in art circles. When the downtown district burned down again in 1952, the Bear Totem Store was lost.

A replica of Chief Shakes House was constructed in 1939 as well as the establishment of the Wrangell Institute that same year.

The Bureau of Indian Affairs, in 1932, set aside 500 acres for the Wrangell Institute, a coeducational boarding school for a hundred selected Native American children from eighteen villages throughout Southeast Alaska. Vocational training was the Institute's primary goal preparing students to live in a white man's world. The school was a continuation of Young's Fort Wrangel Tlingit Industrial School founded in 1878. The campus had large multi-storied wood structures making up the teachers' quarters, dormitories, a hospital, and classroom buildings all painted in a brilliant white along the shoreline.

Here students with diseases and malnutrition were treated, but not without a price. Many were severely beaten if they spoke their native language rather than English, sometimes with a razor strap administered by the two largest students in the school. By 1968, the school had roughly 120 students. It was finally closed and sold to the Cook Inlet Regional Corporation in 1978. The campus was then leased to the U.S. Forest Service for their Young Adult Conservation classes until it was deeded to the City of Wrangell in 1995.

Former students persisted with rumors that the school structures are haunted.

The 1950s saw only one riverboat, the 64-foot *Judith Ann*, navigate the Stikine. She was built in Wrangell and owned by Al Ritchie. Her captain, Sid Barrington, became a Wrangell fixture. When old age caught up to Berrington, Edwin Culbreath bought the *Judith Ann* operating it for three years in the 1960s before replacing it with his own 65-foot *Margaret Rose*. The vessel handled shipping on the Stikine for two more years before lack of freight shut her down. The *Margaret Rose* was the last of the Stikine riverboats.

Wrangell was dubbed the Lumber Capital of Alaska in the 1980s when high tech mills were opened near the town. The Alaska Pulp

Corporation, the largest of these lumber mills and Wrangell's main employer, shut down in 1994.

For centuries rose red garnets had been gathered in a 38-acre area along a ledge of the Stikine River. It had been mined by America's first all-women corporation when former Wrangell Mayor Fred Hanford obtained ownership. He deeded it to the children of Wrangell in 1962.

Japanese corporations invested heavily into the Wrangell economy from the late 1980's into the 1990's. Because heavy equipment had to be brought to Alaskan locations and the Jones Act forbade foreign ships from hauling American goods between American ports, Alaskan lumber could not compete with Washington State or Oregon lumbering interests in the United States. Alaskan lumber taken from the forests around Wrangell could be shipped in Japanese ships to Japan at competitive prices.

Japanese firms also invested in Wrangell's fishing industry, principally salmon roe which brought high prices back in Japan. Japanese firms valued it so much they sent their own people to the Wrangell canneries to grade and pack the roe.

The federal government listed the Wrangell Institute a contamination site due to leakage from the school's fuel system. The City of Wrangell removed all the fuel tanks by 1999 and demolished the campus in 2001. The federal government in October 2003 announced the soil was still contaminated. The State of Alaska, with the City of Wrangell as a partner, set aside $2.35 million for the cleanup. Wrangell began promoting part of the site as an industrial park.

The beginning of the 21st Century saw Wrangell in conflict with its neighbors Petersburg and Kake over the creation of a borough government. The three communities had been in the Wrangell-Petersburg Census Area. The City and Borough of Wrangell was formed in 2008 without Petersburg.

The James and Elsie Nolan Center with art, exhibits, and historical displays of Wrangell was opened in 2004. Wrangell is also the location of Muskeg Meadows, a regulation USGA rated golf course.

One of the last two major sawmills in Southeast Alaska was in

Wrangell, Silver Bay Logging. The sawmill closed down in 2011 but was able to reopen in 2015 after securing a six million loan from the Alaska Industrial Development and Export Authority.

PETERSBURG

IT IS HARD TO BELIEVE THAT set in amongst the fog shrouded inlets and isles of Southeast Alaska is such an unusual ethnic community as Petersburg, Alaska's Little Norway.

Approaching Petersburg through early morning mist, one cannot help sense here is the quintessential Alaskan fishing community. The smell of brine hanging over wooden docks, weathered wooden buildings, men working on boat decks preparing to go out to sea serve to reinforce this conclusion.

The community is located on the northern end of both Mitkof Island and the Wrangell Narrows. The Wrangell Narrows runs for 21 miles separating Mitkof and Kupreanof islands with more than 60 lights and buoys for ship navigation. At some points, the Narrows is only 300 feet wide.

Formerly a Kake fish camp, carbon dating indicates the nearby petroglyphs are over two thousand years old. Some of the Kakes, including Chief John Lot, were reported to have stayed at the camp as year-round residents. The island itself is inhabited by wolf packs, Sitka deer, black bear, and moose. The hills are low lying with the highest elevation just above 3,000 feet. Muskeg dots the landscape.

Petersburg was the last of the major Southeast Alaska towns to be founded. The Russians visited the region in the 1850s in order to harvest icebergs from nearby LeConte Glacier and ship the ice to San Francisco, but they established no settlements.

Prior to its settlement, the area was known as the site for the fabled Lost Rocker Mine. In 1867 the Hudson's Bay steamer *Otter* came across a canoe adrift near Mitkof Island containing a near dead prospector. On the prospector, Fred Culver, were huge gold nuggets worth $1500. Culver was not only near starvation but had a man-made wound. As he gained his strength, he told how he and his partner had been testing the streams along the mainland when they came across the gold nuggets. Hiding their canoe, they climbed upwards and inland until they came upon a small lake. Surveying the lakeshore, they decided to test one of the many streams emptying into it from the Coastal Mountains. They came across huge placer gold deposits and quickly built a "rocker" which helped them sift through stream gravel.

For two weeks they worked the site when they were attacked by Indians. Culver's partner was killed. Wounded, Culver grabbed his poke of gold and made a run for it. With the Indians giving chase, he made it to the canoe launching it into the open water where he drifted as his wound festered.

There was no mistaking the gold Culver had with him. Returning to Port Townsend, Washington Territory, excitement over his gold find caused the creation of the Fred Culver and Associates Corporation. He and his new partners sailed back to Alaska in 1868 but could not locate the site nor the small lake.

Years later when Culver died, he gave the exact location to a friend, Mike Powers, who was working his own claim during the Juneau Gold Rush. Powers was killed in a cave-in at Gold Creek soon afterwards never revealing the location to the Lost Rocker Mine.

Prospectors roamed the mainland near Petersburg for decades trying to locate the mine without success.

A second local legend centered around Thomas Bay on the mainland. Known as the "Bay of Death" by Tlingits due to a landslide in 1750 that wiped out a Native village, prospector Harry Colp claimed he and three others encountered "strange" creatures chasing them that appeared ape-like in 1900.

What is odd about Colp's story is that he did not record the incident until 1925, when more sightings were taking place in the Thomas Bay area, becoming known as Devil's Country. He kept what he had written a secret. The incident was not generally known until after Colp's death in 1950 when his daughter found a manuscript in her father's personal belongings speaking of the encounter. Virginia Colp had the account published titled *The Strangest Story Ever Told* in 1953. The account is still in circulation.

When Peter Thams Buschmann arrived in Seattle from his native Norway in the 1890s, he learned Southeast Alaska was experiencing a salmon boom. Assigned to construct a saltery at Taku Inlet in 1897, Buschmann slowly sailed through Southeast Alaska on his *Annie M. Nixon*. After going through the Wrangell Narrows, he dropped off his son August and a workman to start a homestead at the north end of the Narrows.

The location had many things going for it as a site for a cannery: Ice was available from LaConte Glacier just seventeen miles away, the Narrows saw steamboat traffic serving Southeast Alaska pass through, and the rich halibut fishing grounds of Frederick Sound were close by.

At the time, Juneau was the only Alaska port shipping fresh halibut to Seattle, iced from nearby Taku Glacier. Buschmann himself shipped 15,000 pounds of halibut from Juneau that fall.

Buschmann built the Icy Strait Packing Company at Petersburg in 1899 which remains in operation and is one of the oldest continuously operated canneries in Alaska. Buschmann drove the pilings for the pier himself allowing fishing boats to tie up during salmon season. Sail powered fishing craft from Puget Sound arrived during the winter months to fish for halibut giving Peter's Burg an edge over rival Juneau. A sawmill was soon set up providing boxes for shipping fish. A few scows were maintained nearby at what became known as Scow Bay so fishermen could ice and box their catch.

Fishermen lived on their boats. Buildings and other structures did not start to appear until the arrival of women a few years later. A post office was opened in 1900 with Buschmann's son, Christian, as postmaster.

Buschmann continued to invest heavily in Alaska. Besides the cannery at Peter's Burg and the saltery at Taku Inlet, he built additional canneries at Sitkoh Bay and Swanson Harbor in 1902. Within a year, financial losses took a mental toll on the Norwegian. He committed suicide in Tacoma, Washington, on May 6, 1903, leaving behind a widow, five sons, and four daughters.

But news of a Norwegian settlement in Alaska drew other Norwegians from Seattle. By 1905 Peter's Burg had not only a cannery and sawmill, but a machine shop and shipways. The 1910 U.S. Census showed the now named Petersburg having a population of 585. April that same year Petersburg incorporated as a city. Two years later, thirty children were attending the local school.

The Scandia Hotel was built in 1910 and rebuilt after a devastating fire in 1995. The Sons of Norway Hall was built in 1912 and was placed on the National Register of Historical Sites in 1979.

Eventually five city blocks evolved along the waterfront with most of the older section of town connected by Indian Street, later called Sing Lee Alley. Along the alley way can be found Variety Theater and skating rink constructed in 1912, the Enge Building built in 1901 containing a restaurant and store, and the local fishermen's watering hole, Kito's Kave.

Within twenty years, only Juneau and Ketchikan could report more gross revenue than the Norwegian settlement. The main reason for this was Petersburg's concentration on the halibut market during her early years. The bottom fish was prized on the world market.

Earl Ohmer and brother-in-law Karl Sifferman formed Alaska Glacier Seafoods in 1916 in order to process a distinctly flavored shrimp found in the surrounding waters. Petersburg raised the money for a hydroelectric plant and a bank in 1925. The bank remained locally owned until 1971. The new hydroelectric plant allowed a cold storage facility to be constructed in 1926.

Petersburg processors were shipping fillets directly to Germany, roe to Japan, and smelt to Great Britain. The town boasted a herring catch of ten million pounds annually.

The Knudsen brothers, in 1911, opened a sawmill for the manufacture of barrels needed for shipping fish across the Narrows from the Petersburg docks. It became the nucleus for West Petersburg. The Yukon Fur Farm opened in the 1920's first raising fox before shifting over to mink. It was the first mink farm in Alaska.

Eventually West Petersburg had a general store, post office, a clam cannery, an outboard motor repair shop, a gaff hook factory, and a ship repair dock. It was too close to much larger Petersburg. By 1950, it had only 60 residents. Ten years later even though both the Knudsen mill and the Yukon Fur Farm were still in operation, its population was only 26. Fearing being annexed by Petersburg, the town incorporated in 1975 taking the name Kupreanof after the island. Today residents go to work and shop in nearby Petersburg by skiff.

The creation of the Tongass National Forest by President Theodore Roosevelt in 1907 saw Petersburg becoming a major administrative center for the Forest Service. One aspect of this was the need for forest rangers to traverse the dense growth and many remote islands of the region. The answer was the construction of a ranger fleet.

The first ship, the 64-foot *Tahn*, went into service in 1908. The next year, the Forest Service made the addition of floating bunkhouses called "wanigans" that could be towed by ranger boats to remote sites and remain for months. The ranger boats were of wood construction and designed to take on heavy seas. Being the only federal boat in an area a lot of times, their duties included search and rescue, taking the U.S. Census, mail delivery, troop transport as well as an office and a workstation for Forest Service personnel.

Often painted yellow with red trim, the fleet peaked with eleven vessels in 1928. The *Chugach*, built in 1925, was transferred from Cordova and the Chugach National Forest to Petersburg and Tongass service in 1956. It has been assigned to Petersburg ever since. In 1992, the vessel—the last surviving member of the Tongass Fleet—was placed on the National Register of Historical Places. *Chugach* is still listed on active duty though the role the ranger boats played has been filled by float planes and other aircraft.

Petersburg by the 1930s had a population of 1,500. The town had plank streets, brilliantly painted house boats in the harbor, and Alaska's only traffic light. It had a weekly newspaper that eventually went out of business, replaced by the *Petersburg Pilot,* which began printing in 1974. In 1937 a 24-foot channel was dredged to the wharves, a small boat harbor was built, and the harbor improved.

The University of Alaska opened an experimental fur farm in 1937 to assist the 60 fur farms in the area. Fur farming was active in the region until 1972.

Tourists discovered Petersburg in the 1930s. Local pranksters had set up a box labeled "Red Bat: Dangerous when Flying." Visitors would peer inside only to find a brickbat.

The town made headlines in 1963 as the State of Alaska's new ferry fleet came online. An eight by seventy-foot gash was ripped across the hull of the *Taku* in April that year as she hit a rock while docking during low tide. Late summer of the same year, two boys were able to sneak into the *Taku*'s wheelhouse and hit the controls sending the engines full forward. The result was the 180-foot loading plank tumbling into the harbor and dock repairs that took three months.

Based on volume, Petersburg ranks 15th among U.S. fishing ports with 101 million pounds of fish and shellfish passing through her docks in 2011 with an estimated value of $65 million. Petersburg fishermen do not stay in local waters. A large number travel a thousand miles west each year to make up part of the Bristol Bay fishing fleet.

Petersburg united with its smaller neighbor Kupreanof (West Petersburg) in forming the Petersburg Borough in 2013.

Today Petersburg's Norwegian descendants hold the Little Norway Festival on May 17th, the date Denmark granted independence to Norway, with its own Scandinavian inspired Leikarring dancers. The tradition of Julebukking is held every Christmas Eve as merchants offer food and spirits to their customers. Several town structures are decorated with Rosemaling, a traditional Norwegian art form.

KAKE

BEFORE THE ARRIVAL OF THE EUROPEANS, the fierce and war-like Kakes, a Tlingit subtribe, controlled Kupreanoff and Kuiu islands, a choke point for controlling trade among Tlingit clans. The Kakes charged a toll on intertribal trade through the surrounding waters. Control of these trade routes became the basis of Kake prosperity until broken during the Kake War with the United States.

Yet, when English explorer Sir Frances Drake arrived at Kake in 1579, he reported the Kakes to be a friendly people.

Throughout the late 1700s and 1800s though, American and English traders and sea captains reported attacks by Kake warriors. The Kakes may have participated in the attack on English explorer George Vancouver in 1794 when he unintentionally ventured into their territorial waters while mapping Revillagigedo Island near modern day Ketchikan. The Kakes may have also participated in the Tlingit multi-clan attack on the Russian outpost of Redoubt Saint Michael, near modern Sitka, in 1802. The occurrences laid the seeds for their reputation as a warrior society among the Europeans.

The U.S. and British governments had several run-ins with the Kakes during the mid-ninetieth century. Members of the Alaskan coastal tribes, such as the Kakes and Haidas, often traveled south to look for work in Puget Sound during the summer.

In 1856, after a series of Indian raids, settlers in the Seattle region became alarmed by a rowdy group of Kakes and Haidas and called on the U.S. Navy for assistance. The *USS Massachusetts* was dispatched to subdue the offenders, ultimately killing some twenty-seven Kakes. A Kake retaliation the following year, in which Col. Issac Ibey was beheaded at his home on Whidbey Island, left relations tense.

Many native Alaska tribes—including the Kakes—were unhappy when the United States purchased the territory in 1867. Two years later, a sentry at a trading post in Sitka killed a visiting Kake. The Kakes in turn killed two prospectors, setting off the conflict known as the Kake War.

The warship *USS Saginaw* sailed into Kake territory and bombarded three Kake villages, destroying homes, boats, and food supplies. The Kakes scattered. Some were taken in by surrounding clans while others roamed Kuiu Island in small bands. For more than twenty years, they remained a displaced people without a home.

The Kakes finally returned to their native land in 1889 and constructed one communal village. In 1891 a store and a Bureau of Indian Affairs school were built in the village, and soon afterward the Society of Friends, commonly known as Quakers, started a mission there. Civilization was overtaking the old ways.

A post office opened in 1904, and in 1912 came Alaska's first modern cannery, which operated continuously until 1940. Today the Kake Cannery is listed on the National Registry of Historical Places.

After World War II, logging became the main stay of Kake's economy; more than 120 miles of logging roads penetrated the surrounding forest. The town was incorporated in 1952.

When Alaska achieved statehood in 1959, state officials seized one of four salmon traps that had been given to the Kakes nine years earlier by the federal government, the state constitution forbade the use of such traps. Officials also arrested the president of the Kake Village and the foreman who supervised the traps. The raid became a watershed for the issue of tribal versus state sovereignty. The Kakes sued the State of Alaska claiming tribal sovereignty taking the case all the way to the

United States Supreme Court. That body ruled in 1962 that the state was within its rights in regulating fishing on what had been traditional tribal waters since the Kakes had no reservation.

In 1967, in honor of the centennial of the U.S. purchase of Alaska, the village commissioned Chilkat artists to carve the world's largest totem pole. The 137 and a half foot tall totem pole was shipped to Japan in 1971 for the World's Fair. It remains on display in Kake today, and the town is still home to many Tlingit artists.

In 2000, the dam at nearby Gunnuck Creek, which supplied water to Kake, failed, and since then, the town has relied on a makeshift system of emergency pumps.

SITKA

THE ROCKY KNOLL NEAR DOWNTOWN, today called Castle Hill, is why Sitka exists.

The Kiksadi Tlingit clan migrated into the area from Wrangell selecting the rocky knoll with its splendid view of the two harbors for a fortification called Knootlian.

Sitka itself is a Tlingit word meaning near the sea.

The Russians were the first Europeans here. Part of the Vitus Bering Expedition led by an officer named Aleksei Chirikov lost two boat loads of men along the coast in 1741. Tlingit oral history about the visit tells how a chief had lured the Russians to their death disguised as a bear.

A Spanish expedition arrived in 1775. The Kiksadi Tlingits informed the Spanish they were welcomed ashore, but they expected to be paid if the Europeans filled their casks from streams belonging to them. The Catholic explorers did so then erected a cross claiming the land for the Spanish monarch. As soon as their ship sailed over the horizon, the Tlingits yanked the cross down.

Captain James Cook sailed by Knootlian naming the small volcano nearby Mount Edgecumbe, but he did not land. When French explorer Etienne Marchand landed in 1791, he noted the Kiksadi had two copper coins minted in Massachusetts, evidence Yankee traders were here first.

When Russians finally began visiting the region in 1799, they were met by Captain Richard Cleveland of Boston already harvesting otter pelts. The Boston men, as Tlingits called Americans, had been trading in Southeast Alaska since the end of the American Revolution in 1789.

Alexander Baranov

Fearing both the growing influence of King George men, as the British were called by the Tlingits, and the never-ending need for more furs, the Russians, led by Alexander Baranov, came to Sitka in 1799.

Baranov asked permission from the Chief of the Kiksadi for constructing a Russian outpost six miles north of Knootlian. Seeing the advantage of European trade, the Kiksadi agreed.

Baranov put up a stockade, warehouses, and roughhewn homes. When winter began settling in, he ordered his Aleuts back to Kodiak leaving behind twenty-five Russians and fifty-five Aleuts. He named his new settlement New Archangel or Archangel Mihail for Our Protector.

A party of Baranov's Aleuts made camp between Baranov and Chichagof Islands along a narrow strait. Discovering small black snails in shallow water in great abundance, the men feasted through the night. Morning found over a hundred Aleuts dead. The snails had been poisonous. To keep a warning of the area alive, Russian mapmakers christened the waterway Peril Strait.

It has never been satisfactorily explained why the Kiksadi attacked New Archangel. There were many advantages for them in having a Russian fort nearby; trade being the first. But, with European goods so close at hand, other Tlingit clans became jealous of the Kiksadi. The Kiksadi lived in a warrior's world fighting neighboring Tlingit clans. With the Russians as their newfound ally, the balance of power in tribal warfare had tipped in the Kiksadi's favor.

Yet, for unknown reasons, a growing hostility grew between the Kiksadi and the Russians.

Boston men and King George men had a trading post to the south of the Kiksadi. There the whites traded everything, including muskets and cannons, with all the Tlingit clans in exchange for pelts. A new Tlingit village evolved by the post led by Chief Kaniagit. Kaniagit began putting together an alliance for an attack on New Archangel.

Around two in the afternoon on June 24, 1802, a Russian hunter named Abrosim Plotnikov went to check on cattle. The other hunters had all left. An hour later when he returned, he came upon hundreds of Tlingit warriors rushing into the stockade with the bodies of two headless Russian sentries laying on the ground.

For eight days Plotnikov hid in the forest until he saw three British ships arriving in a nearby harbor. He managed to board the *Unicorn*. After telling the story of the massacre, the British captain invited local chiefs to come on board to discuss trade. Once the chiefs were on the *Unicorn*, Captain Barber said he would hang them unless they returned what Russians they had captured.

Though Britain was at war with Russia at this time, Barber oversaw the freeing of three Russians, two Aleuts, eighteen Kodiak women, and thousands of beaver pelts. The *Unicorn* then sailed for Kodiak.

Anchoring off the then Alaskan capital, Barber sent a note to Baranov reading, "Although I belong to a country at war with Russia, I have sympathy for human beings. I brought these poor people out of the hands of barbarians, clothed, and fed them, spent all my activities to bring them to you."

Barber ended the message demanding fifty thousand rubles for the return of the survivors to make up for his losses. Baranov negotiated with him to accepting furs worth ten thousand rubles.

The Battle of Sitka

In mid-September 1804, a small fleet consisting of a small Russian warship the *Neva* and 250 kayak-like bidarkas manned by 500 Aleuts sailed out of Kodiak Harbor crossing the stormy Gulf of Alaska with Knootlian as their destination.

Electing a new chief, Katlian, the Kiksadi built a reinforced log fort just to the south of Knootlian along the Indian River as a fallback position.

Katlian purchased cannons from the British traders and stocked the new fort with enough food to hold out for a long siege.

The Battle of Sitka was a series of fights spanning several days. Baranov had his Aleuts tow the *Neva* with their bidarkas into the narrow harbor at the base of Knootlian's rocky knoll. There the Russian warship brought her cannons to bear on the native fortification. After a long bombardment, Baranov and the Russians charged the knoll only to be repulsed by volley fire from the Tlingits. Baranov was badly wounded, and twelve Aleuts were killed. A second attack found Katlian had withdrawn to the log fort.

The Russians then assembled for a frontal assault on the Tlingit fort a few miles to the south. Katlian slipped out from the back of the fort with selected warriors. Crossing the river, Katlian and his men were now behind the Russians. The Kiksadi had been holding their fire on the Russian advance. When they received a signal from Katlian, they fired into the Russian line. The Aleuts who were leading the advance broke and ran. As panic began taking hold, Katlian and his men hit from the rear. The Russians were in disarray and in retreat.

For the next two days, Baranov tried negotiating a surrender from Katlian. Katlian entered talks while his men sought more gunpowder from the British traders.

Late on the second day, the Kiksadi discovered that Baranov was bringing cannons ashore from the *Neva*. Still without supplies, Katlian made the decision to lead the clan out of the fort during the night. Now in flight, the Kiksadi retreated to Peril Strait and from there eastward until they were on the eastern shore of Baranov Island. From there, they sailed off to neighboring Chichagof Island. Their homeland and town of Knootlian was abandoned to the Russians.

A few days later, the Russians entered the fort finding a ghastly scene. To ensure their flight would not be discovered, the Tlingits had killed their infants and dogs leaving the bodies behind.

In winning the Battle of Sitka, Baranov ensured the islands and fjords in this part of the Pacific Northwest coast would be Alaskan and not eventually part of Canada.

Baranov chose Knootlian as the site to rebuild New Archangel. The governing house was constructed on top of its rocky knoll. Kiksadi lodges were destroyed, and cabins built. The *Neva was* sent back to Kodiak for more supplies as Baranov had his men dig into tree trunks, logs, and the like to recover fired shot. Katlian's two cannon were added to the Russian arsenal.

Captain Urey Lisiansky of the *Neva* reported that within a year of the battle, New Archangel consisted of eight buildings, four cows, two calves, three bulls, three goats, one ewe, and a ram along with pigs and chickens.

The next year, 1805, Japanese fishermen, blown off their course, became shipwrecked on Japonski Island in Sitka's harbor. They were returned to Japan in 1806. The Russians later built a magnetic observatory on the island.

Baranov moved the Alaskan capital from Kodiak to his New Archangel. From 1808 to 1906, Sitka was the capital for the vast territory of Alaska.

Baranov's New Archangel

Over the next fourteen years, Baranov made Alaska profitable to its share holders. Crippled from arthritis, Baranov could fly into a savage rage. His justice was simple, death or torture for breaking company rules and rewards and wealth for following them. He treated the Tlingits with the same simple harsh code by which he ruled his own people. Baranov made a fortune, but gave most of it away building schools and churches for Russians and for Natives along with the offspring of the two peoples.

Sitka resembled an armed camp during its first year with sentries posted day and night. Buildings were nothing more than logged hovels. Baranov's office and quarters were made of heavy logs with a partially sod roof. It was damp, dark, and always filled with smoke due to poor ventilation.

Worse, starvation seemed the fate of the Russians as their first winter set in. Aleut and Russian did not stray far from the protective walls of New Archangel fearing Tlingit ambush.

Baron Nikolai Rezanov arrived that first winter direct from the court of Czar Alexander to inspect Russian holdings in North America.

Shocked by the suffering in New Archangel, Rezanov sailed for San Francisco to obtain grain and beef for the colony from Spanish California. On March 28, 1806, he entered San Francisco Bay and was greeted by Commandant Don Jose Eario Arguello. The Spanish commander invited the forty-year-old Baron to dinner at his private residence. Rezanov was immediately taken back by the Commandant's young fifteen-year-old daughter, Maria.

Her father granted the supplies Rezanov asked for as the Baron and his daughter fell love. Rezanov approached Don Arguello for her hand. The Commandant said such a union was impossible; he was Orthodox, and his daughter was Catholic.

Rezanov though was determined to have her. He told Don Arguello he would go back to St. Petersburg for the Czar's permission then to Rome to see the Pope if his daughter would wait.

On June 1, 1804, Rezanov's ship sailed for New Archangel loaded with cattle and grain saving New Archangel from being abandoned. The Baron then went on to Siberia that September. Traveling across Russia, Rezanov came down with fever after becoming soaked crossing a river. He died in March 1807.

Maria would not learn what had happened for forty years. During this time, her father had become Governor of California. Maria joined the first convent in California established by the Dominican sisters where she died on December 23, 1857.

The Rezanov affair was a turning point for New Archangel. New California trade secured a food source for Sitka. Life began improving. Baranov built a more commanding home with a 1700 volume library. The house even contained a piano as well as valuable paintings. Though New Archangel was known as a rowdy, rough and tumble port of call for those plying the Pacific trade, Baranov tried bringing to it touches of grace and eloquence.

Under Baranov, New Archangel became a trade center for the North Pacific with her own blacksmiths, coppersmiths, and coopers. The small capital now had icehouses, sawmills, salteries, brickyards, flour mills, and shipyards. The first steamship on North America's west coast was designed and constructed here. Hardware and metal goods were manufactured and exported along with lumber and fish.

All this resulted in a growing population involved in world trade. New Archangel soon had five schools, many financed out of Baranov's own pocket, a museum, a lighthouse, and a magnetic observatory. It was now earning the name Pearl of the Pacific.

Baranov's downfall began when he filed charges of insubordination against various naval officers in New Archangel. The Navy, through influential friends in the Czar's court at St. Petersburg, had Baranov reprimanded instead.

Naval officers went to the Czar claiming the Alaskan Governor General had pocketed 5,000 Spanish piasters, that he had misruled Alaska, and that the Navy could rule vast Alaska with far more efficiency.

Dismissed in disgraced in 1818 and ordered to St. Petersburg to answer charges, Baranov became fatally ill on the voyage and was buried at sea near the East Indies. His son-in-law replaced him as Governor General of Alaska. A review of the account books revealed no funds had been misappropriated and that Baranov for years supported public education in Alaska out of his own pocket.

The Pearl of the Pacific

The Governor Generals who followed Baranov brought their highborn families and subordinates to New Archangel. By the 1820s, the small capital was the site for gala balls, dinner parties, and amateur theater. Wines challenged vodka as New Archangel's drink of choice. What became known as Baranov's Castle was built in 1837. There Civil servants and military officers met for tea every Sunday at five in the afternoon.

The Cathedral of Saint Michael, which dominates the heart of Sitka, was dedicated in 1848 after taking four years to build. A second hospital was built a few miles south of the capital when hot springs were discovered in the area. An orphanage was opened in 1842, the same year the Russian Bishop's house was constructed.

Ioann Veniaminov was the Bishop of Alaska in 1841 after serving as a missionary, earlier in the Aleutians, and later, among the Tlingits in 1834. Seeing himself first and foremost a Russian Orthodox priest, he continued missionary work in Southeast Alaska. He eventually converted more than 10,000 Natives. Noted for his works on the Aleut and Tlingit language and culture, he later became the Metropolitan of Moscow and eventually Saint Innocent, one of the four Orthodox saints for Alaska.

Despite the continued ambushes and hit and run warfare between Tlingits and Russians, Tlingits were invited to return to Baranov Island in 1821. Hundreds settled just outside the log walls of New Archangel.

Hostilities with Tlingit clans grew until the Russians lost control of the situation. In 1852, Tlingit warriors attacked the colonial hospital located at the hot springs where modern Goddard is today. Three years later, a mass attack on New Archangel itself by Tlingit warriors was stopped by Russian cannons.

The stockade that protected Sitka from the Tlingits had three Russian blockhouses, that can be seen today. A church was also built along the wall, Trinity, with an entrance to outside the stockade for Tlingit Christians and one inside the stockade for Russian converts. It is through this door in 1855 that Tlingit warriors charged into Sitka. By the end of a two-hour battle, twenty Russians and sixty Tlingits were dead. The warriors were driven out by point blank cannon fire. When the Governor General discovered he did not have the manpower to drive the Tlingits away from the wall, an uneasy truce settled in.

The U.S. Purchase

The 1867 treaty of purchase by the United States made provisions for Russians living in New Archangel. Transportation back to Russia was to be provided if they decided not to become American citizens.

Major General Jefferson C. Davis with 250 troops arrived for the ceremonial transfer of the territory. Accompanying Davis was William

Summer Dodge, the future Collector of Customs for the new District of Alaska.

On October 18, 1867, Governor General Prince Maksoutoff, his wife, Princess Maksoutoff, eighty Russian soldiers, and several Tlingit chieftains stood on the rocky knoll under a flagpole, behind them the tidy homes of Sitka all painted bright yellow with red roofs. Captain Alexei Peschouroff stood representing Russia. Facing him were General L. Rousseau representing the United States, General Davis, and Dodge. As New Archangel's population of one thousand watched, the flag of Czarist Russia came down. Russian warships in the harbor fired a salute to their double eagle flag. Then Rousseau's son raised the Stars and Stripes.

The American warships in the harbor fired a salute and New Archangel cease to exist, replaced by a new name Sitka, capital of the U.S. Customs District of Alaska.

Americans flooded into Sitka giving it the atmosphere of a boom town. Stores and homes sprang up as did businesses ready to trade for the famous Alaskan pelts from the Tlingits. A total of 800 Americans made it north, mixing in with the many Russians who stayed.

The boom ended abruptly within two years. Congress had made no provisions for civilian government for the District of Alaska. It did not even have enough population to quality for territorial status. H.H. McIntyre was sent by Congress to Alaska to investigate possible civil rule. McIntyre's *Report on Alaska* noted there were only 125 legal voters in the entire District in 1869 of which fifty were in Sitka. The report recommended that civil government not be granted. McIntyre stated the population did not warrant the expense.

Due to this report, there was no mechanism in place to purchase or own title to land, homes, or businesses. Sitka police discovered it had no authority to legally make arrests. The city council failed to build a jail when it discovered it did not have the legal power to tax.

General Order Number 1, issued on October 29, 1867, placed governing Alaska, under the U.S. Army with some authority given to Collector of the Customs. The Army had the biggest payroll in town. It also acted as a social safety net as General Davis made sure needy families, in particular the Russians, were given Army rations.

The Russians found they were faced with a desperate situation. General Davis was under orders not to hire them as part of his civilian work force, and yet to also provide protection for them as stipulated in the purchase treaty. The Russian population had formerly either worked for the colonial government or for the Russia American Company. After the transfer of Alaska to the U.S., they found themselves unemployed. Russian families began selling off furniture and even their clothing to make ends meet.

Sitka's newspaper, the *Alaska Times*, began running editorials on their plight. Many Russian Americans left Sitka within three years after the purchase, either for other Alaskan communities like Kodiak or into the unknown Alaskan Interior where American authority had not been established.

Davis was also not blind to Tlingit traditions and sense of justice. Under Tlingit law, the punishment for murder was either death or payment in goods at the value of the life taken. When an American named Parker killed a Sitkan Tlingit, Davis had him arrested to stand trial. The problem was a civilian court could not be legally convened. To avert an assault against the city walls, Davis handed out twenty-five blankets to the relatives of the murdered victim.

Sitka began to noticeably suffer under American rule. The 1870 census showed the capital's population had fallen to a mere 391. Worse, of the 86 adult women, 33 were listed as known prostitutes.

The U.S. Army decided to withdraw its troops from Alaska to aid in the fight against the Nez Perce in the Pacific Northwest. Troops in Sitka boarded a steamer southbound on June 14, 1877.

As soon as the soldiers were on board ship, the Tlingits and Russian creoles went on a rampage looting government building and tearing down parts of the protective wall Baranov had erected.

Sitka in peril

With Sitkan Chief Annah Hoots trying to persuade his people to retake Sitka and portions of the wall gone; the white population panicked. They sent word to San Francisco for help fearing they would be massacred. In mid-August, the U.S. Revenue steamer *Thomas Corwin* visited Sitka, and later in October, so did another U.S. Revenue steamer *Wolcott*. Both captains reported that Tlingits living near the wall numbered around 1500 with only 24 Americans, five Russians, 270 creoles, and two illegal breweries making up the city of Sitka.

Then in the spring of 1878, six Tlingits drowned after being hired by an American as part of a sealing party and the Tlingits demanded payment for the lives lost. Frustrated as the Americans dragged their feet over the question of reimbursement, Sitkan Chief Katlean demanded six white lives.

A mail boat slipped out of the harbor for Victoria, British Columbia asking for help from British authorities. On March 1, 1879, the British warship *Osprey* arrived with her guns trained on the Tlingit settlement outside Sitka's walls. The following day the *USS Wolcott* arrived. HMS *Osprey* stayed in Sitka until relieved a month later by the U.S. warship *Alaska*. The *Jamestown* relieved *Alaska* on June 14, 1879, and from then on, the U.S. stationed a warship in Sitka for twenty years giving the U.S. Navy responsibility for governing the District of Alaska.

Even while under imminent attack, Sitka was beginning to have growing pains. After unloading heavy equipment on the docks in 1878 for a cannery, Tlingits lined the waterfront not allowing eighteen Chinese workers to disembark. A quick agreement was worked out whereby the Tlingits would catch salmon exclusively selling them to the new cannery where the Chinese would be working.

A new Collector of Customs, M. D. Ball, took full advantage of this rebirth by confiscating liquor entering Sitka. Alaska was officially classified as Indian country by the federal government. Liquor was forbidden. Ball was confiscating the liquor and then reselling it to the saloons popping up in the capital.

Ball was finally replaced by William Gouverneur Morris who reported, "There are in this country as God-abandoned, God-forsaken, desperate and rascally a set of wretches as can be found on earth."

Morris made an honest effort to enforce prohibition in Sitka with the aid of the Navy. Ball and his supporters passed a petition around Sitka trying to get his old job back. When the petition drive failed, the tall softspoken Ball and his men tried gathering the majority of the thirty votes in Sitka to send him to Congress. Men were kidnapped, forced to vote, and then given a thank you beer; much to Morris' disgust.

Congress refused to recognize the red-haired Ball as the District's delegate but voted him fare back to Sitka.

Enter the Missionaries

Into this whirling scene stepped American missionaries who stabilized the situation. The Russian Orthodox Church had remained in Sitka after the purchase while the first Protestant church on the Pacific Coast was founded in Sitka in 1840, the Lutheran Church, by Governor General Adolph Etolin, a Lutheran Finn.

Literally at the same moment the Army was withdrawing in 1877, five feet four-inch Sheldon Jackson, from the American Missionary Society, came ashore. He fell in love not just with all Alaska as well as Sitka, but with the Native culture whether it be Tlingit or Aleut. The Tlingits were impressed with how Jackson and other missionaries entered their villages alone, armed only with their Bibles. It was Jackson who opened the door to a changing attitude among Tlingits towards Americans. It was difficult. After the Navy shelled Kake in the 1880s, Sitka harbor was filled with Kake war canoes threatening retribution.

During a visit to New York, Jackson persuaded Rev. John A. Brady to come to Alaska with him. Brady arrived in Sitka on March 13, 1878; two weeks after the *Osprey* had possibly prevented a massacre. In spite of this, he shared a fascination with Jackson for the Tlingits. Both collected totem poles, war canoes, and artifacts.

Brady founded the Sitka Industrial and Training School in 1878 utilizing old, military, barracks to advance Native education. After the barracks burned down in 1882, Jackson raised funds for a new school. When Jackson died in 1910, the school was named in his honor. A boarding high school existed on campus from 1917 to 1967. The school began offering college programs in 1944. The school became the foundation for Sheldon Jackson College.

Major fires plagued Sitka as the 19th Century closed. Baranov Castle burned down in 1894. The Russian landing warehouse near the docks where trade goods from around the world such as hides, tea, chocolate, spices, and snuff were stored, burned down in 1917.

President William Howard Taft created the Sitka National Monument in 1910 along Indian River where the Tlingit fort had been. Over sixteen historical totems were restored and placed at the site. Later, a studio for totem artists was established and is still in operation.

Both the Alaska Native Brotherhood and the Alaska Native Sisterhood were founded in Sitka in 1912 to combat racism.

The massive Alaska Pioneer's Home was rebuilt and opened in 1935. Skagway Bill Fonda, who had been part of the vigilante committee that drove the Soapy Smith gang out of Skagway, posed for the statue, *The Prospector*, in front of the building before his death that same year. The site had been where the Russian log barracks were located. The U.S. Marine Corp was moved into the barracks in 1879 where they remained until 1913.

No longer the Capital

Once the government had moved out of Sitka for Juneau, the small city turned to fishing for a living. In 1936, commercial fishing brought in $5 million. The next year a thousand commercial fishing boats were registered in Sitka. By the end of the 1930s, Sitka had a population of 1,600 and growing.

Military preparations began in Sitka even before the attack on Pearl Harbor. The U.S. Army began the construction of Fort Ray in January 1941 taking portions of "G" Street in Sitka proper and harbor islands.

Today underground ammunition magazines near Cascade Creek and a dam and a pipeline is what is left of Fort Ray in Sitka proper.

Much of the military buildup took place on Japonski Island and a small chain of islands stretching out from it. The U.S. Navy had a presence on the island since 1902 when it had a coaling station.

From July 1941 to 1943, the U.S. Army constructed a series of harbor fortifications on these small islands, Forts Pierce, Rousseau, and portions of Ray, with a causeway fill linking them together. Fort Babcock was built on the other side of the channel. Meanwhile, the U.S. Navy brought in 30,000 personnel for the construction of an air base on Japonski. Four ferries carried people back and forth from Sitka to the island. The ferries continued operating until 1971 when the O'Connell bridge was constructed, the first vehicle cable-stayed bridge in the Western Hemisphere.

The military withdrew in 1944. Buildings on Japonski Island were turned over to the Bureau of Indian Affairs for the Mount Edgecombe school in 1946. The State of Alaska opened Mount Edgecombe High School for rural Alaskans in 1986 after the BIA closed the facility in 1983.

Old hangers were turned into the Sitka Community College in 1962 eventually evolving into the Sitka campus of the University of Alaska Southeast in 1987. The Southeast Alaska Regional Health Consortium opened Mount Edgecombe Hospital in one of the former military buildings.

Along Swan Lake, a row of houses had developed for prostitutes servicing Southeast Alaska's fishing fleet. In the early 1950s, many wanted these homes torn down to clean up Sitka's image. Others felt the women were a necessity.

One town meeting became a flash point between the two groups. One man stood up saying that the descent women of Sitka would not be safe in a community of unrelieved fishermen. He would not raise his family in a town where there were no whores.

"Don't say that again," said his wife jumping to her feet, "Or you won't have no wife to worry about."

Swan Lake's houses of ill repute were closed.

Sitka became a borough in 1963 and expanded its borders to include most of Baranof Island in 1971 save for Port Alexander on the southern tip of the island.

In 1966, Sheldon Jackson College earned official accreditation as a four-year college. Author James Michener stayed at the college as he wrote his epic novel *Alaska*.

That same year tragedy struck Sitka as Saint Michael's burned down only to be restored again using the original plans. The historical icons of the church were saved during the fire. Saint Michael's is one of the top ten tourist attractions in Alaska.

In 1977, the U.S. Coast Guard moved from Annette Island opening Air Station Sitka on the northwest sector of the island along with a Coast Guard cutter.

To stimulate the economy, town fathers offered a Japanese firm tax-free status for ten years if it opened a pulp mill. The firm agreed bringing Japanese personnel to Sitka. With them came their children and Sitka experienced a jump in enrollment and expenditures at their public schools without an increase in tax revenue. The Japanese offered to pay the Sitka school system $75,000 to offset costs. Then local workmen went on strike for higher wages even before production began. To bring about an end to the strike, the Japanese opened a commissary selling workers food and consumer goods at cost. The strike ended, but the commissary arrangement hurt local merchants.

The mill turned out 175,000 tons of pulp from Sitka Spruce and Western Hemlock annually for shipment to Japan and its rayon plants.

Sitka's Alaska Raptor Center began in 1980 and by 1991 was in a new facility covering 17 acres. Sitka expanded her boat harbor in 1992 to 1,150 berths: half of them taken up by commercial fishing boats.

The community took a blow in 2007 when historical Sheldon Jackson College closed due to financial pressures.

Still by 2005 Sitka became Alaska's fourth largest city with a population of close to 10,000 and more than 22 buildings listed on the National Register of Historical Places.

It is the home of mystery writer John Straley.

Sitka is also the site for the famous April Fool's Day hoax. In 1974, Porky Bickar flew hundreds of old tires into the volcanic cone of Mount Edgecombe and lit them on fire. The black smoke billowing from the cone convinced Sitka residents the mountain was about to erupt. Many evacuated the city.

ANGOON

ARCHEOLOGICAL DIGGINGS INDICATE ANGOON MAY BE one of the oldest, continuously, inhabited sites in North America. The Tlingits have lived in the area for only a few hundred years. Native legend has it they were shown the site by a magical beaver.

Kootznoowoo, the Tlingit name for Admiralty Island, means fortress of the Brown Bear. Those Tlingits who settled on Admiralty did so because the island receives less rainfall than the surrounding islands. They became known as the Kootznahoo Tlingits. Angoon or Aangoon means isthmus town in Tlingit.

Today it is estimated that anywhere from 1500 to 1700 brown bears inhabit Admiralty. One oddity is the fact that their DNA does not exactly match the DNA of their brown bear cousins on the mainland though their DNA does match that of brown bears on nearby Baranof and Chichagof islands. An explanation of this may be that the three islands were not covered by the last ice age. They were ice free lands called Refugias. When the ice sheets retreated on the mainland, their distant brown bear cousins migrated up from the south after the gene pool had been separated for thousands of years.

Admiralty Island itself is the seventh largest island in the U.S. covering 1,646 square miles. It was proclaimed the Admiralty Island National Monument in 1978.

The first historical record of Killisnoo (Xootz-Noo) as Angoon was earlier known, or for that matter of the Kootznahoos, was in 1804 when they went to the aid of the Kisadi (Sitkans) in their epic battle against Alexander Baranov and the Russians.

For decades until Russia sold Alaska to the U.S., the main industry was collecting and selling furs in Sitka to the west.

A flare up between the U.S. and the Kootznahoos took place shortly after the American purchase of Alaska. Three white traders of possible Russian descent were murdered in Angoon in 1869. Saginaw Jack, chief of the Kootznahoos, was taken prisoner and held at Mare Island, California, on board the *USS Saginaw* for a year before his release, thus the chief's nickname. By this time, Angoon and the Kootznahoos had gained fame for an alcoholic concoction they brewed called Hoochinoo or Hootch.

The Northwest Trading Company set up a post and a whaling station on nearby Killisnoo Island hiring Angoon residents for whale hunting. To make Killisnoo attractive for relocation, the trading company arranged for a Bureau of Indian Affairs school and a Russian Orthodox Church to open at the new site. The original school burned down in 1894.

A whaling vessel's harpoon misfired in 1882 killing a Tlingit shaman who had been hired on as a crewman. The village demanded 200 blankets for the deceased family. Refusing to pay, the Northwest Trading Company turned to the U.S. Navy in Sitka as the mood grew ugly. The Navy sent the revenue cutter *Thomas Corwin* which shelled both Angoon and a summer fish camp nearby. Six children died during the attack from smoke inhalation. Some eighteen homes and forty canoes were also destroyed.

In 1973, Angoon won a $90,000 settlement from the United States government for the 1882 bombardment.

The Northwest Trading Company switched from whaling to herring processing shortly afterwards. A post office was opened in Killisnoo in 1884. The 1890 census had 29 families living at Killisnoo. Their school had a student enrollment of 15 boys and 20 girls who were taught by a female teacher.

Surprisingly, despite the gold rush underway in Juneau and Douglas, there were no mines opened near Angoon nor on Admiralty Island during this period.

So many Angoon residents moved into Killisnoo for work that Angoon became abandoned. Then in 1928 a fire burned the entire community of Killisnoo down forcing the Tlingits back to what was left of Angoon. A post office was established in Angoon that same year. Angoon was organized as a city in 1963.

Angoon chose to prohibit the possession of alcohol which is enforced today. The local school has an estimated 130 students. A shellfish farm has been started up through state and federal funding. There are 55 fishing permit holders in the village for hand trolling of king and coho salmon.

Inside Passage North

The difference between the north and south portions of the Inside Passage is the collision of the Yakutat tectonic plate against the North American plate. The resulting uplift of immense glacier-clothed peaks and ice fields in the north are not found in the southern end of the Inside Passage.

Mount Saint Elias with her mountain range is the fastest rising mountain in the world. This uplift is also responsible for such natural wonders as Glacier Bay.

The average visitor though has a different take on the difference between the north end of the Inside Passage and the southern end—sunshine. Whereas Alaskans in Ketchikan and Petersburg measure rainfall in feet, residents of Juneau and Haines speak of rain in inches.

The Tongass forest here is different too. In the southern section of the Inside Passage, the canopy of her rainforest barely allows in light in many places. Here in the northern region, the forest breaks up allowing for meadows and fields. Farming exists though not to the extent it had a century ago. Dairies and truck farms once crowded the landscape between Auke Bay and Juneau. Skagway still calls herself Alaska's Garden City. Gustavus began as a farming community and Haines' landscape is marked by a number of farms.

There are still colossal islands here, but the maze of waterways that carve and divide up the southern portion of the Inside Passage do not exist here. With only four exceptions, nearly all of the major communities of the north end are on the mainland.

It is still a land cut off from the world. The vast ice fields such as the Juneau Ice Field and towering glacial peaks separate this land from the rest of North America. Juneau is the only state capital one cannot drive to. Yet, there are road connections out of Haines and Skagway. An individual cannot do the same in the southern end where nearly all the communities reside on islands.

Icy Straits, running from the Pacific towards Juneau, offers the best whale watching in Alaska while the town of Haines is famous for the largest winter concentration of bald eagles in North America.

There are more wolves in this section of the Inside Passage and less Sitka deer. Unlike the southern portion, due to the glaciers and ice fields, one now and then can spot a phase bear also known as a Ghost Bear or Spirit Bear. In truth a black bear, their coloration has been transformed by nature to blend into the world of ice around them. They are usually spotted around Juneau, Skagway, and Yakutat. The Russians called them Saint Elias Bears for the mountain, at one time considered the highest peak in North America. The Tlingits believed sighting one was an omen.

The Russians had very little impact in this part of Alaska nor did salmon. Very few communities here are primarily fishing communities. To one extent or another, gold was what gave birth to most of the towns of the north end whether from mining such as Juneau and Douglas, transportation to the gold fields such as Skagway and Haines or a place for miners to winter such as Tenakee Springs.

Lack of Russian activity in this area of the Inside Passage meant a lack of sea charts. After the purchase of Alaska, the United States neglected the Inside Passage including its sea lanes. When the Klondike Gold Rush broke loose, there were no charts at all for this end of the Inside Passage. From 1900 to 1920, some one hundred ships sank in these waters due to striking submerged rocks.

The Lynn Canal thirty miles north of Juneau was the scene for one of America's worse maritime disasters.

On the morning of October 24, 1918, the *SS Princess Sophia* ran aground on Vanderbilt Reef with 288 passengers and 61 crewmen. Most of the passengers were men and their families from the Interior gold rush town of Ruby going off to enlist for World War I. Family members had traveled along to wish them farewell. At first the captain did not feel alarmed and rescue efforts were going at a slow pace when a combination of stormy seas and high tide caused the passenger ship to slide off the reef straight for the bottom of the sea. Everyone went down with the ship. There were no survivors. Among those lost was the first man to have stood on the summit of Denali, Walter Harper.

Sentinel Island Lighthouse marks the spot of the tragedy today.

A series of wood structured lighthouses were built up and down the region as quickly as budgets would allow. Nearly all but one was replaced in the 1920s and 1930s with more substantial structures in the Art Deco style. The Eldred Rock Lighthouse as one approaches Haines is the last of the wooden structured lighthouses. The Five Finger Island Lighthouse has been a base for whale researchers since 2011.

The crown jewel of the region is the 3.3-million-acre Glacier Bay National Park and Preserve, more astonishing if one considers that physically the mammoth bay did not exist in 1794.

The State of Alaska also maintains a string of five marine parks along the Lynn Canal running from Pavlov Harbor near Tenakee Springs north to Haines, part of 17 state parks and historical sites in the area.

TENAKEE SPRINGS

A GENUINE HIDDEN TREASURE, THIS SMALL PORT of a hundred souls offers much in charm whether from its Gold Rush-era buildings such as the Snyder's Mercantile which serves as the town's general store and still using a 1917 hand cranked register, the equally old Shamrock Building, or the newly restored St. Francis Chapel.

One has to stoop when entering the two-room cabin called the Blue Moon Cafe as the owner, Rosie, who has lived in Tenakee Springs for over 60 years prepares for her usual lunch crowd. Most of the homes and businesses are on wood pilings over the sea.

A three-mile-long gravel road paralleling the beach serves as the town's only road. Motorized vehicles are not allowed in town save for the 1980 Chevrolet truck that is used by the volunteer fire department. Pumps are available to be rushed to the beach using salt water in case of an emergency.

The local school is built on a small mountain top accessible by walking up 146 metal steps. Built in 1987, the school won an architectural award in 1988 and services thirteen students.

The word Tenakee stems from tinaghu, a Tlingit word meaning coppery shield bay. The name stems from a Tlingit legend that three valuable copper shields were lost at sea nearby during a storm.

The reason for the town's existence is due to the sulfur hot springs reaching temperatures of 108 F. It was quite the draw during winter months. Prior to the Klondike Gold Rush, prospectors, trappers, and fishermen would wait out the dark, cold winter months camping by the springs. The construction of a large tub building to ensure warmth during the winter marked the beginning of the community.

Tenakee was one of the first Alaskan communities to witness the practice of taking a "winter wife." A winter wife was a prostitute hired for the duration of the winter for taking on the duties of a domestic partner in exchange for a percentage of the trapper or prospector or fisherman's income. Come spring the couple would go their separate ways. This arrangement worked well as long as the women did not mix with respectable society.

However, the town was scandalized when winter wives were discovered at a high-society masked ball held in Tenakee's only dance hall.

As the Klondike Gold Rush got underway, Tenakee saw the influx of even more people. Even members of the infamous Soapy Smith gang out of Skagway soaked at the hot springs. Ed Snyder built his Snyder's Mercantile in 1899 to service the needs of those camped around the springs as well as supplying the saloons and gambling establishments that had popped up. A post office opened in 1903. At first the community was simply called Tenakee, but by 1928, it became known as Tenakee Springs.

The Superior Packing Company opened a cannery in 1916 soon followed by two other canneries. At the height of canning operations more than 200 seasonal workers lived in the community. Superior closed in 1953, but cannery operations hung on until 1974. A logging camp operated at Corner Bay near town for quite some time.

The facilities at the hot springs were added in 1915 and in 1929. The current bathhouse was built in 1940. A local tried enlarging the basin of the hot springs using dynamite only to stop the flow of the springs for a worrisome three days.

By the 1930s, the town had grown to 200 in population and home for two general stores. Cherry trees from a tree farm in Sitka were planted downtown along with Norway Maple. A nearby portage connects Tenakee Inlet with Port Frederick and the village of Hoonah.

The town has not escaped tragedy. In 2003, 19-year-old Maggie Wigen was last seen walking her dog. A three-day search found her murdered body in a fresh grave only 50 feet from her cabin. A 26-year-old man from a local family was convicted of the murder.

In 2007, Tenakee lost its 911 emergency service because there were not enough people to operate it.

The community almost lost its school in early 2009 when student enrollment dropped to only nine students. The town went on Craigslist looking successfully for a family with children in order to keep the school open.

Tenakee Springs gradually evolved into a retirement village for Juneau and Sitka residents. Drinking water comes from either nearby streams or from wells. A water ambulance christened *Maggie's Wake*, in honor of Wigen, went into operation in 2008.

The town has a Farmer's Market with produce from surrounding gardens.

Renowned Alaska artist Rie Munzo maintained a home in Tenakee Springs.

JUNEAU

Juneau's history nearly became something different than what it is today.

The Russians granted the Hudson's Bay Company the right to trade along the banks of Taku Inlet just south of present-day Juneau. Hudson Bay men landed at Taku in 1840 constructing Fort Durham and a trading post in Taku Harbor.

Trade with the Tlingits was not as profitable as the British had hoped for. Within a few years, Hudson Bay gave up Fort Durham.

An American settlement in Taku Inlet began in 1912 and lasted until 1945, but by then, both Juneau and Douglas were well established towns.

Sitka Origins

Four men, Richard Harris, Joe Juneau, George Pilz and Chief Kowee of the Auk Tlingits created Southeast Alaska's largest city.

Pilz had been a mining engineer in Germany. Always in poor health, Pilz had his successes. He had built a copper smelter and a stamp mill for gold in California when he was only twenty-four. He was recuperating in San Francisco when he was hired to manage a gold mine at Silver Bay near Sitka at age thirty-three.

Succeeding in the construction of a stamp mill in Sitka in March

1879, he began looking for miners with experience in sinking a shaft through the quartz rock. Sorting through dregs and rift raft in Wrangell, he found two such men, Harris and Juneau.

Harris was an Irish immigrant from County Down. After fighting in the Civil War, he drifted West and into Mexico as a miner. He had come north to search for gold in British Columbia's Cassiar country.

Harris met Joe Juneau there. Juneau was from Quebec, and though he could speak English (with a strong French accent), he could not read nor write.

The two struck up a friendship, deciding to try their luck searching for the Lost Rocker mine north of Wrangell. The two had gone broke in the Cassiar Gold Rush. They had just returned to Wrangell to raise a grubstake for the Lost Rocker search when they learned Pilz was hiring.

They took the mail steamer *California* after promising the purser they would stake a claim for him if he gave the two free passage.

Sitka's Silver Bay mine had pinched out. Pilz was faced with being unemployed. He knew that a Captain J.W. White of the cutter *Wyanda* had filed a mineral report covering the north end of the Inside Passage. Once in possession of the report, Pilz sent prospectors out in all directions while offering 100 Hudson Bay blankets to any Tlingit that brought him evidence of gold.

Auk Chief Kowee came to Sitka for the reward. Harris and Juneau were hired to investigate Kowee's find. The two took three Tlingit workers, supplies for three months, and a boat. Harris was to be paid sixty dollars a month for his services. Juneau a little less. Pilz would receive title to the first and second locations of all quartz lodes the two uncovered. Harris and Juneau would have title to the rest.

Led by Chief Kowee, on August 17, 1880, the two followed "color" in a stream emptying into Gastineau Channel. They returned to Sitka, got more provisions, and returned to stay a year in the area.

With Tlingit workers, the two went up Gold Creek on October 3rd into an area called Silver Bow, named by Harris after a Montana mining district. They decided to pan a little before breakfast. They were shocked when they uncovered the richest diggings they had ever seen as prospectors. "Streaks running through the rock and little lumps as large as peas and beans," Harris wrote. On October 18th, the two hauled a thousand pounds of gold-bearing quartz rock over a mountain to the beach.

The two sat down with their three Tlingit workers. Mining law required five miners in order to form a mining district. With a district formed, they could file legal claims protecting what they had just found. Juneau could not read nor write nor could the three Tlingits who were now being legally described as miners. Harris scribbled out a draft on a piece of paper for the new mining district becoming its secretary and recorder. Juneau would be the president of the miners' meeting. The new district was christened the Harris Mining District.

Now with the force of the miners' law behind them, the two staked out claims for themselves, Pilz, and for the purser on the *California* who had given them free passage earlier. After digging out a half ton of gold ore, they set to work laying out a town site.

Chief Kowee had a different version of the story though.

The Kowee version claimed that Juneau and Harris traded their supplies for homemade alcohol (hootch) and female pleasures while boasting that as soon as they found gold, they were going to head south for Wrangell, and from there, to Victoria, British Columbia.

The two arrived back in Sitka with the half ton of ore on November 17, 1880. It set off a stampede. The *USS Jamestown* transported Pilz, Harris, and Juneau to Gold Creek on condition that a claim would be filed for her Naval Captain, Henry Glass. The *Favourite*, a Northwest Trading Company vessel, transported even more stampeders to the new town of Harrisburg. On board was an already framed house which Pilz erected in the new town site, the first house in Juneau.

Harrisburg

The winter of 1880-81 was spent building a town of logs and the infrastructure needed for heavy mining. By March 1881, the region was dotted with 293 placer claims and 131 lode claims.

The legality of Harris' authority soon came into question. His miners' laws were rejected.

The Navy sent Lieutenant Commander Charles H. Rockwell with a detachment to keep the peace and the miners showed their gratitude by renaming the town Rockwell. The post office, however, still used Harrisburg. After Joe Juneau continued to buy everyone drinks through the winter, a miners' meeting changed the name again, this time to Juneau.

Juneau moved on to other diggings. Harris stayed marrying a Tlingit woman of the Huna clan named Kitty and fathered four children, two of which died in infancy. Kitty died in 1893 at age 26.

Richard Harris went broke from financially defending Pilz of fraud charges. All of Harris' Juneau property was sold to satisfy financial claims. He was left with only his Juneau home. Suffering from yellow jaundice and going blind, he was registered into a home operated by the Masonic Order in Portland, Oregon, where he died at age 73 in 1907.

Pilz built the first ore reduction plant in Juneau only to be forced to sell it off to pay debts. After the fraud conviction, Pilz ventured into the Alaskan Interior dying in the town of Eagle at age 81.

Joe Juneau roamed from gold strike to gold strike in the North country making and spending several fortunes before dying penniless in Dawson in 1899. Old timers put together the money to bring his body back to the town named after him.

Chief Kowee died in 1888 after serving as the police chief for Juneau's Native village. Juneau, Harris, and Kowee's graves are located in Juneau.

Prostitution brings territorial status

By the summer of 1881, Juneau/Harrisburg had a population of 150 whites. Stephen Ushin, a Russian who stayed in Sitka after the U.S. purchase noted Harrisburg had five stores, a restaurant, several saloons, and a guardhouse manned by five officers, soldiers, and a few marines.

The Navy maintained a military presence to keep the peace and assist the Deputy Collector in trying to stop the flow of liquor to no avail.

The Deputy Collector's excuse for not being able to stop the liquor trade was that it was smuggled ashore while he was asleep. In a report to the Treasury Department, his boss complained that the Deputy Collector must be asleep all the time!

Liquor became the spark for a push for home rule. As long as Alaska was under military rule, liquor was prohibited.

During the long winter months, miners met to do away with prohibition, they invited other Southeast Alaska communities to send delegates to Juneau. There at the convention former Collector of Customs, Sitka's M. D. Ball, was elected to go to Washington and push for territorial status for Southeast Alaska. He failed, but Congress did pass the 1884 Organic Act setting up a court system in Alaska, law enforcement, and education.

Yet for all the talk about prohibition, neither the City Brewery in Juneau nor the Douglas Brewery saw no disruption to their business.

A "beer tent" went up within weeks of the arrival of the prospectors. The first real Juneau saloon was the Missouri, later known as The Louvre, proudly advertising it was Alaska's first and finest saloon "in spite of prohibition." James Carroll, Alaska's first mail captain and eventually its delegate to Congress, bought the Occidental which had been in operation since the founding of Harrisburg in 1881 and was built on pilings along the shoreline.

Carroll decorated the place with expensive mirrors and renamed it the Crystal Palace and Ballroom. Liquor was brought in through a trap door in the floor during high tide while the girls "entertained" in the Kensington Rooms. The Palace remained in operation until 1954.

The Juneau Opera House broke all attendance records in 1895 when Violet Raymond, the Queen of Burlesque, performed at age sixteen. Two years later, she was a high-class prostitute in the Klondike Gold Fields.

Gertie Joseph handed out invitations' city wide about her services the following year, but the powers that be would not let her branch out from the designated area of town.

Canadian Robert Service got off the boat in Juneau for a couple of days on his way to the Yukon Territory. There he learned of the killing of the local Juneau gambler Dan McGrew. The gun play that brought about McGrew's end was witnessed by Dr. Leonard Sugden in 1897. As in the poem, Sugden stated a stranger walked into the saloon and started playing the piano. Suddenly he stood up calling McGrew out. The bartender turned out the lights hoping it would spoil their aim. It didn't. They both lay dead on the floor when the lights came on. The famous Lou may have been good time girl Lulu Eads.

A few years later, Service put the killings on paper in the form of his classic poem *The Shooting of Dan McGrew*.

U.S. Attorney John J. Boyce and Judge Melville Brown, disciples of the Progressive Era philosophy, were determined to clean Juneau up. To do so, they decided to convict Fred Rassmussen for his prostitution operations. In October 1902, they had his wife arrested for operating a whorehouse. Rassmussen was personally charged rather than his wife for the crime.

When the Rassmussen case ended in a hung jury, Judge Brown had him tried by a petit jury of only six men as allowed by federal law in unorganized territories. Found guilty, Judge Brown ordered Rassmussen to serve a year in jail and pay a $2,500 fine.

His attorney, W.E. Crews, appealed right up to the U.S. Supreme Court stating that his client had been denied the right of having a twelve-man jury. In 1905, Rassmussen and his attorney won!

The U.S. Supreme Court ruled that though Alaska was an unorganized territory, a citizen still has full constitutional rights.

The ruling changed Alaska's official legal designation from being a district to a territory.

Expelling the Chinese

Inexpensive Tlingit and Chinese labor that eased operational costs for the mines and the labor shortage. Juneau saw 450 Tlingit workers laboring for a dollar a day.

The Chinese though were another matter. Like everywhere else in the American West, the Chinese became on unwelcomed element. In

1886, miners were forcing all Chinese workers aboard a ship bound for Wrangell. John Treadwell in Douglas refused to fire his Chinese. A Juneau mob of over a hundred crossed the Channel forcing their way into Treadwell's mining complex grabbing 87 Chinese workers. They were placed on two small boats bound south.

China Joe was soon the only Chinese resident left in Juneau. A baker by trade, the miners allowed him to stay for the help he gave during a starvation winter in the Cassiar gold field.

Treadwell was furious. He had his tug, the *Lucy*, intercept the boat with 15 sacks of rice to feed the exiled Chinese and then sent an urgent message to Alaska District Governor A.P. Swineford.

Swineford sent a Navy ship, *Pinta*, with a U.S. Marshal and law enforcement officers to disperse the mobs and allowed the Chinese back into Juneau. The miners lined the waterfront with shotguns and refused to let the Chinese workers back.

In the end, Treadwell and the other mine owners had to hire more Tlingit workers.

Bart Thane

Juneau was unique. At no other time in Alaskan history save the Nome gold strike, were the gold fields so close to the sea for easy access. Juneau's Silver Bow became an area of tunnels, shafts, stopes, and drifts. Small independent mines dotted the landscape along with residential homes, saloons, churches, and dry goods stores.

Juneau and Douglas were in strong competition with each other for prominence. For many years, the Treadwell Mines of Douglas were the richest in the world. But when the mines collapsed in April 1917, Juneau's Alaska-Juneau Gold Mining Company obtained that honor. The A-J Mine had opened a year before the Treadwell disaster. It churned out $80 million in gold before its closure in 1944.

Just to the south of Juneau, a third town sprung up, Thane.

The Alaska Gastineau Mining Company began operations there in 1914 after Bart Thane had a two-mile shaft chiseled through Mount

Roberts to the Perseverance Mine near Gold Creek. Led by Foreman Paddy O'Neil, a hand pick crew of 14 underground drillers, all second generation Irish, bore a 10,000-foot tunnel through the heart of Mount Roberts. Then a crew of 70 men working three-hour shifts cleared out the tunnel in 16 months. Thane had tracks laid so a train could haul raw ore through the tunnel to the mill along the coastline.

First called Sheep Creek, but the name was changed to Thane in 1927 in honor of the man who caused the town to come into being after he died of pneumonia. The mine though gave out and the town became a bedroom community of Juneau.

Bart Thane by then had seen to it that Juneau had both water and enough electricity to grow into a city.

Thane had the 175 feet high, 648 feet wide, Salmon Creek dam built north of Juneau in 1912; the largest of its kind in the world. Thane did not believe the newly created lake would be a large enough source for electrical power, so he had the Annex Lake hydroelectric plant constructed eighteen miles from Juneau.

Juneau passes the competition

Juneau had outpaced Sitka in population by 1884, having half of the white population in the District of Alaska. More than 150 million dollars in gold was taken from the region.

The Juneau-Douglas region held more than 150 small individual mine operations producing gold. A small fleet of colorful ferries based in Douglas with names like *Marion, Julia,* the *Lone Fisherman,* and the *Sealion* (was to be *Sea Lion* but the painter became intoxicated) hauled mine workers back and forth across the Channel until the Douglas Bridge was constructed in 1935.

Besides mining, Juneau in 1909 could boast of a halibut fleet of thirty vessels. Within two decades, a cold storage facility and eleven canneries opened.

Eloquent hotels were now springing up. The owners of the Alaskan Hotel and Bar hired part of the ferry fleet to bring people over for their grand opening. During the dedication, they tied the keys for the front door to balloons releasing them. As the balloons and the keys drifted away, they told the crowd that the doors to the hotel would never close.

Up Franklin Street from the Alaskan, the Baranof Hotel opened its doors with a national radio broadcast in 1935.

Downtown though was still a dangerous place.

Local Juneau pimp Robert Stroud, known the world over as the Birdman of Alcatraz, began his crime spree here in 1909 by murdering a bartender over the services of a prostitute named Kitty O'Brien.

The red-light district along South Franklin became so dangerous that in 1914 District Attorney John Rustgard ordered marshals to close every whorehouse down along the boulevard. Four months later the bawdy houses were open again and the killings began anew.

Alaska's third capital

Congress designated the gold town the District of Alaska's capital in 1900, but the administrative offices remained in Sitka until 1907. The bunker style Federal Building (now the state capitol), home for the Territorial legislature and the U.S. District Court, was completed in 1931 at a cost of a million dollars. The Governor's Mansion was completed in 1913.

Six years after the capital was physically in Juneau, the Organic Act of 1912 not only created the Territory of Alaska but named Juneau the capital.

By 1939, the A-J Mine was employing 900 men with an annual payroll of $1.5 million and boasted of being the largest gold mine in the world based on tons of rock mined.

Juneau had an electric sawmill and fourteen canneries processing salmon, halibut, herring, shrimp, and crab. Fox farmers dotted the surrounding islands. Six local dairies kept the city supplied with milk products. Community churches sprouted up as early as the 1890s with the Presbyterian Church made of logs in 1891 and St. Nicholas Orthodox Church was built in 1894.

Just before World War II broke out, the city also boasted of two newspapers, tennis courts, and baseball diamonds. Thane even had a nine-hole golf course dubbed the "million dollar" having been laid out over the tailings of the closed Alaska Gastineau Gold Mine.

Mud

Built at the base and along the slopes of Mounts Juneau and Roberts, the danger of avalanches lurks year around. In the last decade, snow avalanches have brought down power lines putting the city in the dark. In the summer and fall, rain transforms topsoil into mud along the mountain slopes, and from time to time, it comes thundering down.

One of Juneau's deadliest mudslides took place the night of November 22, 1936, after receiving more than 20 inches of rain. One man was taking a bath in the Matson boarding house when he heard the descending mud. He threw a towel around himself, grabbed fifty dollars and his cello, and jumped out of the window.

Fifteen dead were the result of a wall of mud that ended at Franklin Street 20 feet deep and 75 feet wide. Among the dead was a Mrs. Erickson. But her caged canary was dug out alive and unharmed.

In 1962, a mudslide destroyed some 24 homes along the slopes.

All was not grim. Locals got a laugh out of a bull terrier named Patsy Ann as she met arriving vessels at the dock in the 1930s and 1940s. The town dedicated a bronze statue in her honor.

World War II

Mining as a major player for Juneau ended with World War II. President Franklin Roosevelt ordered all mining operations in the United States halted so that materials used for mining could be funneled into the war effort.

Early in the war, Juneau became infamous for the number of all-night fights taking place—especially on Franklin Street. The avenue was lined with bars sporting names like Bloody Bucket and Blacky's Bar. Mixed in with the bars were houses of prostitution with actual red lights and women showing off in picture windows to attract customers.

The Coast Guard had enough sending Quartermaster Red Holloway and a seven-man shore patrol team up from Ketchikan to restore order.

Holloway, who later owned several Juneau taxi firms and the Prospector Hotel, restored order after what seemed like a non-stop three-month fight. A makeshift jail was set up on South Franklin with cots and vomit buckets. Skin sheets detailing why personnel were arrested accompanied them back to their ship. It was up to the discretion of their captain if sailors were punished.

More respectable single women had their choice of thousands of military personnel to select for dates. To make sure none of Juneau's young women got into trouble, policewomen were hired to keep an eye on them as they were taken on dates to fraternal organizations such as the Elks and Moose.

Calls to move the capital

After the war both Anchorage and Fairbanks passed Juneau in population. Attempts were made to move the state capital out of Juneau in 1960 and 1962; both fueled by Robert Atwood, owner of the Anchorage Daily News. The argument used for moving the capital from Sitka—isolated and hard to get to—was now being used against Juneau by the newer population centers.

In a statewide vote in 1974, an initiative to move the capital from Juneau pushed by Atwood won with 57 percent approval. Willow was chosen as the new capital in 1976. However, in 1978, voters rejected a $966 million bond for physically moving the capital and it remained in Juneau.

Again in 1982, Alaskan voters were asked to move the capital to Willow at the cost of $2.8 billion. It was rejected.

A new Juneau

With the closure of her mines, Juneau had to find other ways to grow. Commercial fishing looked like the answer at first. From 1946 through 1960, an average of 2.5 million pounds of halibut were hauled out of Juneau waters. Then there was a sudden drop off until only 500,000 pounds of halibut was caught in the late 1970s. The Juneau Cold Storage finally closed in 1983.

Juneau prosperity started coming off cruise ships as early as 1964 which saw 60,000 tourists visiting Juneau and Southeast Alaska. By 1979 that number had reached 350,000.

Two small events in Juneau's post war history had major long-term effects.

The Juneau-Douglas Community College was founded in 1956. With impressive enrollment numbers, the community college was transformed into the University of Alaska Southeast with its Auke Bay campus in 1987.

After the Alaska Steamship Company closed in 1954, the State of Alaska took over the small car ferry operating between Tee Harbor and Haines. The move was the forerunner to the Alaska Marine Highway System. Voters approved a $63 million ferry bond, and by 1963, the first of the blue canoes, *Malaspina* pulled up to Juneau's dock with the local high school band playing before a large crowd.

Juneau today

Home of the Alaskan Brewing Company, 21st Century Juneau's skyline is dominated by the Federal Building (1962), the State Office Building (1974), and the State Court Building (1975) along with the Capitol Building mentioned earlier. The capital's 60 plus restaurants are scattered along with shopping from downtown to residential areas such as Mendenhall Valley where the last dairy closed in 1965.

State government and tourism are now Juneau's main employment sectors.

Juneau's commitment to the tourist industry is evident in downtown Juneau by the docks. The iconic Red Dog Saloon was moved from its location on Franklin Street down to near the docks. A tramway was constructed along the docks as well so tourists may travel to the top of Mount Roberts.

World renown artist Rie Munoz had her studio near the airport.

DOUGLAS

For a while it appeared Douglas would be the dominate city along Gastineau Channel and not neighboring Juneau.

British explorer George Vancouver mapped the seventeen-mile-long island in 1793 naming it after John Douglas, Earl of Salisbury.

The first gold shipment from Gastineau Channel did not come out of Juneau's Gold Creek, but from Douglas Island. In December 1880, a party heading for Harrisburg (Juneau) was forced to make camp on Douglas Island. Poking around, they found gold on the beach and kept the discovery quiet.

The party took in a thousand dollars in gold. They did not file a claim until mid-February when miners revolted against Richard Harris' rule in neighboring Juneau and drafted a new code for the Harris Mining District. In this new draft, miners added Douglas Island to the district. By then, the Douglas group was ready to ship the first ore out of the Harris District.

Having made this first shipment, Douglas became just as attractive as Juneau for incoming prospectors. Arriving from San Francisco in the summer of 1881, John Treadwell thought so. He had a few claims near Juneau before buying a Douglas claim known as the Parris Lode from Pierre Joseph "French Pete" Erussard for four hundred dollars.

By this time, a mining camp had already been established on the island called Edwardsville after a local miner, H.H. Edwards.

Treadwell was known as a likable man and a hard worker, but his lack of vices such as drinking, and smoking kept him socially apart from others in the rough makeshift camps. He worked the Parris lode while buying up two other neighboring claims trying to follow where the gold vein ran.

Finally, when Treadwell had 22 sacks of samples, he headed off for San Francisco for a mill test. The samples showed all three claims were rich in gold. On December 27th, he formed the Alaska Mill and Mining Company selling stock to five California mining men raising $10,000. Treadwell bought a five-stamp mill transporting it to Edwardsville, now finally called Douglas, and set up shop a mile southeast of town.

Discovering the gold vein wider than he anticipated, he bought two more claims from D.W. Clark. His stamp operation was too small for the volume of gold being uncovered. He sold the old stamp to mining interests in Juneau who set the equipment up along Gold Creek for a mine later known as Little Treadwell.

The Treadwell Mine grew into the Treadwell Complex connecting four mines into one massive gold operation. Besides the Parris Lode, Treadwell now possessed the Ready Bullion, the Mexican, and the Glory Hole. Nor did Treadwell have the only mine on Douglas Island. Others popped up, some just as rich as his own.

Multiple mining operations and an ever-growing Douglas needed more water. The Treadwell Ditch, five feet wide and running sixteen miles, was dug in 1889 from Fish Creek near the current Eaglecrest ski resort into Douglas. The "Ditch" today is a hiking trail cluttered with mining relics.

By then, Douglas had secured a post office (1887). It was at this moment that John Treadwell decided to sell his mining interests. He found a buyer in one D.O. Mills of New York for $1.5 million in 1889.

Treadwell moved on to California where he made some investments. Business dealings with his brother did him in. The two formed a trust company which became infamous for the Bear's Nest Swindle, a local mine. In 1914, Treadwell had to file for bankruptcy in New York owing $2.9 million. He died in a New York hotel room at age 85 on November 6, 1927.

The Treadwell Complex and Douglas continued to grow. A school was opened in Douglas in 1891 and a fire department in 1898. Though the District of Alaska was officially under prohibition, the Douglas City Brewing Company was founded in 1899, becoming the largest of the four in the region.

The town incorporated in 1902. Douglas also became the site for St. Ann's Hospital. A 1900 Fourth of July photograph of Douglas shows main street lined with two-story buildings as crowds gathered to watch such events as sack races, wheelbarrow races, greased poles, and the featured event of jack hammering steel bits into boulders.

The town boasted of an opera house and one of the finest dens of prostitution in the District of Alaska, operated by the infamous Dutch Kate Wilson.

A two-foot narrow gauge railroad was built connecting all the mines just south of Douglas including those of the Treadwell Complex. The rail was used to haul men and equipment back and forth as well as into town and down to the ferry docks.

Even the savage fire that swept through Douglas in 1911 did not keep the town down. Douglas was the home to 15,000 miners in 1915.

The Treadwell Complex began running shafts under the Channel going wherever the gold veins led them. Some of the mine shafts were more than 500 feet below sea level. Treadwell pioneered deep tunneling going as far as 2400 feet into the earth with mining techniques that would later be employed in South Africa. The mines not only employed men, but teams of horses and mules pulling carts of ore and debris from below ground. More than 960 stamps were in continuous operation, sometimes with deafening effects in Douglas, Juneau, and Thane.

Treadwell provided its employees a $100 a month salary, among the highest wages earned in the world then, a medical health plan, a swimming pool, Turkish baths, tennis courts, a bowling alley, a gymnasium, and a 15,000-volume library. Miners were brought over from their homes in Juneau and Thane by a fleet of small ferry boats, one of them being the noted *Lone Fisherman*. Mine tailings dumped into the Channel eventually formed Douglas' Sandy Beach. Here vessels in need of repair were beached and refurbished.

The Treadwell Mine Complex was a city onto itself. Its general store was better stocked than those in neighboring Douglas with its own butcher shop, wide assortments of teas, sweets, and fresh fruit such as bananas. The complex boasted of electric lights, a wall telephone, and dining halls that seated 300 miners at a time with rolled napkins, fresh flowers, and tablecloths.

But Treadwell had also gained a reputation for having one accidental death per day when it first began operations. The Glory Hole was given its name because so many workers were sent "on the road to glory" in the open pit mine. A third of the miners' salaries were deducted to pay for room and board which led to strikes in 1907 and 1908.

Treadwell became the world's largest low-grade gold mine. With 2,000 men on payroll, it produced $68 million in gold while the rest of the mines in the Juneau-Douglas region were producing a mere $4 million. A hundred tons of gold were mined out of the Treadwell Complex making it the second greatest producer of gold in Alaska to date.

All this activity had its effects on Douglas. The 1910 census showed that Douglas had become the largest community in Southeast Alaska, larger than her sister community of Juneau across the Channel.

Prosperity came to an end on April 21, 1917.

Geological shifts were noted underground in 1909 and 1913. Management realized Treadwell's production was beginning to decline in 1916 and ordered "pillar robbery," the mining of untouched ore in the pillars supporting the roof to take place.

On April 21, the ceiling of the mine began collapsing forming a sink hole that devoured the gymnasium, the swimming pool, and the fire hall. It was suddenly discovered that the sink hole was below the high tide line. A frantic evacuation ensued before the tide came in. Only one man was reported missing, and he was later found in a nearby tavern. Twelve horses and a mule were lost as sea water filled the shafts running under the Channel.

One mine was spared the flooding, the Ready Bullion, which stayed in operation until December 1922 employing 500 miners before it petered out.

Eight years after the closing of the Ready Bullion, Douglas had a mere population of 593 with residents now crossing the Channel working for the Alaska Juneau mining firm. A smaller Douglas contained a Native school, a school for white children, and a high school. A salmon cannery and the Alaska Juneau foundry were located in Douglas. The foundry was Douglas' main employer producing 65 tons of iron, 32 tons of steel, and a ton of brass each month. A major portion of the business district was consumed by a 1937 fire.

After skis were used in winter for the laying of transmission lines through the island's mountainous interior, the Forest Service built a four-mile ski run on the island that became an attraction bringing some business to Douglas.

The struggle for Douglas to maintain its own identity began with the construction of the Douglas Bridge over the Channel in October 1932. On the island side of the bridge, housing soon went up creating West Juneau. Lawson Creek was recognized as where West Juneau ended and Douglas began.

Douglas continued to hang on to its identity, refusing to be swallowed up by the much larger Juneau. Her high school basketball team, the Douglas Huskies defeated the Juneau Crimson Bears by one point, 47-46, to win the Southeastern championship in 1952. But, even then, it was becoming apparent that from a financial standpoint, the school systems should merge into one.

Douglas fought hard against it. A region wide vote for merging the schools carried due to West Juneau voting in favor. Douglas High School was closed as students were transported over the Douglas Bridge to a new Juneau-Douglas High School.

Douglas began losing its identity as a separate community in 1970 when its residents agreed to be part of the City and Borough of Juneau.

But Douglas as a community began making a comeback in 1979 when Molly Smith organized the Perseverance Theater in downtown

Douglas. The town soon was drawing people who wanted to sample the small-town Alaskan lifestyle with the Douglas Cafe and Louie's Douglas Inn Bar. Perseverance Theater became Alaska's flagship theater producing more than 60 plays, many by Alaskan playwrights.

Though Douglas Island has a population of 5,000; there are 2,000 living in the town itself. The rest are in West Juneau or scattered throughout the island.

HAINES

Stone tools uncovered at nearby Ground Hog Bay date back some 10,000 years demonstrating that the Chilkat Peninsula was on a migratory route into North America.

The Chilkats had four villages around Deshu, the original site of Haines; Klukwan, Klaktu'h three miles downstream from Klukwan, Yindes-tuk-ki where the Chilkat River empties into its inlet and Chilkoot (The North Wind Does Not Strike Here) on the shore of Chilkoot Lake. Klukwan is considered the original village for the Chilkats.

Traditionally, Natives living west of the Chilkat River called themselves Chilkats while Natives east of the river were known as Chilkoots.

The Chilkats had competing trails into the Interior with the Chilkoots for trade. Other tribes were not allowed on these trade routes. The clans were often at war over the Chilkat monopoly.

The Chilkats were strikingly different from other Tlingits. They did not build their villages near the ocean. They depended on game rather than fish.

The arrival of whites only meant new customers for the Chilkat trade with Interior tribes. Guns, copper plate, iron tools, cloth, blankets, food, and whiskey were hoisted onto the backs of porters for the steep climbs over the passes. The most valuable trade commodity they transported was eulachon oil from candle fish. Thus, these trade routes became known as "grease trails." The porters returned with huge bundles of furs strapped to their backs.

Interior tribes, including the Teslin and Atlin Tlingits, regularly ran out of food and needed this connection to the bounty Southeast Alaska possessed.

Prized throughout the Pacific Northwest and the Interior were Chilkat blankets.

Chilkat blankets were weaved from the wool of three to ten mountain goats, the inner side made from yellow cedar and sinew. A loom, consisting of two upright poles, held a narrow piece of skin. Cedar covered with wool was hung and bound together by wool threads. A black dye made from alder bark was added along with green dyes made from lichen and a bluish green created from copper ore. In the central part of the blanket a totemic figure was traditionally placed while the rest of the design was left to the creator's imagination.

The blankets were used for ceremonial dances and for funerals.

Tlingit legends claim the concept of the Chilkat blanket goes back to a time when animals could remove their skins at will.

A girl came across a handsome stranger as she was returning from gathering wild celery. She went with him to be his wife, but soon found he was in reality a grizzly bear, and that his other wife was a lynx. She watched as the lynx wife weaved a blanket skin for herself. She eventually learned from the lynx wife how the blanket skin was made.

One day the Great Raven visited the home. He was given the blanket skin as a gift, which in turn he gave as a gift to his people, the Tlingits.

Thus, the concept of the Chilkat blanket was born.

Early Chilkat contact

In 1794, English Lt. James Whidbey with the Vancouver Expedition explored Lynn Canal. Whidbey had a confrontation with Chilkats armed with brass blunderbuss, a telescope, and a trumpet. When the Chilkats got the worse end of the fight, they tried luring the party onto shore by having a nude woman stand on the beach. The ploy failed. Whidbey named the spot Seduction Point.

On April 21, 1811, Captain Samuel Hill with the Boston brig *Otter* sailed into trade and had to fight his way out. The cluster of villages was the northern terminus for the Hudson Bay trading ship, the *Beaver*, the first steam ship to operate in the North Pacific. She traded with the Chilkats until 1865. Two years later, after the U.S. purchase of Alaska, regular monthly boat service was established between the Chilkats and Sitka.

The tribes' reputation for violence against outsiders was beginning to wane. George Davidson with the US Coast and Geodetic Survey visited in 1869 to study a total solar eclipse without incident. The first American governor for Alaska, General Jefferson Davis, persuaded the Chilkats to carry mail into the Interior to Hudson Bay posts.

Edmund Bean and a party of miners located the Chilkat Pass in 1880. German scientist Aurel Krause studied the Chilkats in 1882 and was permitted to use the Chilkat Trail into the Interior. Lt. Frederick Schwatka in 1883 hired Chilkats to carry his supplies over Chilkoot Pass to the source of the Yukon River.

S. Hall Young and John Muir sailed into the land of the Chilkats in the fall of 1879 hoping to set up a mission. Excited, Chilkats carried their canoe from shore to the clan house of Chief Don-na-wuk, known as Silver Eye. He had been given spectacles years earlier by a Russian officer. Muir and Young were feasted through the night. The next day Young began reading the Bible to them. The Chilkats agreed to allow a mission at Deshu (End of the Trail) because it would give them added status among the Tlingits and the education provided by the mission would help them in dealing with white traders.

The Northwest Trading Company had also decided to open a post at Deshu under the management of George Dickinson. His native wife, Sarah, had obtained an education in Portland and was now teaching at the Wrangell Mission School. Young immediately appointed Sarah as the new teacher for the mission. A room at the trading post was set aside as a school.

The Haines Mission

Denied funds by the Mission Board of the Presbyterian Church, Sheldon Jackson obtained a personal loan to send Rev. Eugene S. Willard and his wife and daughter to Deshu. Dickinson disliked the Willards and refused to sell them supplies or even use the company ship to obtain supplies. For nine years they relied on the Chilkats for food until a child died, they had tried to save. The Chilkats blamed them for the child's death and stopped selling them food as well. The Willards finally had to leave.

Jackson then renamed the town Haines after Mrs. Francina E Haines, secretary of the Women's Executive Committee for Home Missions.

She had crusaded within the board circles of the church for reimbursement of the personal loan Jackson had taken out for the Willard family move. A local post office opened in 1882, and by 1884, began using her name for the town. It was now handling mail not only for the mission and the trading post, but for two canneries now in operation. Haines had a white population of twenty.

The Porcupine Gold Rush

Jack Dalton, from the Cherokee Strip of Oklahoma, arrived around 1886 putting together a trade route from the cannery docks near Haines inland for 246 miles to Fort Selkirk on the Yukon River.

While following the Dalton Trail to the Klondike, Silva Mix, Ed Finley, and Perry Wiley hit a gold strike on Porcupine Creek, 36 miles inland, on October 10, 1898. It started a small gold rush under the shadow of the much larger one taking place in the Klondike.

Twelve days later the Porcupine Gold District was officially organized.

Dalton saw an opportunity. He received a federal license to operate a toll road in 1899 with fees ranging from a dollar for foot passengers to $2.50 for each horse. Chilkat packers could use the toll road free of charge.

The town of Porcupine was laid out covering 150 acres with a population of 200. Dalton opened a store there, but he had competition. Besides a post office, the new town had four saloons, a three-story hotel, a sawmill, and a general store owned by the Porcupine Trading Company.

In spite of the saloons, Porcupine was still a lonely place.

Five miners ran an advertisement in the *Seattle Times* on January 4, 1899, looking for wives.

There is a sudden demand for women at Chilcat and is a great chance and one that should not be overlooked by Seattle old maids.

The first applicant for a wife was J.C. Brown who simply posted a description of his two mining claims and noted he was not particular how the woman looked as long as she was "nice."

Within two years, Dalton brought in heavy equipment into the Porcupine District. He also bought into the Porcupine Trading Company which in turn constructed a thousand-foot-long wooden flume and created an artificial lake by damming the Porcupine. Soon two rival mining companies were at work, the McKinley Creek Mining Company and the Cahoon Creek Mining Company. Both were accused of conducting petty sabotage on the other including rolling boulders down the Cahoon Creek flume.

Then in 1905, the Porcupine was struck by a major flood. Most of the infrastructure was demolished. A new firm, the Porcupine Mining Company sawed two million board feet for an 8,000-foot flume that was 40 feet wide in places. A 1915 flood destroyed it.

August Fritsche bought up most of the property claims in 1926. A decade of gold clean up produced $1.7 million before Fritsche died in 1936. The claims then reverted back to smaller operators.

The 1905 Flood brought an end to Dalton's connections with Alaska. He left moderately wealthy. He went on to British Guiana (today's Guyana) opening diamond mines. He died in San Francisco in 1944 at age 89.

Small scale gold mining is still active in the Porcupine District.

When Jo Jurgeleit, a peg-legged miner who worked a claim in the Porcupine District, died in 2002 at age 91, she had already been featured in National Geographic. Living in a corrugated metal roof house near Haines, when she became ill, she received a get-well card from billionaire J. Paul Getty. Jurgeleit was a symbol of the independent, small mining operator now working the Porcupine District.

The Moore family comes to Haines

Meanwhile, the Northwest Trading Company opened a cannery at Chilkat Inlet. Canneries were also opened at Pyramid Harbor and near Chilkoot.

Bernard Moore, Billy Moore's son of Skagway fame, married Klinget-sai-yet, daughter of Shathitch of the Klukwans in a Tlingit ceremony. The Willards gave the Moores a Christian wedding in Juneau for the sake of legalities.

John Healy from Dyea opened a second trading post in Haines. Sol Ripinsky opened a third. F H Poindexter of the Chilkat Cannery Company was selected as justice of the peace with Healy as town marshal.

The Dalton Trail caused Haines to grow acting as a third supply point for gold prospectors after Skagway and Dyea. Haines was incorporated as a city in 1910, but by then, its population had declined, losing freighting business to the White Pass and Yukon Railway operating out of Skagway in 1900.

The original surveyor's site for Haines was found beneath the Harbor Bar when they renovated the establishment.

Around 1900, Charles Anway won international fame for a giant hybrid strawberry called Burbank. A strawberry festival was held annually until it evolved into today's Southeast Alaska State Fair.

Boundary dispute

The Canadians pushed hard for ownership of Haines during talks with the United States over the disputed Alaskan border. The border had always been vague. In 1871, the Dominion of Canada requested a survey of the border after British Columbia joined the Confederation, but the U.S. rejected the notion.

The Canadians felt an urgency to settle the border issue once gold was found in the Klondike. Canadian citizens were being chased out of Haines and prevented from making land claims. In 1898, the U.S. and Canada came to a compromise for the border only to have it rejected by British Columbia. Then President William McKinley suggested that the Canadians and British Columbia have a permanent lease port near Haines, but that offer was rejected.

The Hay-Herbert Treaty of 1903 declared that the border would be settled through a six-member tribunal made up of three Americans, two Canadians, and one British representative.

During the talks, the Canadians stated they would give up their claims to Skagway in exchange for Haines. Worried, the United States quickly selected Haines as the site for the planned Fort William Seward. The military post was built in 1904 on land donated by the Haines Mission.

Troops were transferred over from Camp Skagway. The 400 officers and men soon found their duty at the post summed up as "practice plow, and parade." Only once were the troops called into action. Alaska's governor in 1907 ordered them to intervene with a strike at the Treadwell mines in Douglas.

Finally, under President Theodore Roosevelt, the current border was accepted in a four to two vote by the tribunal; Britain's representative sided with the U.S. in the dispute.

The fort was later renamed the Chilkoot Barracks in 1922. It was in Hotel Halsingland, then, the commanding officers' quarters, that Elinor Dusenbury, author of Alaska's state song "Alaska's Flag," once lived.

Two military ships, *Peterson* and *Captain James Fornance*, allowed Haines residents to ride free between Haines and Juneau as the two 125-foot crafts hauled freight, mail, and military personnel on leave.

With a military post nearby and thirsty Alaskans, Lu LaMoore opened what later became the Bamboo Room and Pioneer Bar. It served as a combination bar, brothel, and bootlegger operation during Prohibition.

By 1939, Haines had a population of 344 primarily servicing the various gold camps of the Porcupine District. Freighters used the fort's dock facilities for off-loading cargo. Fur farming was a large part of the local economy. Schools were segregated between Whites and Natives with the Presbyterian mission maintaining an orphanage for Native children.

World War II

The war saw the construction of the Haines Highway in 1943 connecting Haines with the Alaska Highway. It was restricted to military use only until it was opened to the public after the war. Fort William Seward was the staging area for construction of the Haines Highway upon the arrival of 1500 African American troops in November 1942. The highway itself was a successful attempt to relieve some of the congestion away from the Skagway docks where supplies and equipment for building the Alaska Highway were piling up.

Designated a foreign duty post, the U.S. Army closed Fort William Seward in 1945. Private citizens then raised the money buying the fort in 1946. They christened it Port Chilkoot and attempted to make it a cooperative community of 200 families. As a port, the founders hoped it would compete with Skagway for shipping goods into the Yukon Territory. When that plan failed, residents organized the city of Port Chilkoot with their own mayor and city council in 1956. They remained a separate town until 1970 when they finally merged with Haines.

Birthplace of the Alaska Marine Highway System

The Alaska Marine Highway traces its roots to Haines.

Steve Homer, Robert Sommers, and Ray Gelotte began operating a converted LCT-Mark 6 landing craft in 1948 they dubbed the *MV Chilkoot*. For three years, they hauled freight, passengers, and vehicles between Haines and Tee Harbor, a minor port for Juneau. The Territory of Alaska bought their business in 1951. The *Chilkoot* continued operating until 1957 when it was replaced by the *M/V Chilkat*. This one craft was the entire Alaska Marine Highway fleet up to 1963. The *Chilkat* eventually found its way to Seldovia, a thousand miles to the west.

Currently, the Juneau-Haines-Skagway portion of the Alaska Marine Highway ferry system is the only profitable section of the entire system.

In 1972, the former military post office was designated a national historic site and the name Fort William Seward was restored. That same year the last of the original canneries was closed due to a decline in fish stocks. The fort was designated a National Historic Landmark in 1976 and a number of barracks, officer housing, and the parade grounds are maintained though the complex is under private ownership. Several of the structures are leased out to businesses and restaurants.

A timber boom took place in Haines in the early 1970s, but it did not last long. The sawmills were closed in 1976.

With a collection of used dairy equipment from Minnesota as well as a homemade kettle, Paul Wheeler opened the Haines Brewing Company in 1996, Alaska's oldest and smallest brewery.

Walt Disney Films came to Haines in 2000 building sets for the filming of *White Fang*. Afterwards, a dozen structures with the look and feel of the Klondike Gold Rush were incorporated into the local fairgrounds. The fairgrounds are the site for the Southeast Alaska State Fair.

Haines is the home for the Alaska Indian Arts housed in Fort William Seward's restored hospital with its renown Chilkat Dancers, the Sheldon Museum and Cultural Center, and the Hammer Museum, dedicated to the history of the hammer in human society. The unusual museum houses more than 1800 hammers including a Roman battle hammer. Nearby Davidson Glacier has become the site for heli-skiing adventurers.

In 2002, the Haines Borough was created taking in both Haines and surrounding communities such as Porcupine and the two Tlingit villages of Chilkoot and Chilkat in Klukwan.

The nearby Chilkat Bald Eagle Preserve is home to the world's largest concentration of bald eagles feeding from hot spring-fed rivers. Established in 1982, the 48,000-acre preserve is the home to nearly 3,000 bald eagles.

Haines received some notoriety from local author Heather Lende's book *If You Lived Here I'd Know Your Name* (2005) portraying life in Haines. She wrote it while in a Seattle nursing home recovering from injuries she received in Haines after being run over by a truck while riding her bicycle.

Haines is noted for its unusual climate. Unlike the rest of Southeast Alaska, Haines is classified as having a much drier and warmer humid continental climate. Summer temperatures have reached 98 degrees Fahrenheit. That has not affected snow fall, however. Haines saw 309 inches of snow during the winter of 2007 and 360 inches of snow during the winter of 2012.

Discovery Channel's reality program *Gold Rush* was filmed in Haines and nearby Porcupine Creek.

SKAGWAY

Few Alaskan towns are draped in as much myth and legend as Skagway. Its very name conjures up prospectors, gunfights, and a true Alaska.

There will be those who will tell you gold made Skagway. Perhaps, but that is not the reason Skagway exists today. Gold made Dyea too and today there is hardly anything left of Skagway's sister city only a few miles away. What made Skagway and saved Skagway was the railroad.

The name Skagua is Tlingit for the Place of the North Wind.

Captain Billy Moore

Skagway was the brainchild of Captain William Moore. He came to the United States from Germany in 1822 and served in the Navy during the Mexican War. From Mexico, he tried finding his own gold in California in 1851 and then to the Queen Charlotte Islands when gold was discovered there. He was briefly in Peru before returning to British North America to participate in the Caribou Country Gold Rush in British Columbia.

A person with energy, Moore was always building and sailing steamships. He participated in the Cassiar Stampede. Failing to find color, he turned to what he knew—steamboats. He piloted men and supplies up the Stikine river from Wrangell making a fortune. He and his family lived in grand style in a beautiful home in Victoria, British Columbia. But his money ran out when Cassiar gold ran out.

Down on his luck, William Ogilvie hired him to be part of the surveying party going into the District of the Yukon. Ogilvie felt Moore's knowledge of boats might prove useful once they reached the little-known Yukon River.

Moore heard of a pass near the Skaguay river. Oglivie had taken his men up the Dyea Trail and through the Chilkoot Pass to reach the Yukon. When Moore told the Canadian official of the possibility of another pass, Ogilvie sent him to investigate. The 65-year-old German adventurer followed the Skaguay river up into the Coastal Range through a pass that was less difficult and lower than the Chilkoot. Moore named the pass, White Pass, in honor of the Canadian Interior Minister, Thomas White.

For the remainder of the journey in the Yukon, Moore kept telling Ogilvie that they were in gold country. And the logical place for a port to serve this new country was at the mouth of the Skaguay river at the base of White Pass. Ogilvie told Moore he was too old for such dreams.

But, on October 27, 1887, with his youngest son Bernard, Moore landed at the mouth of the Skaguay with tools and supplies to begin homesteading. They left mid-November, but they got their 160-acre homestead started. For nine years, the Moore family made improvements such as a wharf and a family cabin. Moore laid out streets calling the place Mooresville.

Since the Lynn Canal was in disputed territory, he filed title to his land with the U.S. office in Sitka and with the Canadian government.

In February 1895, his son Bernard persuaded seven prospectors traveling together into the Yukon to take the White Pass route. The party transported five tons of equipment over the pass without major problems.

Moore soon secured financial backing in 1896 to develop Mooresville pointing out to investors the site's deep-water harbor in contrast to the mud flat approaches of Dyea. Though now 74 years old, Moore won the mail contract from Juneau to the town of Fortymile in the Yukon from the Canadian government. His contract called for at least three round trips of fifteen hundred miles each during the summer of 1896. A round trip usually took him or Bernard fifty-one days.

Moore found Fortymile, a ghost town, when he arrived in early September with the mail. Even the Mounties stationed there were gone. They had taken their official leave to join other prospectors tearing up the land along Klondike Creek in a frenzy. Moore realized what had just happened. He stood to profit from his 160-acre waterfront homestead. Still, he found he was going to have to compete with Dyea established by former Montana lawman John Healy.

The Chilkoot Trail was more difficult but was only twenty-five miles long as opposed to the forty mile long White Pass Trail. Many preferred the Chilkoot due to swamps along the White Pass trail once one crossed the mountains.

Fifteen miles out from Dyea, the Chilkoot Trail follows a narrow valley crossing a river fifteen times. At timber line, another town began growing up, Sheep Camp. From Sheep Camp, it was another six and a half hours with 1500 steps cut into the ice as prospectors carried the one ton of supplies required by the Northwest Mounted Police before being allowed to cross the summit into Canada.

Sheep Camp was the site of the Palm Sunday avalanche in April 1898 when over fifty prospectors were buried in a snow slide that covered ten acres and in many spots was 30 feet deep.

Dyea rivaled Skagway in size and importance and made Healy a very wealthy man. The town's population ranged anywhere from 5,000 to 8,000, milling around some 150 business that ranged from attorneys to undertakers along with saloons, barber shops, a hospital, restaurants, and at the time, Alaska's largest brewery.

But Mooreville saw the first stampeders.

The White Pass and Mooresville

When the first ship with gold seekers arrived off Dyea on July 31, 1897, Healy's men told them the Chilkoot was closed due to a summer snowstorm. Instead of returning south, the ship docked at Mooresville. Moore and his son helped offload seventy-five tons of cargo in twenty four hours as a gale struck the Lynn Canal. Moore had built his wharf into the face of a rock cliff with no connecting road to the valley.

Now with the cargo off, Moore transported it by boat to the beach charging a dollar a ton.

The prospectors learned more disheartening news. It would take more than forty days to transport their heavy loads from Skaguay to Lake Bennett where the Yukon River flowed from. By the time they reached the lake, it would be frozen over. They had the choice of try beating the freeze or camp the winter in Mooresville.

Eleven days later, Mooresville had four hundred people living in one hundred tents. Despite lawsuits filed in Sitka by Bernard, people began staking out lots on Moore's land asserting squatter's rights. Because of a shorter turnaround time, more ships selected Mooresville over Dyea to drop off their human cargo.

Within only a few weeks, saloons, dry goods stores, and offices sprang up to serve the estimated 8,000 temporary residents of Skagway. A thousand prospectors were passing through the port to the White Pass every week.

A city council was elected. Taxes were levied. Frank Reid was empowered to start surveying off city lots to be sold at five dollars apiece. Corner lots sold for ten dollars. Reid had been a surveyor for the City of Bellingham, Wash., and had stolen the city's surveying equipment when he went north.

Dr. H. B. Runnals set up a private post office using the name Skagway, a corruption of the Skaguay River. The U.S. Postal Service adopted Runnals' post office and its name, never using Mooresville.

The Outlaw Soapy Smith

Skagway with its teaming transient population seemed ideal for Old West outlaw Jefferson "Soapy" Smith.

Finding Skagway lawless, Soapy and his men took full advantage.

At first, he simply had his men rob people in town and along the trail. He took over some of the more lucrative saloons. A vigilance committee was organized when two men, including the local town marshal named Rowan, were gunned down. The killer was a known member of the Smith gang. Smith sent his men away until the situation calmed down.

Committee members moved on into the Klondike. Soon Soapy was back in business. Murders began taking place again. When two murders—one on the docks and one along the trail—occurred at the same time, citizens like Frank Reid organized the Citizen's Committee of 101.

But they did not have the law behind them. The U.S. Marshall and the town's prominent newspaper, *Daily Alaskan*, were part of Smith's growing criminal empire. After the Committee made a few saloon raids, Soapy posted an announcement on the wall of the Pack Train Saloon. "We, the people of Skagway are running this town to suit ourselves. The committee can go to hell."

By now Soapy had a system in place. News reporters working for his paper would interview people as they got off the boats. Those who seemed to have money were identified. Smith's cronies ran a series of confidence schemes to separate newcomers from their funds. When that did not work, Soapy stationed men along the trail to ambush and rob.

On the other hand, Smith gave financial assistance to the widows his men created, bought would be millionaires who had lost everything a one-way ticket southbound, and organized a charity for the ownerless dogs roaming the streets of the town.

He justified his actions in a comment saying the North was about the survival of the fittest. If a man could not protect himself in Skagway, how could he protect himself in Dawson? It was best a person found that out here where one had the means of getting back home rather than along a lonely trail in the Yukon wilderness.

The killing of Soapy Smith

Smith's prominence peaked during Skagway's Fourth of July celebration in 1898. Playing host to Governor John Brady, Smith led the procession on horseback.

Three days later a prospector arrived named J. D. Stewart from the Yukon seeking passage on a steamer home. He deposited some $2,700 in the safe at Kaufman Brothers clothing store. Stewart then walked into one of Smith's saloons. There "Old Man Tripp," one of Smith's shills, got Stewart involved in a card game. Winning, Stewart ran back to the clothing store getting the rest of his money.

The Smith gang claimed Stewart came back and lost the entire amount in a card game. Stewart, however, told everyone that the gold was yanked from his hand by a thief who ran out of the saloon with it.

Skagway's merchants had enough. The town's reputation for murder and stealing was already causing many leaving the Klondike to either go down the Yukon River to Saint Michael or cross the Chilkoot Trail for Dyea. Both were preferred rather than brave the gauntlet of Smith men in Skagway. Smith was even interfering with the construction of the White Pass and Yukon Railroad under the direction of Michael Heney.

First Stewart went to the town marshal who brushed him away. Then Stewart went to Dyea to tell his story to United States Commissioner C. H. Sehlbrede. Sehlbrede in turn advised Smith to see the money returned, warning there was a growing public anger over the incident. Smith refused.

Reid confronted Smith on July 7th asking what he was going to do about Stewart's complaint. Smith said nothing, and if he didn't like it, he could step into the street and face him. Reid walked off.

It was decided that a general meeting would be held after dinner at the Skagway wharf on State Street. Reid, J. M. "Sid" Tanner, and two others were appointed to guard the approaches to the wharf so the meeting would not be disrupted. Smith was reported to have a hundred-armed men.

Drinking all day, Smith took a few of his men and headed for the wharf. Several warned him not to go.

Leading far ahead of his men, Smith walked towards the meeting only to be challenged by Reid. Sporting a .44 Winchester, Smith told Reid to get out of his way. When Reid blocked his way, Smith tried hitting him with the barrel of the rifle. Reid knocked the barrel aside while firing his pistol. The first shot from Reid was a misfire with a second shot hitting Smith in the leg. Smith got off his only shot as Reid fired a third time. Reid hit Soapy in the heart while Smith's bullet struck Reid in the groin.

However, rumor had it that it had been Jesse Murphy firing from a hidden location who had killed Soapy Smith. Railroad bosses may have wanted Smith's control of the town to end.

Tanner and others rushed up with Smith lying dead and Reid down lying in his own blood shouting "I got the son of a bitch. I got the son of a bitch." Reid was carried to a doctor's office where he died a few days later.

Tanner and his men arrested twenty-six members of the Smith gang sending thirteen, including the marshal, to Sitka to stand before a grand jury. Stewart got his gold back. In appreciation, he had a solid gold lawman's badge made for Tanner.

There was much talk about simply kicking Smith's body into the sea. But a Christian burial was arranged for the outlaw with only three in attendance.

Reid's funeral in contrast was an elaborate affair topped by the laying of a marble slab over the grave site with the inscription reading: "He gave his life for the honor of Skagway."

Railroad town

With Smith gone Skagway grew. Within three months of the shooting, the community could boast of fifteen general stores, nineteen restaurants, four meat markets, eleven feed yards, six drugstores, a bowling alley, a sawmill, eleven saloons, six lumberyards, nine hotels, five hardware stores, two shoemakers, eight bakeries, three furniture stores, seven doctors, six lawyers, two barber shops, three laundries, ten grocery stores, and four clothing stores.

Much of this growth was due to Mike Heney employing some 35,000 men in constructing the White Pass and Yukon Railway. By July 1899, Heney was able to ship half a million in gold into Skagway. On July 29, 1900, the 110-mile rail line reached Whitehorse at the cost of $10 million and 450 tons of explosives.

Heney's railroad killed Dyea. With rails now going over White Pass, the torturous Chilkoot Trail was abandoned. Dyea dried up. Its post office closed in 1902. In 1964, sole resident Emil Hanousek dubbed himself the Mayor of Dyea. He had built a house in Dyea in 1949. Ironically, his brother, Ed Hansousek, became mayor of Skagway.

Not all the women who came to Skagway in the early days were prostitutes. The Depression of the 1890s sent many single women, several being widows with children, north to the Klondike.

Ma Pullen arrived on Skagway's docks with children and no money. She hired out as a cook baking pies on the side. She was so successful with her pies that she went into business for herself. From her earnings, she sent for her three sons, horses, and supplies. She had decided to go into the freight business packing people over White Pass. But she suffered a setback when her equipment was stolen. The Smith gang may have been the culprits. She baked more pies and raised more money going back into the packing business.

Still, she knew the days of packing stampeders over the pass were numbered. Heney's railroad would be operational soon. She opened the Pullen House, a combination hotel and restaurant. With gardens and small ponds, it was one of the most elegant in the district of Alaska with fresh vegetables and dairy products brought in from farms around neighboring Dyea.

Another woman of note was Vernie Woodwards in Dyea. When the gold rush began, she chose to operate near Healey's trading post in Dyea rather than off Moore's wharf in Skagway. She backpacked supplies over the nearly vertical Chilkoot Pass when her five horses could not handle an entire order. Along this trail, a Mr. Joppe had set up a grub tent with food and lodging. There Vernie spent a considerable amount of time.

On April 3, 1898, the construction gang from the Chilkoot Tramway came running down the trail warning everyone of possible avalanches. Joppe and his partner Mueler rushed to inform prospectors camped above Sheep Camp. The two began guiding people out along a rope line. They had gone just a quarter of a mile when a wall of snow came down hitting them.

The force of the impact knocked Mueler into the safety of a nearby powerhouse. Next to him was Joppe's lifeless body. His body was laid in the row where the dead awaited burial.

Vernie hurried to the disaster. Mueler stated what he witnessed next was nothing short of a miracle. Vernie undid Joppe's shirt rubbing his chest and then his arms. She began breathing into his mouth, forcing air into the man's lungs. She refused to accept that Joppe was dead.

She kept this routine up for hours on end until around three in the morning when Joppe began breathing on his own. He opened his eyes looking at the large, roughhewn woman and said in a quiet voice, "Vernie."

She collapsed from exhaustion having saved his life.

Skagway grows up

In 1900 Skagway became the first Alaskan town to become incorporated, beating Juneau by one day. The newly established Alaskan courts recognized Captain Moore's homestead claims awarding him sizable damages. Most of Skagway's business district was now on Moore's original homestead.

The town's first stone structure went up housing the new McCabe College. A YMCA was formed to hold a debating club. The Skagway Literary Society and the Skagway Tennis Club were organized. Fundraisers were held in the form of masquerade balls. Now with a population of 1600, it had electricity, running water and plumbing.

The effects of dwindling gold production in the Klondike though had its effect on Skagway. By 1903, the town had only 500 residents.

The college lasted only until 1901. U.S. Army troops of Camp Skagway were housed in the Pack Train Building until they were ordered to Haines in 1904.

Residents seemed to have taken all this in stride. At age 14, Bobby Sheldon built the first automobile in Alaska and drove it in the 1905 Fourth of July parade.

The Rasmuson family opened their bank in Skagway in 1916. They pioneered branch banking in Alaska and eventually grew into the largest banking firm in the state.

Fire began claiming the old Skagway when the roundhouse and workshops of the White Pass and Yukon Railway burned down in 1932. Rebuilt, they would burn down again in 1969.

Tourism

The first tourists to come to Skagway was the Christian Endeavour group arriving on the first ship into port in 1897. Tourism began having an economic impact on the town by the mid-1920s.

The first heavy promotion of Skagway and that of Soapy Smith is credited to Martin Itjen in the 1930s.

He converted an old Ford bus into a tour wagon, even rigging a mechanical Soapy to salute visitors as they drove by. Itjen bought Jeff's Parlor transforming it into a Soapy Smith Museum. In 1935, he shipped the bus and the mechanical Soapy to Hollywood trying to drum up interest in Skagway. He ended up posing with actress Mae West. He published a book in 1939 titled *The Story of the Tour on the Skagway, Alaska Streetcar* which went into detail on the Soapy Smith shootout.

Hollywood always wanted to film the story of Soapy Smith, but every time it was attempted, the studio in question faced a lawsuit from his son Jefferson Randolph Smith III then living in St. Louis. His first lawsuit was in 1919 over the movie *The Girl Alaska* which was filmed in Skagway. Both *Honky Tonk* with Clark Gable in 1941 and *The Far Country* with James Stewart in 1955 had to be rewritten due to fear of litigation.

Itjen was not the only one trying to gain fame for Skagway through Soapy Smith. The local chapter of the Eagle held dances in the1920s to raise funds for the local hockey team. Local actors from the show slowly transformed it into *The Days of '98 Show* about the shooting of Soapy. Funds from the program are used for improvements to historical structures, scholarships, and for monies to local charities in Skagway.

The town was also being promoted as the "Garden City of Alaska." The town had its first city wide gardening contest in 1902. A 1905 railway brochure on Skagway highlighted its flowers, trimmed lawns, and prolific gardens. Local jeweler Herman Kirmse soon began sponsoring an annual gardening contest. The contest and Skagway's gardens captured national attention. It sent flowers to the 1909 Alaska-Yukon Expo held in Seattle. The Blanchard Garden with its photographed dahlias, sweet peas, begonias, geraniums, pansies, and nasturtiums was the most famous of the group. In 1929 the garden produced the world's largest dahlia.

World War II

Most of the gardens were abandoned during World War II when the city was overrun by 3,000 U.S. Army troops for the construction of the Alaska Highway. Army barracks were scattered all over the small town. The railway was relocated off Broadway so that some 20 trains could run per day over the pass.

The Army took over the duties of fire protection without much success as fires damaged major landmarks during the war years. However, the U.S. Army is given credit for having prevented Skagway from being destroyed by floods from the Skagway River in 1943 and 1944.

Still, the town of Skagway presented the War Department with a bill of $177,500 for damages due to military occupation of the town.

Reverend G. Edgar Gallant opened a boarding school for Native children, St. Pius X Mission, in 1933. During the war, student enrollment doubled to 80 and high school classes were added. The school eventually closed in 1959 though services were held in the building up to the 1970s. A fire destroyed the structure in 1985.

Shortly after the war, it looked like Dyea was going to come back to life again through the efforts of ALCOA (Aluminum Company of America). The corporation laid out a plan in 1952 to reverse the flow of the Yukon River by way of a dam at Whitehorse. Water would have been diverted from the lakes formed by the dam through two tunnels down the Chilkoot Trail to Dyea where a massive $400 million smelter would be constructed. It was forecasted that Dyea would eventually have a population of 20,000 rivaling Juneau, and possibly Fairbanks, in size.

However, ALCOA failed to win over Canadian officials who nixed the project in 1953.

Skagway sustained major damage in 1967 when the Skagway River breached its dikes during a flood. The White Pass and Yukon rail line suspended passenger service in 1982 only to reinstate it in 1988. In 1994, the railway won designation as on International Historic Civil Engineering Landmark.

That same year the city dock collapsed creating a small tidal wave that destroyed the state ferry dock killing one worker. Five years later, the White Pass and Yukon Railway settled with the state for damages caused by the dock's collapse at the cost of $1.8 million.

The Klondike Highway to Dawson opened in 1979 costing $14.4 million for the U.S. side and $12.2 million on the Canadian side.

Unlike other Southeast Alaska communities, Skagway has no fishing fleet nor canneries nor pulp mills.

Though Skagway today serves as a rail terminus for Yukon mines with lead, zinc, and copper loads coming in from the Interior, summer tourism is the major source of revenue. An average of a million tourists visits the town each summer. A 1999 Economic Impact Study concluded that more than 51 percent of all businesses were not owned by year around residents.

In 2007, the municipal government was dissolved and replaced with a borough government.

The Red Onion and other sights

Home to the Klondike Gold Rush National Historical Park, created in1976, Skagway's historical district has 100 buildings from the gold rush era.

One of the most prominent landmarks from this era is the Red Onion Saloon. The combination saloon and bordello opened in 1898. The second floor was made up of ten small cribs, ten feet by ten feet, with three exists. Among the famous women who worked the second floor was Klondike Kate.

In 1914, the Red Onion was moved from the corner of Sixth and State streets to where it is located today using one lone horse. Surprisingly enough, the front and back of the Onion had to be removed to switch them around. The establishment had been dragged to its location backwards.

The Red Onion's history in many ways reflects modern Skagway. During World War II, the structure was a troop barracks after which it became a laundry, a bakery, a union hall, a television station and finally a gift shop. Jan Wrentmore reverted the building back into the Red Onion in 1980.

The Arctic Brotherhood Hall is one of the most photographed structures in Skagway. The Arctic Brotherhood was organized aboard the *City of Seattle* as it approached Skagway on February 26, 1899. Their motto was "No Boundary Here."

The hall was built the same year the AB was organized. Charley Walker and other lodge members collected 8,800 sticks of driftwood and nailed them to the front in 1900 to give it today's appearance. The Brotherhood entertained President Warren G. Harding within its walls when he came to Alaska in 1923.

The White Pass and Yukon Route operates a narrow-gauge train in the summer for the tourist trade. When built, Mike Heney's railroad was the most northern on the continent. It still has one of the steepest grades on the continent climbing 2,885 feet in 20 miles as it approaches White Pass.

Dyea still is a destination for hikers who wish to walk the Chilkoot Trail over 3,739-foot Chilkoot pass to Lake Bennett. The trail attracts around 3,000 hikers each year.

HOONAH

THE NORTHERN REACHES OF THE INSIDE Passage contain the Tlingit's largest village, Hoonah, home of four Huna clans.

British explorer George Vancouver charted the area in 1794 finding the Huna living in twelve fortified villages along Icy Straits vigilant of possible attack from nearby Chilkats and Auks. The largest of these "forts" was Hoonah. Originally the village was called Gaawt'ak.aan meaning "village by the cliff." The name changed over time to Huniyaa meaning "in the lee of the north wind." Huniyaa transformed into Huna.

Clan warfare between the Huna and their neighbors were brutal and savage as a classic attack by the Huna on the Chilkats underscored.

Because of a poor salmon season, Hunas planned to attack the Chilkat for their salmon. The Chilkats offered the approaching Huna warriors' food as a gesture of friendship which the Huna accepted. Then, after taking the Chilkat gift, the Huna launched an attack anyway. The Chilkats defeated the Huna warriors. They then beheaded their Huna captives throwing the decapitated bodies off a rock cliff near present day Klukwan.

Even after the American purchase, the Huna ranged far and wide. A young Army lieutenant, part time poet, part time adventurer, Charles Erskine Scott Wood, reported running into Huna canoes heading north toward Yakutat to harvest potatoes in the summer of 1877. Wood and his party took shelter from a gale at a small Huna fishing camp along the coastal route to Yakutat a few days later.

Two years later naturalist John Muir began his detailed study of Glacier Bay. He noted that Huna hunters prowled the expanding bay taking seals and mountain goats. Glacier Bay had become the primary location of food for the surrounding Huna villages.

Looking for a site to build a trading post, the Northwest Trading Company selected Hoonah opening a store there in 1880. A Presbyterian Home Mission and school were located in Hoonah the following year. Gradually Huna from the outlying villages migrated to the larger Hoonah. Within seven years of the opening of the trading post, some 500 Huna were wintering at the community. A post office was set up in 1901. A cannery was built one mile north of town in 1912, the Hoonah Packing Company. Hoonah Packing canned an astonishing 2.3 million cans of salmon in 1914 taken mostly from Icy Straits.

Elsewhere American fur farmers were seizing Huna lands around the other village sites driving the Tlingits off. With nowhere else to go, many of these displaced Huna relocated in Hoonah.

By the 1930s, Hoonah had a federal school for Natives, two general stores, two churches, two canneries, and a sawmill.

A devastating fire consumed the town in June 1944. The Coast Guard hurriedly evacuated residents to the nearby cannery, but priceless Tlingit artifacts were lost in the blaze. War time housing in transit to Hawaii was diverted to Hoonah and set up amongst the ashes of downtown. Several of these homes are still standing and are called "war houses" by locals. The federal government continued sending aid and assistance in rebuilding the community which was incorporated in 1946.

A second cannery opened during the war years. When salmon prices nose-dived in the 1970s, both canneries turned to crab.

Logging also was a mainstay of the economy with a system of logging roads webbing across the northern portion of Chichagof Island. Much of the area around Hoonah was clear cut during this time. Gradually additional communities, Whitestone Logging Camp and Game Creek, sprung up within Hoonah's municipal boundaries.

The Huna and the National Park Service became locked in an ongoing fight over the harvest of gull eggs. Gull eggs had been a traditional food source for the Huna before the purchase of Alaska by the United States. More than 9,600 eggs were collected in 1943 alone. The traditional site for collecting eggs was the Marble Islands in Glacier Bay. Huna tradition dictated that nests were to be left alone if three eggs were found, but the eggs were to be collected if the nest contained only one or two eggs.

But, in 1960, the National Park Service banned the collection of gull eggs by the Huna.

The creation of Glacier Bay National Monument in 1925, and later its expansion as it transformed into Glacier Bay National Park and Preserve in 1980, covered most of the traditional Huna lands. Hunas have labeled park regulations the "Second Ice Age." A compromise was reached whereby the Huna were allowed to collect gull eggs on Middle Pass Rock in Icy Strait. But Huna elders complained strong currents at the compromise location are a danger to children traveling along on such outings.

The Farm

Three miles southwest of Hoonah a separatist religious sect called The Move founded the community of Game Creek in 1975.

Called "The Farm," the commune is operated by Whitestone Farms (Church of the Living Word Inc) and was part of an end-time movement founded by former Florida Baptist minister Sam Fife. Preaching that the second coming of Christ was close at hand, Fife told his followers in 1971 to go out into the wilderness in order to find salvation through sinless perfection. His followers built communities in Alaska, Canada, and Colombia.

Fife died in a plane crash in Guatemala in 1979, but Game Creek has been successful enough for the movement to establish a second community by Haines. An account of life in Game Creek can be found in "Wilderness Blues," written by former commune member T.B. Botts who raised his seven children at Game Creek before being banished as a "blemish on the community."

By the early 1990s Hoonah's lodges, stores, and high school's swimming pool along with a modern harbor, boat builders, welders and mechanics made it an attractive lay over for fishermen after selling their catch to local packers. Logging was still the mainstay of the economy. So much so that the U.S. Forest Service opened a large district office in Hoonah.

But as timber prices fell and the political climate on logging changed, Hoonah began thinking of tourism. The town has always been known for its traditional Tlingit Mount Fairweather Dancers.

Point Adolphus, to the west, is a highly active feeding ground for whales as nutrients are washed out from Glacier Bay. The National Park Service counted 161 whales in 2007 in comparison to 41 whales in 1985. Taking this into account the local native corporation, Huna Totem with 1300 shareholders, purchased the historic Hoonah Packing Company cannery in 1996.

Under the leadership of Huna Totem's Bob Wysocki, the old red cannery was transformed into a historic theme tourist attraction offering shops, dining, excursions, and traditional Huna dances. Opened in 2004 and renamed Icy Strait Point, 32 cruise ships docked the first year. Within three years, 80 cruise ships docked in Hoonah. The facility itself grew to a hundred employees with a ninety percent local hire.

An incident took place during a high school basketball tournament in 2008 that underscored the character of the Hoonah community.

The Hydaburg Alaska basketball team was staying in the high school while participating in the tournament. While the team was away, someone broke into the school and stole the team's money and belongings. The next night after the Hydaburg team had finished their game, ten Hoonah elders stood up and walked across the court to the Hydaburg coach handing him $950 to make up for the loss.

However, tragedy struck Hoonah in 2010 when two police officers were killed from ambush by a local resident.

GUSTAVUS

THE MOUTH OF GLACIER BAY HAD been a fertile plain bordered to the north by a massive glacier. Here the Chookaneidi Clan (People of the Grass) built a singularly large village on a dune that rose from out of the plain. Then sometime between 285 to 210 years ago, what the Chookaneidi called the Black Glacier made a rapid advance devouring the grasslands as an ice wall marched to the sea.

The advancing glacier forced the clan to split into numerous villages as their ancestral land became entombed under thousands of tons of ice.

British explorer George Vancouver reported nothing but a wall of ice along the coast in 1794. He did find Huna summer fishing camps along the edges of the glacier ice going back for miles. The fame Glacier Bay still did not exist.

U.S. Army Lieutenant Charles Erskine Scott Wood discovered Glacier Bay in 1877. Wood had been under orders to assist in Charles Taylor's quest of scaling Mount St. Elias, then believed to be the highest mountain on the continent. After Taylor gave up and returned home, Wood returned to the area to attempt scaling the mountain himself.

His Tlingit porters abandoned him after they encountered a Ghost Bear along the foot of Mount Fairweather. Starving, Wood stumbled across a Huna village near a massive bay choked with icebergs.

Glacier Bay was just beginning to form while Wood was there. He noted the Huna villagers attached wooden false sidings and false bows to their canoes for voyaging through the ice field. The Huna chief informed Wood the bay did not exist when he was a child.

The Huna made Wood their medicine man, but the young officer made his escape back to Sitka after a patient died. He brought along his report of Glacier Bay.

Two years later, John Muir conducted an extensive scientific survey of Glacier Bay. He noted the Huna roamed the vast glacier waterway taking seals and mountain goats. Glacier Bay had become a major source of food for the Huna.

One of the interesting side effects of Muir's writings was that fact that Glacier Bay became a tourist destination by the 1880s when most of Alaska was still largely unexplored. The bay itself was given its name not by Muir or Wood, but by a Commander Beardsley in 1880.

Excursion boats then were able to sail right up to within a few hundred feet of the mammoth glaciers; in particular the 200-foot ice wall of the Muir Glacier. Then, in September 1899, one of the most powerful earthquakes to ever strike North America hit Yakutat Bay to the north. Chunks of rock and earth were raised up anywhere from 30 to 40 feet.

The Yakutat Earthquake's effects on Glacier Bay were equally impressive. It was as though the glaciers had been glass and now shattered. Where there had been clear waters, the bay was choked with ice being discharged from the surrounding glaciers. Vast quantities of ice have choked Glacier Bay ever since then.

By 1916, the principal glacier, the Grand Pacific, had receded back some 65 miles from where Vancouver had reported its face. Nowhere else in the world have glaciers been recorded retreating at such a rapid rate.

Americans did not venture in to settle until 1914 when three newly married couples started farms after just arriving in Alaska. They soon left. Three years later, Abraham Lincoln Parker arrived setting up a homestead along Good River with his wife and six children. Other homesteaders soon followed, putting in crops and raising cattle. Six canneries in the area provided seasonal employment for the homesteaders. They also sold strawberries, crops, and beef to the cannery workers.

Parker used a steam driven motor in 1924 to open a sawmill for the community. Besides farming and cannery work, many tried their hand at gold prospecting. The only commercial gold mine, however, was the Leroy opened in Glacier Bay by Abraham Parker and his son Leslie in 1938.

Muir's writings on Glacier Bay and the constant tourist flow to Alaska in order to see the region resulted in President Calvin Coolidge creating Glacier Bay National Monument on February 26, 1925, taking in 1,820 square miles.

By 1925, Strawberry Point had become Gustavus, named after Point Gustavus seven miles to the southwest. It had a post office, a general store, and a school. The general store, the Gustavus Dray, is a pre-World War II replica of a Mobil gas station, still in operation, selling fuel as well as being the local gift shop and museum.

Thirteen families lived in Gustavus when President Franklin Roosevelt enlarged the Monument's boundaries in 1939 taking possession of all unpatented land around the community. Roosevelt's actions land locked the farms and prevented further growth. It also brought the brown bear preserve dangerously close to the cattle herds.

Locals complained that the Park Service was attempting to strangle their livelihood and drive them out of the area. Abraham Parker's son, Charles, soon began a relentless letter writing campaign trying to have local homesteading restored. President Dwight Eisenhower issued a presidential proclamation in 1955 returning 19,000 acres to Gustavus from the Monument.

World War II saw the military building an installation at nearby Excursion Inlet and an airport at Gustavus in 1942. A road was finally built connecting the town with Bartlett Cove in 1956. Two years later, a dock and some port facilities were constructed. Today, the dock remains a one-way wooden dock with a "sliding" dock for boats to tie up at its end.

Moose began appearing in the region for the first time in the 1960s.

Tourist curiosity in the town has grown as tourism into Glacier Bay has grown. The 48 room Glacier Bay Lodge was constructed in 1966. With an airport and a dock, the town soon became known as the "gateway" to Glacier Bay. The town itself has become an attraction.

With the passage of the Alaska National Interest Lands Conservation Act in 1980, Glacier Bay became a national park with an additional half a million acres added giving Glacier Bay National Park a total of 3.3 million acres and twelve tide water glaciers.

Gustavus became an incorporated town in 2004 boasting a nine-hole golf course, a clinic, restaurants, art galleries, and a taxi service.

Gustavus was linked to Juneau through ferry service for the first time in 2011.

PELICAN

ONE OF THE LAST OF THE old rubber boot working class communities in Alaska, the first Pelican was founded by the survivors of a shipwreck. A Russian ship following the usual route between Sitka and Kodiak foundered in Cross Sound. Survivors took their lifeboat down a long inlet now known as Lisianski.

The Russians built a makeshift settlement in one of the coves put in a garden and hunted game to stay alive. The survivors claim they put together a shipyard and constructed a ship to sail back to Sitka. Tlingit tells how they came across the half-starved Russians while gathering food in winter and took them back to Sitka.

Decades later, American hunters and trappers found the clearing made by the Russians and some iron and copper tools in shallow graves. For some odd reason, they named the abandoned site Sunnyside.

Gold miners began peppering the area. Hjalmor Mork, Jack Ronning, and Hjalmor's oldest son opened the Mork Mine near Sunnyside. Across the inlet, the Apex Gold Mine came into being producing 18,000 ounces of gold. A third, developed by Jack Koby, came into being at the head of the inlet with a fourth near the inlet's mouth.

They were the sole inhabitants in 1938 when Kalle (Charley) Raatikainen sailed into the inlet with his boat *Pelican* looking for a site to start a town. Raatikainen was tired of buying fish and running them to distant Sitka with its cold storage facilities. He wanted a location closer to the fishing grounds to cut his run time in half.

He had been friends with Hjalmor Mork and thought he might know of a good site. Mork in turn led him to Sunnyside with its small harbor, and a large lake with a waterfall.

A corporation was quickly formed as a crew went to work transforming Sunnyside into a living community. Alaskan historian Bob DeArmond came to work as a timekeeper and storekeeper. Eli Rapichin was hired as camp bull cook. A.P. Walder and his wife came with their trawler. Raatikainen brought in his fish scows with two more trawlers following him. He beached one of his scows to act as a mess house with living quarters. A second scow was anchored at the end of a floating walkway leading to the beach. It became a warehouse and workers' quarters.

He christened the site Pelican City after his boat.

Four Paddock brothers came operating a pile driver with a donkey engine that cleared timber for the construction of the cold storage unit. Men from the Mork Mine cleared rock away at the site. The first structure set up on shore acted as a Finnish steam bath and the store and offices for the new corporation. When the Paddocks and Raatikainen built their residential homes, Pelican began taking on the appearances of a town. Arthur Silverman from Sitka opened the town's first bar shortly afterwards.

In late Fall 1938, the *Tongass* unloaded a large amount of lumber and pilings for the construction of the town. Raatikainen waited for the cargo to be completely unloaded before informing the captain he had no funds to pay him. After a tongue lashing, the captain had to agree on payments for the cargo.

Costs of raising a cold storage plant, obtaining diesel engines, and a water and electric system during the Great Depression forced Raatikainen to obtain loans from individuals in Seattle. Fishermen and laborers did work in exchange for food, tobacco, and stock in the corporation. A fire destroyed the bath/store building. The building was rebuilt, eventually becoming the town's school. Arvo Wahto was its first instructor teaching generations of Pelican children until he retired in the 1960s.

A multipurpose building was built serving as a combination kitchen, mess hall, office, and store. When a post office was established in 1939 with Bob DeArmond as the first postmaster, it was located in the multipurpose building as well. Gus Servile built the local dam. The Paddock brothers oversaw construction of the wharf, fish house, and the beginnings of a boardwalk as the main thoroughfare.

A small sawmill was started up for lumber for the growing number of residential homes. The demand for housing increased in 1940 when A.R. Breuger from Wrangell set up a floating cannery moored to the dock. In 1941, the Cape Cross Salmon Company, owned by Larry Freeburn and Pros Ganty, opened with canning equipment producing 17,000 cases per season. Cape Cross opened a cannery next to the cold storage plant bringing the total number of canneries to three.

With such a large number of Scandinavians residing in Pelican, the community had the nickname "Finn Town" for years during the Great Depression.

World War II brought change to Pelican. Refrigeration equipment was brought in, a hydroelectric power plant was finished, and a new office and storage building were added to the cold storage plant.

Pelican grew from a population of 48 in 1939 to 180 by 1951 peaking in the 1960s at around 250. Fishing allowed for the development of a grocery, a laundry, and two bars and restaurants. Businesses and wooden homes with fuel storage tanks alongside developed. The boardwalk serves as the town's only road. Nearly all the town's structures are on pilings.

The 1980s were good to Pelican. Salmon, halibut, herring, crab, and black cod were processed year-round. The harbor and ferry dock were improved and expanded. Those just arriving could find lodging in bed and breakfasts, relaxing in a steam bath, and find something to read at a small library.

Residents dubbed their town "closest to the fish" as fishermen took rich catches from the Fairweather fishing grounds to the north. But the 1990s saw a rapid decline in fish processed. Over five million pounds of fish were processed in Pelican in 1995, but by 1999 that figure had fallen to 700,000 pounds. The reason for the decline was a combination of Glacier Bay fishing closures and the Individual Fishing Quota program begun in 1995 to reduce vessel accidents.

A Japanese firm which owned Pelican Seafoods in the 1980s ended up closing the operation in 1995. The Kake Tribal Corporation bought the plant in 1996.

Originally planning on transforming the Pelican Seafoods plant into a lodge, the Kakes ended up operating the local processing plant and cold storage facilities. They also became owners of Pelican's hydroelectric plant, general store, and fuel dock as well. There was much disgruntled talk among residents on how their community had become nothing more than a "company town."

A raw fish tax was the main source of revenue for the city government. Recent years have been hard on Pelican.

The Kakes closed Pelican Seafoods and the cold storage in 2004 due to low fish prices. The facilities were leased out to a private operator in 2006 reopening the plant. But the operator ended up having cash flow problems unable to make payments to fishermen for their catch. The plant closed in 2009 along with the general store. The Kakes agreed to keep the ice processing plant in operation, but stated their intent is to pull their business interests out of Pelican.

Part of the problem in operating the processing plant in such a remote location had been fish buying tenders from other processing plants. Operating near the mouth of Lisianski Inlet, they approached incoming fishing boats about selling their catch before they arrived in Pelican.

In August 2009 heavy rains caused the wooden water flume to collapse, the source for community's water. The hydroelectric plant had to be shut down due to the flume collapse with diesel generators serving as backup.

Pelican has 15 students enrolled in its schools. The Alaska ferry system visits the remote community twice a month in the summer and once a month in winter.

Pelican is the site for the Pelican Boardwalk Boogie, a riotous music festival held every May since 1998. Its roots are from a music festival held as a unity totem pole carved by local students was unveiled.

Rose's Bar and Grill, with its bar top carved with hundreds of names, has been a curiosity destination.

YAKUTAT

Yakutat is the land of the Ghost Bear, of possibly the strongest earthquake ever to strike North America, and a race to a peak of what was believed to be the highest mountain on the continent.

The town is at the foot of one of the the fastest rising mountain ranges in the world, the Saint Elias Mountains, due to the collision between the Yakutat tectonic plate colliding with the North American plate.

The Eyak people from the Copper River Delta inhabited this isolated coast when Tlingit clans migrated up from Southeast Alaska.

By the time Russian, English, French, and Spanish explorers arrived there were several Tlingit-Eyak villages in the area. Monti Bay is a deep sheltering harbor from storms raking the Gulf of Alaska. It became a place of shelter for traveling Tlingits conducting trade with tribes around Prince William Sound and the Copper River Delta.

Yakutat is Tlingit for "the place where the canoes rest" because of Monti Bay.

European explorers

In 1774, the Russian exploration ship *St. Peter* commanded by Alexei Chirikof entered Monti Bay sending two boat loads of men ashore. Neither one returned. Chirikof assumed the men were killed and sailed off cutting his losses rather than investigate their disappearance.

It was shortly after this encounter that French and Spanish explorers reached Yakutat. On June 23, 1786, the crews of the French exploration ship *Boussole* and her escort *Astrolabe* caught the first glimpse of Mount St. Elias.

Three days later, La Perouse lowered three boats to map and explore the massive inlet before them. The survey team was led by Annes-Georges Augustin, chevalier de Monti. After surveying the bay, La Perouse named it after the leader of the French surveying part, Monti Bay.

The Spanish explored Alaska by sending one of their top captains, Alejandro Malaspina. When Malaspina left Acapulco, Mexico, on May 1, 1791, he had onboard astronomers, cartographers, botanists, naturalists, and painters. Instead of hugging the West Coast, Malaspina sailed straight for Mount Saint Elias.

When the Spanish explorer arrived, he set up an observation station that was to fix accurate the height of Mount St. Elias. While the observation station was being set up, Malaspina probed the nearby Icy Bay with his two ships until he was stopped by a massive glacier. Malaspina named the area Puerto del Desengano or Disenchantment Bay.

The huge glacier Malaspina ran into would eventually bear his name thanks to American explorer William Dall in 1874.

Malaspina had onboard renowned artist Tomas de Suria who recorded with pencil etchings and paint Tlingit life and the grandeur of the Saint Elias region.

A Russian colony

The Shelikhov-Golikov Company, forerunner of the Russian American Company, built a small block house in 1795 in Monti Bay just west of the Tlingit village as a safe haven for its trappers and traders as they sought sea otter pelts.

Alexander Baranov had hoped the post could grow crops and eased the chronic food shortage Russian Alaska faced in its early days, but the soil was too rocky.

Some forty criminals and malcontents from Kodiak were sent to man the blockhouse dubbed Glory of Russia or Slavorossiya. A decade later, relations between the Russians and the Yakutats came to a boil when the Russians forcefully prevented the Tlingits from getting to their fisheries. The Yakutats attacked wiping the colony out in 1805.

Three years later, Baranov sent Oliver Kimball to Yakutat to offer ransom for the survivors of the attack. Unknown to Baranov, the Chilkats had attacked the Yakutats the previous year, and after a frightening slaughter, laid claim to the region. Now Kimball, no doubt with Yakutat Tlingit support, attacked the Chilkats taking their chief, Asik, prisoner. The victory ended Chilkat domination of Yakutat Bay.

Baranov saw nothing to be gained by rebuilding the outpost. Smallpox nearly wiped out the Yakutat Tlingits in the 1830s. At one point, their population had dropped to a mere 150.

The Ghost Bear

In April 1877, soldier and poet, Lt. Charles Erskine Scott Wood was ordered to escort Chicago financier Charles Taylor to the base of Mount Saint Elias as he attempted to scale it. Within five days of Yakutat, their Tlingit paddlers refused to go any further. They had heard they were entering the land of the Ghost Bear.

After threats and bribes failed, Wood escorted Taylor back to Sitka so he could catch a boat home. Then Wood returned to the Yakutat region so he could lay claim of "climbing the tallest mountain in the world." He arranged for Huna goat hunters to accompany him. But a week out from their village, a Ghost Bear stepped out from a clearing and went back into the forests. The Hunas refused to go any further and Wood had to call the attempt off.

The Russians had called the creatures Saint Elias Bears. Essentially Ghost Bears, Spirit Bears, also called Phase Bears are black bears with a regressive gene. They evolved from living along the edge and in the crevasses of the ice fields that surround Yakutat. Ghost Bears have a blue-black inner coat of fur with an outer while coat of white with silver tipped fur.

The remainder of the 1800s up to the early part of the 20th century, they were considered a separate species of bear restricted to the ice fields around Yakutat.

After Wood's sighting, there would not be another recorded encounter until 1899. In the 1970s, one was captured in Yakutat and relocated to the San Diego Zoo. In the early part of the 21st Century, Ghost or Spirit Bears were spotted on the outskirts of Juneau coming off the Juneau Ice Field. With the retreat of glaciers and reshaping of the immense coastal ice fields, Ghost Bear sightings are now ranging from Prince William Sound to the west to as far south as Juneau.

The tallest peak in the world

Reports of the immense height of Mount Saint Elias though began creeping into the scientific world. Was it the highest peak in North America?

Nine years after Wood visited the region, explorer and self-promoter Frederick Schwatka attempted to scale Mount St. Elias in 1886 but failed due to bad weather. Harold and Edwin Topham hired a Sitka sealing vessel to take them and their 1,400 pounds of provisions to Yakutat in 1888. From Yakutat, they followed Schwatka's route landing again at Icy Bay and proceeded inland. Continuous avalanches forced them to turn back.

The National Geographic Society entered the picture in 1890 sending geologist Israel Cook Russell and geographer Mark Kerr to Yakutat to find a way to the summit. Russell went to the head of Yakutat Bay and approached Mount St. Elias from the east. While Kerr made incredibly inaccurate measurements of the mountain's height (Kerr set the elevation of Mount St. Elias at an astonishingly low 15,350 feet), Russell became separated from his party and snowed in for six days.

Russell attempted the summit again in 1891. After a twelve-day storm passed, Russell and two packers made it to the base of the mountain at 14,000 feet. They were stunned when they looked to their north and saw nothing but a sea of towering sharp peaks. Again, Russell failed, but he computed Mount St. Elias' elevation at 18,100 (it is now set at 18,008) and that the mountain is within Alaska by two and a half miles. The border with Canada would be adjusted later where it runs right up to the summit.

In 1897, two expeditions, one American and the other Italian, were racing each other to the top of Mount St. Elias.

Wealthy blue blood Henry Bryant led the American team. He had a strong interest in the polar regions as expressed by financing two of Robert Peary's attempts to reach the North Pole. He had also scaled peaks in Switzerland and successfully explored the Great Falls of Labrador.

He was racing against the grandson of King Vittorio Emanuele II, King of Italy, the Duke of the Abruzzi, Lui Amedeo de Savio-Aosta. Though the Duke was in the Italian Navy, he was one of the foremost mountaineers in all of Europe. With him were his climbing partners, all members of the Italian Navy as well.

The Duke and his party moved some 6,600 pounds of provisions to Yakutat and leased a fleet of fast ships to get him there. Money was no object, only the conquest of the mountain. When the Italians reached the fog draped beaches of Yakutat, the Tlingits were there to greet them with torches and bonfires. The Duke discovered one of the Tlingits who was on the beach to greet them had just guided Bryant over to a landing point on the coast ten days earlier.

The Duke wasted no time. Although the Italians were dragging ten iron bed frames to sleep on during the expedition, they made remarkable time. The Duke packed supplies on his back at times and at other times probed ahead for the best route. He was following an earlier route recommended by Russell over Pinnacle Pass. They reached the base of Newton Glacier which comes down from Mount St. Elias in July.

The next day, four men from Bryant's expedition appeared with a note from Bryant. He conceded the race to the Duke and wished him every success.

On July 31st, after climbing 6,000 feet in ten and a half hours, a guide stepped aside so the Duke could be the first to stand on the summit of Mount St. Elias.

It was almost noon, and the day was clear as the ten Italians unfurled their flag over what they thought was the highest peak in North America. They had no idea of William Dickey's discovery of a mountain 2,000 feet higher to their northwest christened Mount McKinley.

North America's most powerful earthquake

The Alaska Commercial Company opened a store trading with the Yakutats and growing number of American trappers in 1884. By 1886 miners were working the black sand beaches for gold. In 1889, the Swedish Free Mission Church opened a school and a sawmill.

It was in this remote setting that North America's most powerful earthquake may have struck on September 10, 1899. Many years later in 1905, the U.S. government sent geologists Ralph Tarr and Lawrence Martin to the Yakutat region to investigate tales of a massive earthquake. They found mussels "resembling clumps of blue flowers" on rocks 20 feet above sea level.

One prospector, A. Flenner, told the investigating team how he and others set up a homemade seismograph using hunting knives hung so their point touched. Flenner told the team they had counted 52 shocks on that September 10th leading up to the big quake. At the time, Tarr and Martin believed the big one was magnitude 8.

They found the seabed had been raised 47 feet and took testimonies that the land itself rolled as though resembling swells at sea. The Tarr-Martin team speculated that one aftershock was a magnitude 7.4.

What was even more remarkable was the fact that there were no fatalities from the event; a testimony to how uninhabited the Yakutat region was at the turn of the century.

The Klondike Gold Rush

Nor did Yakutat escape the effects of the Klondike Gold Rush.

Eighteen New Yorkers studying a map determined the fastest way to reach the Klondike Gold Fields was to land at Yakutat Bay and make their way through Malaspina Glacier. Led by Arthur Dietz, the group which included a doctor and two New York City policemen, landed at Yakutat in March 1898.

The group struggled for three months on the Malaspina. The doctor disappeared down a crevasse with a dog team. Forced to winter it out on the glacier in a makeshift cabin, three died in an avalanche. Some set off to try their luck to reach the Klondike, never making it. With the coming of spring, the party tried getting off the Malaspina only to find themselves going in circles. When the revenue cutter, USS *Wolcott* came across the party, there were only four alive including Dietz.

Astonishingly, when Seattle papers reported the incident, the reporters claimed the party had found a half a million dollars in gold dust!

The Fish Railroad

Seattle's F. S. Stimson and business associates decided in 1903 to invest in Monti Bay in a major fashion. A cannery, sawmill, a general store, and a railroad were planned for Yakutat.

First on the list were the lumber mill and a railroad, the Yakutat and Southern Railroad. Forty-pound rails were laid from the cannery wharf inland for eleven miles to the Situk River. The railroad even had a side spur along Lost River but was abandoned once a road was put in paralleling the track.

The Stimson group soon discovered that canned salmon brought more money than lumber. The nature of the Yakutat and Southern Railroad changed to making stops at the many canneries in the vicinity, taking on loads, and transporting them down to the cannery wharf for shipment. Because of this, the railroad followed a tide table rather than any form of timetable. When the tide came in so did fishing boats unloading their catch at the various canneries.

An open wood platform car was added to the train for passengers to hop on and ride free of charge. This allowed both locals and cannery workers to get around in a wilderness which had few roads.

A 26-ton Lima Prairie locomotive was brought to Yakutat in 1913 for increased loads along the eleven-mile course. It was retired in 1949 after becoming too expensive to operate. The locomotive took two tons of coal for one single round trip.

A second locomotive, a 28-ton Heisler was brought in 1940 after it was converted to diesel. Besides the diesel driven Heisler, two Plymouth locomotives were used along with a Packard sedan equipped with flanged wheels for rail travel. Later, a Chevrolet truck, also with flanged tires, and a homemade gondola were added to the Yakutat and Southern. A hand car was made available for berry pickers and for picnics.

The Yakutat and Southern Railroad ceased operations in the mid-1960s though one of the locomotives is on public display in Yakutat. The railway has slowly been transformed into hiking trails.

Stimson was bought out by Gorman and Company prior to World War I which owned a network of canneries in Southeast Alaska. They, in turn, were sold in 1913 to Libby, McNeill, and Libby, and eventually in 1951, to the Bellingham Canning Company. The original Stimson cannery remained in operation in Yakutat until 1970.

Working in the cannery from 1912 to 1941, Seiki Kayamori took extensive photographs of the Yakutat area that are now in the Yakutat City Hall.

Yakutat had a population of 299 by 1938 and consisted of area canneries, two restaurants, a fox farm, the Swedish Lutheran Church, a Salvation Army post, and a Native school operated by the federal government.

During World War II, the U.S. Army Air Force placed a large aviation garrison at Yakutat with some of the largest hangers then in Alaska. Yakutat soon became a staging field for aircraft during the war. Captain Benjamin Talley and Company B, 28th Engineering Regiment was assigned to construct both the Yakutat airfield and a city dock. Talley would eventually oversee 28 of the 39 wartime construction projects in Alaska.

Douglas B18 Bolo bombers of the 73rd Bomber Squadron were the first to use the Yakutat airfield for their aerial mapping missions.

Exploration of oil and gas took place in the 1970s. Nothing was found and the wells plugged and abandoned. Offshore oil and gas leases were established in 1995, but nothing yet has come of it.

The City of Yakutat was formed in 1948 and a borough encompassing the immediate section of the Gulf of Alaska coast was organized in 1992. State ferry service began in 1998, but due to winter gales, ferry stops were restricted to the summer months.

Geology is a unique aspect of Yakutat whose glaciers are advancing rather than retreating.

The Hubbard Glacier advanced in 1986 and in 2002 damning the entrance to Russell Fiord. Water levels in the fjord rose 83 feet in 1986 and 61 feet in 2002 until the ice dam broke. A pass exits between Russell Fiord and the nearby Situk River. Tests showed that water had flowed over this pass into Situk River up to around 1860 indicating that the Hubbard Glacier may have blocked Russell Fjord for longer periods of time in the past and may have blocked the fjord on a much longer basis 600 years ago.

Nearby, the 2,000 square mile Bering Glacier, the largest mountain glacier in the world, surged rather than retreated in 1993 covering 50 feet a day. It surged again in 1995 and in 2010. Scientists in 2008 estimated that the Bering Glacier spills twice as much fresh water into the ocean as the entire Colorado River system holds.

Currently, North Pacific Processors is the main private employer for the community of 700.

The Yakutat Tlingits received a grant in 2004 from the federal government to teach their language to their young people. A second grant in 2007 allowed the instruction in the Yakutat Tlingit dialect to be expanded in the local school system.

Surfing capital of Alaska

Beginning in the late 1990s, Yakutat slowly began acquiring the title as the Surf Capital of Alaska. The most popular stretch for wet suite surfing is at "the breakers" near the entrance of Monti Bay and at Cannon Beach. Within a decade, Yakutat became the home of many hardened surfers and was receiving national media attention.

Commercial and sport fishing are still the mainstays of the local economy, especially around the Situk River. Several world class fishing lodges have been established around Yakutat.

In 2009, an Oklahoma mining firm laid claim to 60,000 acres after locating a massive gold deposit. Plans calling for an open pit mine raised concerns among Tlingit leaders.

Yakutat also became known for having one of the highest precipitation rates in Alaska with up to 132 inches falling annually including 219 inches of snow.

The Gulf Ports

The coast of the Gulf of Alaska is heavily indented and clothed in thick forests and ice. It is a land of dramatic mountain vistas and tidewater glaciers.

These dynamics are the result of the Pacific tectonic plate colliding and submerging under the North American plate. The collision resulted in an active fault line running the length of Prince William Sound. Because of this, the Chugach Mountains are on the rise with the highest peak, Marcus Baker reaching above 13,000 feet, and many other peaks well over 10,000 feet in elevation.

Yet, the same dynamics are pulling the older Kenai Mountains bracketing the western side of the Gulf down into the sea resulting in the drowned valleys and fjords of Kenai Fjords National Park.

The relatively warm waters of the Gulf of Alaska are uplifted over these rising peaks meeting cold arctic air from Alaska's interior. The clash of temperatures has resulted in the Gulf of Alaska being called the "cradle of storms" by seaman. Snowfall is intense. Many areas of the coast receive 600 inches annually. Thompson Pass just outside of Valdez witnessed 81 feet of snowfall during the winter of 1952-53. Snowplows and shoveling to get back into one's home are a way of life in Valdez.

The snow and rising granite peaks have resulted in an expanse of ice. The Gulf has more than 22 tidewater glaciers pouring their contents out into the ocean along with impressive ice fields such as the Harding Ice Field.

This glacial activity has carved out long u-shaped valleys that serve as highways into the interior. It has also allowed for the mighty Copper River to reach the Gulf dropping her silt and forming the Copper River Delta.

Many of the towns that dot the imposing coastline came about by way of transporting goods into the Alaskan interior by way of these glacier valleys, Cordova, Valdez, Whittier, and Seward.

Nearly all the coast is under federal protection. The Chugach National Forest takes in the most northern temperate rain forest on the continent. Created by President Theodore Roosevelt in 1907, it takes in 6.9 million acres. Its companion, Kenai Fjords National Park, was created by President Jimmy Carter in 1980 covering 1,046 square miles.

The majestic vistas have given rise to most of Alaska's top artists; Sydney Laurence who was a dishwasher in Valdez, Ted Lambert who was a McCarthy dog freighter, Jules Dahlager who was a Cordova reporter, and Eustace Ziegler Cordova's Presbyterian minister. Internationally recognized artist Rockwell Kent earned his fame through the paintings he created during his stay on Fox Island near Seward.

When the Russians came into this land, they found both the Alutiiqs and the Eyaks using kayak-like baidarkas to navigate through the storm plagued waters of the Gulf rather than the imposing war canoes the Tlingits of Southeast Alaska use. Alexander Baranov dotted the Gulf with Russian settlements; Nuchek in Prince William Sound, Resurrection Bay trading post that became Seward, Seldovia, and Alexandrovsk today's Nanwalek. Orthodox missionaries followed finding lasting converts among the Native population.

The gold rushes, the 1964 Good Friday Earthquake and the 1989 Exxon Oil Spill were events that shaped the modern Gulf ports. Interior ore—whether gold or copper—resulted in frantic railroad building and railroad wars. Cordova, Seward, and Whittier are all ports where rails met the sea. Gunfire kept the railroad out of Valdez which had to settle for a trail that became the Richardson Highway and the Trans-Alaska Pipeline.

The 1964 Good Friday Earthquake devastated Chenega and Valdez killing many. It also resulted in serious damage to Seward and Seldovia. Ironically, the Exxon Valdez Oil Spill did not touch Valdez, but nearly destroyed Cordova fishermen's means of making a living.

CORDOVA

On April Fool's Day 1906, a small party of seven men landed near an Eyak village with construction equipment. The men painted the word CORDOVA on a large board as they had been instructed to do by their boss, railroader Michael Heney, and nailed it to a nearby tree. A very brief ceremony was held before the seven went back into their tents.

Thus, Cordova was born.

Centuries earlier, the ancestors of the Eyaks migrated down the Copper River to the sea then fanned out along the coastline. Villages around the modern site of Cordova marked their western expansion while to the east they began settling in Southeast Alaska. There they ran into the Tlingits migrating northward. Gradually the Eyak domain was reduced by Tlingit warfare until only the villages around Prince William Sound and the Copper River Delta remained.

The last full blood Eyak, Maria Smith Jones, died in 2008.

White habitation began when Walter Storey built the first cannery on Prince William Sound on Odiak Slough just south of Cordova in 1887. Two years later, Captain O.J. Humphrey set up a second cannery at Odiak on Cordova's northern flank. After a devastating fire, this cannery was relocated to Orca Inlet in 1895.

The Eyaks set up a village near the Odiak cannery. After whites set up a trading post in the Eyak village of Alagnik, disease broke out killing many of the Eyaks there in 1892. Those who survived joined other Eyaks at Cordova's Eyak Lake.

Eight years before the official founding of Cordova, Presbyterian Minister Sheldon Jackson described the town of Eyak as having "25 White men, 25 Native women, and 25 stills capable of producing 2500 gallons of liquor."

Modern Cordova came into being during a hectic race to build the first railroad to the copper rich Kennecott Mines in the Wrangell Mountains to the northeast. Valdez had already begun constructing a railway as had the oil town of Katalla.

Katalla seemed to have the edge. Oil had been discovered there by Tom White in 1894. In 1902 a huge coal field had been discovered just north of Katalla. For decades, the Katalla Slough had been a minor port of refuge for ships seeking shelter from violent storms in the Gulf of Alaska until the massive 1899 Yakutat Earthquake. The uplift closed off the slough.

Katalla was officially founded in 1903 with rails being laid to the coal fields while oil derricks were going up. The Morgan-Guggenheim Syndicate covered its bets by financing both a Valdez and a Katalla railroad to the copper mines in the Interior.

Michael Heney, who had built the almost impossible White Pass and Yukon Railway at Skagway, saw an opportunity. Though he had limited financial backing, he hoped that by building a rail line from Odiak to Abercrombie Rapids on the Copper River, the Guggenheims would buy him out at a substantial profit.

Heney bought the cannery complex at Odiak from Pacific Packing Company to serve as his headquarters for the construction of his railroad in 1906. He also bought half the village of Eyak the same year which became his Cordova. Also, that same year the U.S. Post Office opened. The entire town of Cordova was moved west to its current site and incorporated in 1909.

Railroad Way Street located on the east side of the slough has many of the old stores and residential homes from before Heney moved downtown Cordova to its current site.

Heney decided to christen his new town Cordova from Puerto Cordova that Spanish explorers had given it in 1790.

Six weeks after his seven men had nailed the town's name to a tree, it had its own newspaper, the Cordova Alaskan, and 500 Irish and Norwegian railroad workers. By September, a 725-foot-long wharf was completed, and by the end of that year, some 30 miles of track had been laid.

Meanwhile, the Guggenheims poured $2 million into Katalla for the construction of a breakwater. But a monstrous storm in November 1907 took the breakwater out flooding the town.

The Guggenheims immediately called a business conference back in New York. There J.P. Morgan banged his fist on the table shouting, "Whatever the route, we've got to bring that copper and coal together!"

The Guggenheims turned to Heney buying his railroad for $500,000. He was then hired to complete the newly named Copper River & Northwestern Railway. Given a budget of $20 million and a free hand, Heney immediately rushed more Irish and Scandinavian laborers to Cordova.

Many believed Heney could not complete the rail line due to the natural barriers confronting it. Ahead of him were 193 miles of rugged terrain. He would have to build bridges for his line in front of advancing glaciers as well as along Abercrombie Rapids and the walls of its canyon. He had to find a way to get supplies to the upper portions of the line. All the while dealing with some of the heaviest snowfall known to Alaska.

The initials for the railway, CR&NW came to be known as "Can't Run & Never Will." But Heney was determined.

As workmen laid track across the swamp-like Copper River Delta, he sent two men from Valdez overland hauling a steamboat. George Hazelet and Jack Meals were in charge of freighting the 70-ton steamboat *Chittyna* halfway up Thompson Pass outside of Valdez and then followed the Tasnuna River eastward to the Copper River. Using horses and sleighs, the boat was divided into four sections with the boiler alone weighed 5,700 pounds. Four days later, Hazelet and Meals were on the banks of the Copper River where the 110 foot long and 23-foot-wide steamer was re-assembled and launched.

It was an amazing feat of endurance and physical skill. Heney now had his boat on the upper Copper able to haul equipment up the line.

Unfortunately, Big Mike Heney would not live to see the railroad's completion. Returning from a business trip in Seattle, the *SS Ohio* struck a rock and went down on August 27, 1909. Heney led the rescue efforts. When he learned there was no more room in the last lifeboat, he hung onto the stern in freezing waters as the boat rowed to shore. He came down with pulmonary tuberculosis and was forced to move into a San Francisco sanitarium where he drew up the engineering plans for the assault on the two glaciers along the route, Miles and Childs.

The plan called for part of the work crew at the base of the new bridge to chop away ice as the rest of the workers worked on the bridge itself. The first span took thirteen days to complete while the second span took six days.

When the railroad workers began the last span, Miles Glacier advanced on the bridge. For forty desperate hours, men worked to complete the bridge as two shifts of 30 men with chisels and ax held off the advancing glacier. Then at the last moment the advancing glacier stopped saving the now completed bridge, today called the Million Dollar Bridge.

A week before his 46th birthday, Heney succumbed to tuberculosis on October 11, 1910. By March 29, 1911, CR&NW reached the Kennecott mines.

On April 8, 1911, a train pulling 32 cars of raw copper ore worth $250,000 came down the line. The contents were loaded onto the freighter *Northwestern* bound for the smelters of Tacoma, Washington. From 1911 to 1938, more than 200 million tons of copper, silver, and gold went through Cordova on the railway Big Mike Heney had constructed.

By then, Cordova had 1,152 residents and nearby Orca had 141. The Eyak village had been torn down in 1908 for its lumber to build Cordova with. Cordova boasted of a newspaper, ten stores, two hotels, two lumber yards, three churches, ten saloons, and a school.

The second building built in Cordova was the famous Red Dragon. The brainchild of a Episcopalian bishop named Rowe and renowned artist Eustice Ziegler, the Red Dragon was a reading room and social clubhouse for railroad workers who did not want to frequent the local saloons. The Red Dragon still stands today in a small grove of trees on a bluff overlooking the south end of Cordova.

Eustace Ziegler was a young Presbyterian minister when he was assigned to the church in Cordova. He took up oil paintings and rapidly won international attention. Cordova also had a second artist by way of its local newspaper when reporter Jules Dahlager took up the brushes. Ziegler took Dahlager under his wing assisting the newspaper man in marketing his oils as well as with his technique.

Before long, the two took in artist Sydney Laurence, a dishwasher in Valdez, and a young traveler named Ted Lambert, who also showed skill with the brush.

Over the years, they became known as the Alaska Four; their oils showing the outside world the life and physical power of the Arctic frontier. (Unalakleet painter Fred Machetanz is often group with them and thus the Alaska Four is five artists.) Ziegler and Dahlager dashed into the Interior by dog team in the 1920s descending the little-known Kuskokwim River to secure visions to paint. Laurence struck out from Valdez homesteading near Mount McKinley painting powerful vistas of the mountain. Lambert eventually lived alone in a cabin along the shores of the Bering Sea painting Eskimo life before he mysteriously disappeared without a trace in 1960.

Alone of the group, Cordova's Ziegler is best known for his portraits of local characters, especially his oil of native Horseshoe Mary, a former slave.

Cordova residents have a history of being vocal in their opinions. When the Taft administration banned coal mining in nearby Bering River Cola Fields, residents held the infamous Cordova Coal Party on May 3, 1911, to show their anger over being forced to buy the more expensive British Columbian coal by shoveling the Canadian coal into the bay.

Though Cordova was clearly a "company" town controlled by the copper mining interests, for a moment in 1913, it was the gateway to the Chisana Gold Rush as prospectors rode the copper trains into the Interior.

Cordova contributed to the mythology of the early Alaskan Bush Pilots by becoming the home base for Merle "Mudhole" Smith, named for one of his unsuccessful take offs, and Harold "No Kill 'Em" Gillam in the 1930s.

Gillam was operating three planes from Cordova, including an amphibian, and lived through six crashes in six months in 1931.

His reputation was cemented that same year when Honest John McCreary impaled himself. The nearest doctor was 125 miles away at Kennecott Mine. With a blizzard raging, Gillam flew McCreary to the doctor and then returned to Cordova for McCreary's son, returning him to Kennecott so he could be with his father.

All totaled, Gillam had flown 375 miles at night through a blizzard over the Chugach Mountains without instruments.

The daring feat caused a Cordova third grader to write a poem about Gillam. "Thrill 'em, spill 'em, no kill 'em Gillam." The handle stuck to the ex-boxer and unflyable weather became known as Gillam weather in Alaska.

Mudhole Smith purchased what would become his Cordova Airlines in 1939 expanding service throughout Gulf of Alaska communities. When the 69 day long West Coast longshoreman's strike hit Cordova with food shortages in 1946, Mudhole Smith flew his DC 3 to Seattle and back with three and a half tons of food and continued such flights until the strike ended.

Eyak Lake became a freshwater seaplane base. In October 1941, the US Navy established a base for a squadron of Navy scout planes in Cordova.

A snapshot of Cordova in 1940 showed it had a population of 1500 with four churches, two banks, a high school as well as a Native school, a theater, library, hospital, two hotels, and proudly advertised it being the home to the Red Dragon. Nearby, the village of Eyak, with its runways, had a population of 366.

Besides copper, Cordova enjoyed a rich commercial razor clam harvest from 1916 to 1958. As much as 3.5 million pounds of razor clams were harvested annually allowing Cordova to call herself the "Razor Clam Capital of the World." But the Razor clams began declining in the late 1950s and a large die off in 1958 brought an end to commercial harvesting.

When the Kennecott copper mines finally did peter out in 1938, only 20 percent of Cordova's work force was employed by the railroad. Cordova's canneries employed 1500 seasonal workers while more than 500 Cordova fishermen ranged out into the Sound and the Copper River Delta.

World War II found Cordova's deep-water port a stopover for military transport ships. At mile post 13 along the Copper River and Northwest Railway, the U.S. Army constructed a garrison for 73 officers and 1,004 enlisted men. The Army repaired the railroad to the garrison site using small gas driven "speedsters" for bringing in supplies from the port. Cordova was doing well during the war with fourteen canneries processing not only salmon, but crab, clams, and shrimp.

After the war, the rail bed became the present road to the airport from town. From 1953 to 1956, the road was extended out on the old rail bed to mile 49 and by 1964 to mile 59. However, when the Good Friday Earthquake in 1964 collapsed a section of the Million Dollar Bridge, the idea of transforming the old rail bed into a highway from Cordova to the rest of Alaska was dropped.

The 1964 Good Friday Earthquake saw the ground thrust upwards as much as six feet ruining Cordova's deep-water port. Large fishing vessels could no longer navigate the mouth of the Copper River for salmon and the uplift destroyed the clam beds.

Local legend has it that graves and coffins were uplifted from a nearby cemetery and flung into Eyak Lake. Every now and then says locals, a few can be seen through the lake water, and occasionally, a coffin pops up to the surface.

The Standard Oil harbor facility went up in flames in 1968 destroying the dock, cargo ready to ship and a nearby cannery. After servicing Cordova for nearly 75 years, the Alaska Steamship Company pulled out. The firm went out of business in 1971.

Though strongly opposed by Eyak Natives, Cordova annexed the village of Eyak or Old Town in 1971 to expand the community's tax base.

In March 1989, the *Exxon Valdez* oil tanker grounded on Bligh Reef northwest of Cordova resulting in one of the most devastating environmental disasters in U.S. history. It greatly affected salmon and herring populations in Prince William Sound causing a recession within the local fishing industry. Cordova fishermen held more than 90 percent of the commercial fishing permits on the Sound just before the Spill. Cordova's raw fish tax brought in $1,294,000. But after the Spill in 1992, the raw fish tax only earned Cordova $561,000.

Cordova reacted quickly when the Spill happened. Her fishermen put together a fleet made up of every boat they could lay their hands. The fleet laid out boomers on the opposite side of Prince William Sound to protect the salmon hatcheries. They proceeded to try sucking and shoveling the thick crude oil up with whatever devise they could conjure up. Their efforts had a mixed to dismal success rate.

Angered by in action over their grievances, Cordova fishermen blocked Valdez with their boats in 1993. The blockade continued until Gov. Walter Hickel agreed to sit down with the fishermen and hear their demands.

A 1994 Anchorage jury awarded the plaintiffs $5 billion in punitive damages which the oil firm was able to have reduced to $2.5 billion in 2007. However, by then some 6,000 of the original 32,000 Exxon Valdez claimants had died.

Standing at the Eyak Native's Ilanka Cultural Center is a totem created by Mike Webber called the "shame pole" demonstrating local feelings towards Exxon.

Gov. Hickel and Cordova had tangled before when Hickel in 1991 ordered the Alaska Department of Transportation to use maintenance funds for the construction of a road to Cordova along the old rail bed. The U.S. Army Corp of Engineers issued a cease-and-desist order which Hickel ignored. His construction plans grinded to a halt when ADOT ran out of funds to continue. When Hickel announced he might use the Alaska National Guard to finish the road to Cordova, legal action stopped the project.

Surveys found Cordova residents evenly split on whether they wanted to be connected with the outside world via road or not.

Cordova is the home of the largest fishing fleet in Prince William Sound and several fish processing plants. This is reflected in the fact that the town's largest employer is Trident Seafoods. Half of all households have at least one person involved in the commercial fishing industry. Cordova's fishing fleet ranges out not only across Prince William Sound, but the Copper River Delta exporting the fame Copper River Reds during salmon runs.

Cordova hosts the annual Iceworm Festival every February. The brainchild of Omar Wehr and Mudhole Smith in 1961, the festival includes a parade, talent shows, oyster shucking, ping pong tournaments, a survival suit race, and the blessing of the fishing fleet. The highlight is the 100-foot long iceworm float making its way down Cordova's main street.

The nearby Copper River Delta, covering more than 500 square miles, sees anywhere from 5 million to 11 million shorebirds annually in early May. Besides Western sandpipers, dunlins, ducks and geese, the delta is the sole nesting grounds for the large Dusky Canadian Geese as well as more than ten percent of all trumpeter swans.

Cordova has taken advantage of this event. Residents in 1990 organized the Copper River Delta Shorebird Festival held in early May.

TATITLEK

TATITLEK, ALONG WITH THE SMALL VILLAGE of Chenega on the western side of Prince William Sound is all that remains of the Chugach Alutiiq people.

Thousands of years ago, Kodiak's Koniag people ventured from their island home northward in their kayak-like baidarkas made of animal skins stretched over wooden frames. After setting up villages along the southern tip of the Kenai Peninsula, they sailed into the island dotted Prince William Sound.

Here Chugach Alutiiqs encountered the Eyaks who were being pushed westward by the expanding Tlingit nation of Southeast Alaska. Prince William Sound transformed into a land of raids and bloody retaliations.

The first European explorers in the Sound such as Captain James Cook in 1778, James Strange in 1786, and Nathaniel Portlock in 1787 visited Tatitlek Narrows as did Spanish explorer Salvador Fidalgo in 1790. English explorer George Vancouver's men mapped the Tatitlek area in 1791.

Vancouver found tree stumps cut by Portlock seven years earlier now underwater. Standing trees in some areas were immersed in ten to twelve feet of water during high tide. The evidence pointed to a horrendous earthquake on the scale of the mammoth 1964 Good Friday

Earthquake. It may have been the very same one that triggered the 1792 tsunami which nearly destroyed the Russian town of Three Saints Bay on Kodiak Island.

Captain Strange traded for sea otter pelts with the Chugach at Tatitlek. Portlock also traded at Tatitlek dealing directly with their chief, Sheenawaa, a man he did not trust. Portlock noted the Tatitlek were "the most powerful tribe about the Sound, hated by all their neighbours, with whom they were continually at variance."

Portlock regarded them as plunderers after they forcibly stole his trade goods from one of his parties. Chief Sheenawaa and two hundred warriors fell upon this small group after they had become beached in the mud.

A Russian expedition under Potap Zailov explored the Sound in 1783. Two small skirmishes with the Chugach reduced the Russians' numbers and killed Zailov. The expedition returned to Kodiak with valuable pelts catching the eyes of Russian fur traders there.

The Russians had two private companies operating in Alaska at the time: the Lebedev-Lastochkin and the Shelikov companies. The new director of the Shelikov Company, Alexander Baranov, personally wanted to see what the Sound had to offer paddling in with thirty-four Russians and a hundred and fifty Koniag Alutiiqs in 1792.

During his journey, one of the Chugach chiefs, very likely at Tatitlek, offered Baranov his 18-year-old daughter. The Russian, in his forties and running away from a wife already back in Russia, refused. The chief then simply abandoned his daughter. Baranov took her in giving her the name Anna Gregoryena.

Anna gave birth to two children, a boy and a girl. Both married into Russian aristocratic society. Baranov was now tied by marriage to the Chugach Alutiiqs.

The village of Tatitlek received its first historical mention in 1847 in the records of the Russian American Company. The village's location moved from place to place several times by 1858. The Russians noted that year it had 39 residents. The first U.S. census of Alaska in 1880 placed the village on the southern shore of Boulder Bay, east of today's location with a population of 79.

When the U.S. purchased Alaska in 1867, Tatitlek trappers prospered due to a boom in furs for the new American Commercial Company now at the old Russian trading village of Nuchek near the entrance into Prince Williams Sound. The 1880 census recorded the Chugach Alutiiqs were down to only four villages from the eight in Baranov's day and that "Tahkhlek" had 73 people. The spelling of the village became officially Tatitlek in 1910 by the U.S. Geological Survey. In that year, the village was recorded at the base of Copper Mountain where it is today.

As Nuchek declined in importance, the American Commercial Company opened a substation at Tatitlek.

Andrew Peter Kashererov, an appointed lay reader for the Russian Orthodox Church, oversaw the construction of St. Nicholas Chapel in 1900. Ten years later, the Russian Orthodox Church opened a school in the village where students practiced their Native customs while learning both Russian and English.

Tatitlek residents found work at the copper mine near Ellamar. A copper ore outcropping was discovered at Virgin Bay in 1897. The first ore was shipped from Ellamar in 1900. Twelve years later, Ellamar was the second largest copper mine on the Sound with a large wharf and several buildings. The mine had a hundred men on payroll with a school and a post office.

Before the mine played out in 1929, it had produced 15 million pounds of copper, 51,000 ounces of gold, and 191,000 ounces of silver. The owners then flooded the eight-level mine that went 600 feet deep and sold the buildings which were later converted into a cannery. Tatitlek's population dropped due to the closure from 187 to 75.

The Russian Revolution and the fall of the Czar ended financial support for Russian Orthodox schools and the school at Tatitlek closed. By 1916, the Cordova newspaper was pushing for one school for all Native Chugach children even though it noted that Simpson Bay Chugachs would not associate with Tatitlek Chugachs. Tatitlek children were refused admittance into the school at Ellamar because of being Native.

Eventually a federal school for Natives was opened in Cordova while Marie Frantzen took it upon herself to teach in Tatitlek.

After the Exxon Valdez Oil Spill and the support money it brought into the Sound, Tatitlek and other small Sound villages gathered to form the Chugach School District. First through ninth grades were required to have "cultural awareness and expression" in the curriculum.

Transportation in and out of the villages improved. During the 1940s, Merle Mudhole Smith's Cordova Airlines made regular amphibious stops at Tatitlek. Tatitlek finally had a ferry dock built by the state twenty years after it had been approved. Prior to the dock's construction, skiffs went out to meet the ferry at night. Passengers were forced to navigate wet and slippery gang planks with their luggage. Many times, winter storms forced the ferry to bypass the village altogether.

The 1964 Earthquake uplifted Tatitlek some five feet making the harbor too shallow for shipping. The U.S. Army Corp of Engineers re-dredged the harbor, but it remains very shallow at low tide. The federal government relocated some of the survivors of devastated Chenega after the 1964 earthquake to Tatitlek.

Native lands at Chenega were forcibly annexed into the Chugach National Forest making Tatitlek's 480-acre Native Reserve the only Native owned land on the Sound.

With the passage of the Alaska Native Land Claims Settlement Act in 1971. Tatitlek became part of the Chugach Regional Native Corporation and its residents' shareholders.

Tatitlek received title to 137,200 acres in 1978, most of which came out of the Chugach National Forest. By the late 1980s, the village was logging again for clients in Japan and China.

Though not directly affected, Tatitlek shareholders agreed to sell critical habitat areas to the newly created Exxon Valdez Oil Spill Trustee Council to protect salmon populations in the Sound.

Tatitlek has been the longest continuously occupied settlement in the Sound. It is the region's only town that has had a continuous census record going back to 1890.

VALDEZ

Tired of shipping canned salmon out of Prince William Sound with their boats returning empty, the Pacific Steam Whaling Company printed fliers and ran advertisements in the Seattle newspapers that Stampeders, as gold prospectors for the Klondike were called, should take the "All-American" route to the Klondike using a trail that began on the ocean side of Valdez Glacier.

The company had a small cannery on the south shore of Valdez Arm. Seeing the potential, shipping firms followed Pacific's example.

This claim was based on an inaccurate report filed by then U.S. Army Lt. W.R Abercrombie during his 1884 Copper River Expedition. Abercrombie had never seen the actual trail.

Ironically the first prospectors to arrive on Valdez Arm were Adam Swan and twenty-two others on the *Salmo* on November 10, 1897, where the Valdez Oil Terminal now stands without booking passage on any of Pacific's ships. Their settlement became known as Swanport.

Eventually thirty-five hundred men and women were dumped onto the beaches of Valdes Arm and told the trail was on the glacier itself. They only had to scale it to get to the Klondike. The average age for the group was 47 and roughly ninety-five percent of them had failed in other business ventures before trying to find their fortune in the Klondike.

Most of the Stampeders tried crossing the glacier between March through June of 1898. The trip over the glacier was difficult and several died in the attempt. The prospectors settled into a series of six semi-permanent camps across the surface of the glacier until the trail they were blazing made it to the shores of the Klutina River in the Interior where a city of 100 tents had sprung up.

This camp had a sawmill for the construction of scows and skiffs for navigating the Klutina. Snow slides, snow blindness, falling into crevasses, and extreme physical challenges were elements encountered. A few may have possibly confronted a rare Glacier Bear as several prospectors returned to the tent city which had sprung up by the sea stating that a creature had come out of the crevasses attacking their party killing one man and injuring others.

One group of prospectors brought a "steam sled" to travel over the ice. But, once steam built up in its boiler, it could not pull its own weight. It was abandoned when it was discovered there was no fuel for the boiler on the glacial ice; an oversight the party had made.

Supplies were transported over the glacier in people-pulled sleds as many as 20 trips back and forth over the steepest legs of the journey were needed in order to get a year's worth of goods over the glacier.

Forced back to the beach, they huddled in for the winter only to learn why there had been no Natives living in the area. Valdez witnesses deep, nonstop snows every winter averaging 25 feet or 330 inches annually. Now buried in snow, their plight seemed hopeless. Many came down with scurvy.

Valdez became the site for Alaska's first hanging on New Year's Day 1898. Doc Tanner shot and killed two of his three partners by firing into their tent. After a five-hour trial, Tanner was taken to a tree to be hanged with his surviving partner, the one putting the noose around his neck.

U.S. Army explorer Captain W.R. Abercrombie arrived on the scene from the Interior and turned the shipping captains into authorities. He found the prospectors huddled from 15 to 20 per cabin, their hair now down past their shoulders and beards covering their faces. The federal government ordered the Pacific Steam Whaling Company and the others to give free passage back to Seattle to the would-be millionaires or face prosecution. Meanwhile Sourdoughs from the Interior came to assist those at Valdez Arm building relief cabins.

Enter the Army

Abercrombie had been ordered to investigate the possibility of a military road from Valdez Arm to the town of Eagle near the Klondike Gold Fields. The McKinley Administration had become worried that Americans going to the gold fields might face starvation and the Army, with or without the British Empire's permission, might have to intervene.

The military took an interest in the Valdez area due to the fact it is the most northern ice free port on the continent. Due to this, Valdez became an entry point for the Interior. The port would witness long sled trains scale Thompson Pass for points in the Interior with as many as six hundred cases of eggs under teamster Jack Spenard who later founded the town of Spenard outside of Anchorage.

Old timers called the community Valdes. But when the U.S. declared war on Spain in 1898, locals let it be known patriotically that Valdez was pronounced VALDEEZ. The odd pronunciation continues to this day.

Abercrombie and his men cut a rough trail through Keystone Canyon and over Thompson Pass. The U.S. Army approved his military road in the spring of 1899 and upgrading work began. Abercrombie then constructed the Trans-Alaska Packtrain Trail to Fort Egbert on the Yukon River, later called The Goat Trail. He built the actual road a little higher along the rim of Keystone Canyon wide allowing for two horses abreast.

The Army constructed Fort Liscum in 1900 where the present Alyeska oil terminal is now located; named for Colonel Emerson Liscum who was killed leading his regiment at the Battle of Tien Tsing in China earlier that year during the Boxer Rebellion. Some 172 men were stationed at the post which included the area's only hospital. The presence of the fort proved a blessing for many. The U.S. Army began setting up a series of telegraph stations to the Yukon River, becoming de facto shelters for weary travelers. In 1905, soldiers helped Valdez residents build dikes to prevent the town from flooding along Glacier Creek. Soldiers also built the first dam and hydroelectric plant at Solomon Gulch.

The trail originally took eight days by bobsled stage to Fairbanks. In 1910, the Ed Orr Stage Company charged $150 per passenger one way between Valdez and Fairbanks, not including food and lodging. Horses were changed every 20 miles with some 37 roadhouses constructed every ten miles. The Wortmann's Roadhouse and Telegraph Station at the base of Thompson Pass had accommodations for a hundred people and boasted of having enough hay and feed for a hundred horses.

The trail evolved into the Richardson Highway becoming the only inland route to Fairbanks until the 1920s when rail service between Seward and Fairbanks began. In 1939, it took an automobile a day and a half. Traces of many of the roadhouses can still be found and several have become private homes.

Prince William Sound mines

After the Klondike Gold Rush cooled, prospectors explored the islands and bays of the Sound uncovering gold, copper, and silver deposits. The more profitable mines were near Valdez. In 1906, H.E. (Red) Ellis discovered what would become the Cliff Gold Mine five miles west of Valdez along the north shore of Valdez Arm. With shafts running below sea level, the mine produced 51,740 ounces of gold and 8,153 ounces of silver. The Midas Mine, in nearby Solomon Gulch on the south side of Valdez Arm, was the fourth largest copper producer in the Sound region. 1912 saw some 48 gold mines and 118 gold claims staked out from Valdez to the Columbia Glacier.

As a transportation port for the Interior, Valdez grew during the first two decades of the 20th Century having a bowling alley, a university for one semester, several breweries, a dam and hydroelectric plant, sawmill, the seat of the Territory of Alaska's Third Judicial District, a bank, two theaters, two newspapers, an Ursuline Convent, a library, a hospital, and schools.

Railroad War

The Alaska Syndicate of Morgan-Guggenheims considered Valdez, along with Katalla, as possible ore ports for the Kennecott Mines.

But when Valdez appeared to be out of consideration, newly arrived H.D. Reynolds touted the concept of an Alaska Home Railroad consisting of an electric tramway from Valdez over Thompson Pass at the cost of $340,000. Many Valdezians invested their entire savings into Reynolds' railroad plans and the Alaska Home Railroad was able to raise $106,000. With the funds, Reynolds bought the town newspaper, a hotel, a bank, and even some of the streets.

To stop Reynolds, the Syndicate in 1907 stationed gunmen in Keystone Canyon. Firing on workers as they tried boring railroad tunnels along the canyon walls, one man was killed and soldiers from Fort Liscum were called out to break up the fight. Held back by the gunmen, the Alaska Home Railroad fell apart. Reynolds hurriedly left town owing a large sum of money and ended his days in an insane asylum. All that was left of his railroad dreams were two tunnels in the walls of Keystone Canyon that can be seen today, some track laid, and 500 unemployed workers.

With the completion of the Alaska Railroad out of Seward in 1924 linking Fairbanks to the outside world, Valdez began declining. The next year, the U.S. Army pulled out of Fort Liscum selling it to the Day family in 1929. The site became known as Dayville and turned into a cannery operation. Valdez' population fell to 500.

Yet, Valdez continued to have political influence in the state. The Egan Brothers, Truck and Bill, guided Alaska's Democratic Party from Valdez's Pinzon Bar through the post war years. Bill Egan was elected as Alaska's first governor when statehood was achieved in 1959 and re-elected in 1962 and 1970.

A spot check of Valdez in 1939 showed the town with a population of 555. The community consisted of several hotels, four churches, a library, and an American Legion Museum along with a weekly newspaper. The main income was from gold mining though there were also fifteen fox farms in the area.

In many ways, this was a golden era for Valdez. The community made its mark in the worlds of aviation and the arts.

The world's greatest pilot and the artist

Determined to find a means of staying in Alaska while trying to paint, Sydney Laurence worked as a dishwasher in one of the local grub houses listening to prospectors describe the landscape of the vast Interior beyond Thompson Pass. His first oils caught the notice of Eustace Ziegler and Jules Dahlager, both prominent living in Cordova. The two offered advice and tutoring. Laurence would make small excursions into the Interior until he was able to save enough to finally strike out and homestead near the base of Denali. The mountain became his favorite subject.

Bob Reeve put Valdez into aviation history.

Reeve had made a fortune flying freight in South America. But he had spent it all on women and parties. He stowed away on a steamer Alaska bound and was thrown off at Valdez with two dollars in his pocket. Valdez had a wrecked Eaglerock biplane. Reeve repaired it, then leased it from the owner for ten dollars an hour.

Valdez is surrounded by gold veins, but there was no way to get heavy equipment up to them. Reeve's plane opened the way. Sometimes he would wrap equipment in mattresses and just drop them over a mining site. Other times he did a "controlled" crash onto a nearby glacier using snowfall to brake himself. Thanks to Reeve, the Rough and Tough, set in a rocky outcropping at the heart of Columbia Glacier, and some twelve other mines opened.

He upgraded to flying a Fairchild charging miners 35 cents a pound. His plane became so battered the floor was patched with grocery boxes, the labels still on them. He used Valdez' mud flats as a runway. On his shack read: "Always use Reeves Airways—Slow, Unreliable, Unfair, and Crooked. Unlicensed and Nuts. Reeves Airways—The Best."

Rex Beach, friend of Wyatt Earp, and author of *The Spoilers* wrote magazine articles on Reeve's exploits. Women wrote letters asking to marry him. He answered one from a Janice Morisette and was shocked to learn she was coming to Valdez to marry him. When she arrived, he hid out in the Yukon Territory for a month. She didn't leave. He snuck back into Valdez. Discovering she was attractive; they were shortly married. Reeve's rambling days were over.

World fame came with the Washburn Expedition. Bradford Washburn hired Reeve to take his mountaineering party to the base of Mount Lucania, the last major North American peak not climbed. Successfully getting the party to the 16,000-foot mountain, he discovered the air too thin for his Fairchild to obtain lift.

Three times Reeve failed to take off. He then asked the mountaineers to help strip the Fairchild of everything as the Sun began to rise. Washburn asked him what he was going to do.

"I'm not a mountain climber," Reeve shot back. "I'm a pilot. You can skin your skunk and I'll skin mine."

Reeve then taxied the Fairchild off a cliff!

"The drop off gave the ship just enough forward speed," Reeve would say later. "It missed a huge crack and sailed into the air!"

When Washburn returned to civilization, he told the world Reeve was the greatest pilot who ever lived.

World War II

When World War II broke out, Valdez' port became vital in getting military hardware into the Interior.

The Alaska National Guard set up a base less than two miles west of town manned by 250 men and 15 officers to keep the flow of supplies to the Interior going. Across the Arm at Dayville, the military housed 40 men in the old cannery bunkhouse with orders to defend Valdez against Japanese attack.

As military personnel began drinking to excess due to Alaska's very liberal bar hours, the military ordered Alaskan port towns to close their bars from 8 pm to 10 am. Valdez kept bars and liquor stores closed until noon as a patriotic gesture.

Congress quickly allocated over $2 million for improvements to the Richardson Highway in 1942. At the start of the war, local truckers had an ongoing, sometimes violent, feud with the U.S. Department of the Interior who had transformed portions of the Richardson into a toll road. Now that the Army needed faster and larger transportation of goods, Valdez truckers' complaints were heard, and the tolls dropped by July 1942. The trucking industry quickly boomed. One firm alone was using a staggering 300 truckers by 1944.

The importance of the Richardson Highway was not forgotten after the war as America faced the Soviet Union in the Cold War. In 1950, $45 million was spent paving the Richardson. A large asphalt storage plant was constructed at Valdez' waterfront taking on hot asphalt from ocean tankers. The plant fell victim to the Good Friday Earthquake in 1964.

With snowfall as deep as 900 inches at Thompson Pass, the Alaska Road Commission and privately owned Alaska Freight Lines joined to keep the pass open during the winter of 1950 for the first time. The efforts worked and the Richardson became a paved, all weather road opened year around by 1956.

The Good Friday Earthquake

The Good Friday Earthquake of 1964 devastated Valdez. Striking on March 27th at 5:36 p.m., the quake lasted four minutes with a measurement of 9.2; the strongest earthquake ever recorded in North America. The epicenter was only 45 miles west of Valdez. Sea level at Valdez dropped some 35 feet before a 30-foot-high tsunami hit killing 32 men, women, and children at the city dock.

Three men on the 400-foot steamer *Chena* unloading cargo also died. The ship rose 30 feet into the air on the crest of a tsunami. Then the *Chena* suddenly found herself sitting on mud flats where the sea had been. Another tsunami came in lifting her up again. This time her captain had the awareness to have the engines come online. He steamed the vessel out into deeper water.

Valdez itself saw a total of four tsunami come in flooding the stricken town; the first two were ten minutes apart while the last two were two hours apart.

The entire town of Valdez was condemned after it was determined the ground was too unstable. It took three years for the U.S. Army Corp of Engineers to construct a new city consisting of 54 houses and buildings, many built and then trucked to the town site. The old town site was dismantled and abandoned after the new site was opened. Some 555 people moved into the new town.

In December 1969, a series of unsolved fires burned down what was left of Old Valdez. Among structures lost were the three-story Hotel Valdez built in 1907 as a bank and retail store, the Valdez Drug and Mercantile constructed in 1898 as a dormitory for the Pacific Steam Whaling Company and the Alaska Communications System Building built in 1904 for telegraph communications with the outside world via cable.

Trans-Alaska Pipeline

Thousands came to Valdez after Congress approved the construction of the Trans Alaska Pipeline in 1973. British Petroleum, ARCO, Exxon, Mobil, Amerada Hess, Phillips Petroleum and Unocal formed a consortium called the Alyeska Pipeline Company with the British controlling 50.1.

Work officially began on April 29, 1974, and eventually employed 70,000 men and women. The 800-mile pipeline had to be built over 34 major rivers and cross three significant mountain ranges as well as swamps, forests, and vertical granite cliffs.

Valdez went from a sleepy community of 500 to 8,000 practically overnight. The man camp for the construction crews assigned building the Valdez Oil Terminal held 3480 beds alone.

The boom town atmosphere drew in crime as well. Nine people were arrested for operating a gambling ring out of a Valdez bar that cleared $1 million in six months. A prostitute known only as April made $100,000 working out of a Valdez trailer house in 1974. Another prostitute, in a hurry to leave town, hired a taxi to drive her the 325 miles to Anchorage tipping the cabbie $5,000. Club Valdez ran an ad in the Seattle newspapers reading: "Tavern Bouncer wanted. Must be 6' 8" or over, ugly, tough, and mean, but diplomatic. pref. 280-300 lbs. The bigger, the better. $50 shift, room, board. Will pay air fare to Valdez, Alaska."

Half of the pipeline was built above ground resting on 78,000 supports to avoid being crushed by permafrost if it had been buried. The pipe itself was coated with zinc anodes preventing corrosion. The total cost of construction was $8 billion, however, the amount of oil coming down the pipeline to Valdez has ranged from 20 percent to 18 percent of total U.S. oil production.

On August 1, 1977, Valdez saw the first oil tanker loaded with North Slope Oil, the *ARCO Juneau*, leave port.

The Valdez Oil Terminal has 18 crude oil holding tanks, each covering an acre. The terminal averages from three to four oil tankers departing each day. Since the pipeline became operational, some 15,000 tankers have left the terminal. The terminal had been a heavy tourist draw. In 2001, before the 9/11 attack, it was the eighth most visited site in Alaska. Due to 9/11, the terminal is now closed to visitors.

Exxon Valdez Oil Spill

On another Good Friday, March 24, 1989, Valdez' fate was determined by a forty-two-year-old Joseph Hazelwood, captain of the *Exxon Valdez*. He had returned to his 987-foot oil tanker after bar hopping in Valdez and went below to sleep the effects of alcohol off. A harbor pilot guided the oil tanker out of Valdez Arm. Hazelwood was then awakened as the pilot turned command back to him. The captain requested from the US Coast Guard the use of the inbound lane going into Valdez. His reasoning was to avoid icebergs calving off nearby Columbia Glacier. Once the Coast Guard gave its consent, Hazelwood went back to bed leaving an inexperience Third Mate in command.

The Third Mate attempted to make course corrections to the plot laid out by Hazelwood which would have taken the oil tanker out of the inbound lane. At 12:04 am the *Exxon Valdez* gave a violent shutter along the full length of the ship as it struck Bligh Reef. Eight of her thirteen holding tanks ruptured as Hazelwood was called to the bridge. Oddly enough, Hazelwood ordered full power forward worsening the situation and did not report to the Coast Guard for more than 23 minutes.

An estimated 11.3 million gallons of crude oil emptied into Prince William Sound. It poured out of the tanker at a rate of over 42,000 gallons an hour. It took Alyeska over five hours to respond to Hazelwood's situation. An empty inbound oil tanker was ordered to the scene and then waited as Alyeska and Exxon officials argued over who was in charge of the cleanup. A sudden blizzard struck sending the oil sheen across Prince William Sound and grounding all efforts at an initial clean up.

Within four days the oil slick covered more than 300 square miles. The spill reached all the way to Kodiak Island and the Alaska Peninsula, over 600 miles southwest of Valdez.

Hazelwood was criminally charged with operating a vessel while intoxicated, reckless endangerment, and negligent discharge of oil. He was fined $50,000 and five years of community service. He was found not guilty of the charge of intoxication

During the months after the spill, Valdez' population exploded reaching 10,000. The town was crowded with clean-up crews, reporters, and government officials as work to clean the beaches and rescue animals in Prince William Sound lasted into the fall of 1992.

A new term came into being, "spillionaires." Though Valdez itself was not affected by the oil spill and was home base to only a small fishing fleet, locals reaped huge profits from Exxon and the government for such services from leasing their boats for shore clean up to providing food and lodging.

Exxon spent more than $2.5 billion dollars on the cleanup effort hiring over 11,000 people and leasing 1,400 vessels and 85 aircraft. In response to the spill, the Alyeska Pipeline Service Company today maintains a ship escort for arriving and departing oil tankers and spill response vehicles at the port of Valdez.

Oil money allowed Valdez to issue start up grants for a hatchery, KCHU public radio, the Valdez Chamber of Commerce, the Valdez Convention and Visitors Bureau, and a grain terminal in hopes of being the exit port for barley grown in the Interior. The grain elevator remains empty.

The city also financed the world's largest floating dock along with an impressive civic center.

Modern Valdez

Valdez' towering snowcapped peaks and snowfields have not been ignored by extreme skiers. The World Extreme Skiing Championships were held in Valdez in the 1990s resulting in WESC champion Doug Coombs moving to Valdez in 1993 to offer heli-skiing guides. Shortly afterwards, a second WESC champion, Dean Cummings, also moved to Valdez opening another heli-skiing firm.

Valdez' Prince William Sound Community College began as one of three regional learning centers operated by the University of Alaska in 1971, the other two being in Cordova and Glennallen. The learning center in Valdez was upgraded to Prince William Community College in 1978 with the other two centers designated as satellite campuses.

When Alaska's community college system shut down in 1986, Valdez decided to underwrite the continuation of the college so poorer members of the community could have the benefits a college offers. The small college became an accredited four-year university in 1989 though it kept the name Prince William Sound Community College.

The college earned international recognition after hiring Dr. Jo Ann "Jodi" McDowell in 1992 as its president. The brusque McDowell immediately used her contacts in the theatrical world to launch the Last Frontier Theater Conference the year she was hired, a workshop involving playwrights and actors. It has drawn such talents as Patricia Neal, Chris Noth, August Wilson, and Edward Albee.

McDowell was also able to persuade Maxine Whitney into donating her collection of Native art, the world's largest private collection, to the college. The Maxine and Jesse Whitney Museum includes Native dolls, a kayak, prehistoric artifacts, and a unique collection of Native carved ivory.

Both triumphs were coops over Alaska's principal universities in Anchorage and Fairbanks leading to conspiracy theories regarding her sudden, unexplained resignation in 2004.

Two impressive totem poles carved by artist Peter Toth grace the campus.

Today Valdez's 4000 residents are involved with transporting goods into the Interior, working on the Trans-Alaska Pipeline and its oil terminal, and such tourism activities as deep-sea fishing, heli skiing, and sighting seeing.

The Steven Seagal film *On Deadly Ground* was filmed in Valdez in 1994.

Valdez' Blueberry Hill, near downtown is the northern most point of the coastal Pacific temperate rain forest. A major excursion attraction is the massive Columbia Glacier 28 miles to the west of town. Named by the 1899 Harriman Alaska Expedition, the glacier is the second fastest moving glacier in the world discharging two cubic miles of ice into Prince William Sound annually. It has receded more than nine miles since 1997. The Columbia is 34 miles long and three miles wide and more than 3,000 feet thick of ice in some places.

The Columbia is the source for most of the icebergs in Prince William Sound including what are known as black bergs; icebergs that break off from underneath the glacier and are black from dirt, debris, and gravel. Black bergs have been known to travel a mile from the Columbia before surfacing without warning. A surfacing black berg ripping off the bow of the fishing tender *Vanguard* in 2001. The crew had only 60 seconds to get off before she sank.

WHITTIER

WHITTIER BEGAN AS A SECRET MILITARY base just prior to hostilities with Japan in World War II.

Chugach Alutiiqs once portaged across the narrow section of land separating Passage Canal along Prince William Sound into Turnagain Arm. The route became part of the Native trade route before the arrival of Europeans in Alaska. But no Native settlement ever existed in the area.

The U.S. Coast and Geodetic Survey named the nearby glacier, Whittier Glacier, after poet John Greenleaf Whittier in 1915.

By 1939, the area was the site for one of the larger sawmills in the Territory of Alaska as demand picked up with World War II looming over the horizon. The United States was beginning to build up its military infrastructure in case of a possible German polar invasion rather than concerns regarding Japan. The port, called Camp Sullivan, was to be a supply point for fuel and military hardware to be offloaded for various sites without fear of attack.

The port and railroad terminus were completed shortly after the Japanese attack on Pearl Harbor. The railroad spurs and tunnels through the mountains to Turnagain Arm were completed in 1943.

The military suspected the Japanese knew about Camp Sullivan though its location made it difficult for the Japanese to mount an air strike. Fame aviator Merle Mudhole Smith made a confirmed sighting of a Japanese submarine near Whittier in September 1941, just months before Pearl Harbor. Because of this, the military reduced the time oil tankers could be in port at Whittier to only a few hours. If they had not offloaded by then, they had no choice but dump their oil into Prince William Sound.

After the war, the U.S. Army intensified its building program at Whittier due to the Cold War. The 14-story Hodge Building, now called Begich Towers, with 198 apartments for family housing and bachelor quarters was completed in 1948. The even more impressive Buckner Building was completed in 1953 with a thousand apartments, hospital, bowling alley, theater, gym, swimming pool, and retail shops. The two were connected by underground tunnels that were heated and well lit. The U.S. Army did everything it could to provide comforts for its personnel under one roof. Whittier sees gales force winds and ten feet of snow annually.

Buckner Building and the Begich Towers became the largest buildings in Alaska.

Later a private concern constructed Whittier Manor in the early 1950s as rentals for civilian employees. When the U.S. Army pulled out of Whittier in 1960, the port town had a population of 1,200. Four years later, Whittier Manor was converted into condominiums while most of the local residents moved into the Begich Towers. The Buckner Building was condemned.

The port was slammed by tidal waves that killed thirteen residents during the 1964 Good Friday Earthquake. The first wave of forty feet swept over the sawmill and a number of houses killing ten people who were attending a birthday party. A second wave of thirty feet killed three others. A wave near town crested at an incredible 104 feet.

The devastating earthquake did have its upside for Whittier. In 1962, the port accounted for a little more than ten percent of all Alaska bound cargo. With the rebuilding and improving of port facilities after the earthquake, Whittier became Alaska's busiest port. A small boat harbor was built in the early 1970s. In 1973, Whittier residents approved bonds for the purchase of the 97 acres military facility in a 66 to 13 vote.

Beginning in the mid-1960s, the Alaska Railroad began offering a shuttle service for vehicles going to and from Whittier. But, by the 1990s, the volume of vehicle traffic made the shuttle system ineffective.

After much lobbying for, the $70 million Anton Anderson Memorial Tunnel was completed in 2000 after two years of construction; in essence, it was a widening of the existing railroad tunnels to accommodate road traffic. The project involved a twelve-mile stretch of rail line between Whittier and Portage on the Turnagain Arm side. It put Whittier on the state road system.

At 13,300 feet, it is the second longest highway tunnel and longest combined highway and rail tunnel in North America.

However, since the tunnel is shared by vehicle and rail traffic, there are waits upwards to two hours for vehicles wanting to travel one way. The tunnel is named for the head engineer who supervised the construction of the railroad tunnel during World War II, Anton Anderson.

A brief construction boom followed as Anchorage investors believed Whittier would become a playground for Anchorage residents. The small boat harbor was expanded handling 360 fishing, recreational, and charter boats.

After asbestos was discovered in the Buckner Building, plans for its demolition were dropped. It was deemed too costly to transport vast volumes of asbestos through the tunnel or shipped out through the port facilities.

Bears have been discovered using the abandoned building as a place to hibernate.

The ice-free port was developed to offer a seventy-foot cargo dock and a sixty-foot floating passenger dock. Summer cruise ship visitation keeps the harbor busy with more than fifty dockings during the summer season. Tourists though are immediately herded onto the passenger train Anchorage bound and are never given the opportunity to explore Whittier.

The community remained below 200 in population. Begich Towers not only has individual apartments, but a bed and breakfast, church, the US Post Office, laundry mat, bakery, tanning, movie rentals, and a barbershop. An underground tunnel connects it with the school where the Class of 2006 consisted of three women.

CHENEGA

THE CHENEGA ALUTIIQS WERE ONE OF the original eight divisions of the Alutiiqs in Prince William Sound.

The first European the Chenega people traded with was Captain Nathaniel Portlock in 1787. Portlock found them so friendly he had no fears in sending out small exploration parties to map the western portion of the Sound.

The original village was on Chenega Island. The name of the Alutiiq village was first recorded in 1880 located on the island's southern tip.

When the American Commercial Company took over the Russian trading post at nearby Nucheck, it opened a substation at Chenega. One of the American traders posted at Chenega taught the Alutiiqs how to brew beer insisting payment for brewing supplies be made with furs. Things soon became so rowdy at the village from all the drinking that Russian Orthodox priest Peter Kashevenov was sent for at Nuchek to calm the village down.

Chenega suffered from archeological theft in the 1880s. Prussian Johan Adrian Jacobsen took stone axes, stone lamps, bead work and jackets of eagle skins for his Berlin Museum in 1886. He noted that during the previous year the Smithsonian Institute had taken bodies from Chenega grave sites.

By 1898, Chenega had a hundred residents with a Russian mission, a small church, a school, and a fox farm. By the early 1930s, it was the largest Native village on the Sound. Employment was primarily through a summer fish camp from which they sold salmon to neighboring canneries. A post office was established in 1946.

During the 1964 Good Friday Earthquake, the entire bay in front of the village suddenly drained down to 120 feet extending some 90 feet from the shoreline. Chenega's school was just getting out while some residents were at the post office at the top of the hill. When they saw the sea rolling back, they ran downhill to their homes to get their children and such valuables as their rifles. It was at that moment the tsunami came crashing in cresting at the base of the school some 70 feet above sea level. When the wave went back out, it took 23 people, 13 being children, out to sea. All but one of the homes were swept away. Most had been constructed on pilings.

The tidal wave left only one home, the school and the post office standing. The Russian Orthodox Church was destroyed, but church relics worth $50,000 were salvaged.

The Chenega Native Reserve where the village had been quickly annexed and added to the Chugach National Forest by the federal government which added to the emotional injury.

Chenega's residents were scattered about. Some ended up in a refugee camp. Others were moved into Anchorage and other towns. Then one family in 1982 moved to the site of the former Crab Bay herring saltery on Evans Island. Other families followed. In the summer of 1984, 21 homes, an office building, a community hall, a school with two teacher residence homes, a church, and a community store were built.

Eventually by 1991 the village had 26 families calling it home.

Every Good Friday since then, Chenega residents gather to remember the victims of the tsunami.

On the 25th anniversary of the original village's destruction, the Exxon Valdez oil tanker struck Bligh Reef on Good Friday in 1989 sending sheets of oil towards Chenega ruining the local economy. The village suffered more than any other community on Prince William Sound.

The passage of the Alaska Native Claims Settlement Act led to the Chugach National Forest to turn over 76,000 acres to Chenega in the mid-1990s.

The Chenega Corporation received $34 million from land sales. The corporation in the past has distributed individual shareholder checks amounting from $30,000 to $40,000. With only commercial fishing, a small oyster farm and village services offering limited employment, there are more shareholders living away from Chenega than in the village.

SEWARD

Alexander Baranov and his men were in bairdarkas, a native kayak, searching for sea otter pelts in 1792 along the fjords of the Kenai Peninsula when they were forced into a 16-mile-long broad fjord to escape the wrath of a storm.

There in the fjord the Russian found a forest of tall trees. When Baranov reached the head of this fjord, he was convinced this would be where he would build his trading post. He named it Resurrection Bay because of the day he arrived, the Russian Sunday of the Resurrection (Easter).

Memories of the thick stands of trees stayed with him. Within a year, Baranov sent English shipwright James Shields to Resurrection Bay to construct the three masts, seventy-nine-foot vessel, *Phoenix*, capable of carrying 180 pounds of cargo. Launched in 1794, it was the first sailing ship constructed in the Pacific Northwest. Word of this feat traveled far and fast. The same year of the ship's launching, British explorer George Vancouver tried putting in at the Russian trading post in Resurrection Bay for repairs utilizing its rumored shipyard, but storms force him into Prince William Sound.

Baranov's *Phoenix* gave him the means to bring supplies to Alaska from Russia and impress the Native population. Though the ship was sealed with a homemade substance in replace of tar, Baranov sent her twice to Siberia for supplies and delivering cargoes of valuable pelts.

Returning on the second voyage in 1799, *Phoenix* went down in a storm taking the newly appointed first Russian Orthodox Bishop of Kodiak, Joasaph Bolotov, with her.

Thus, early Seward came into existence.

For the next hundred years, the small trading post would go through cycles of being occupied and being abandoned, whether by the Russians or by Americans. Then in 1896, after gold was discovered around Turnagain Arm eighty miles to the north, Resurrection Bay became a popular disembarking point for gold prospectors as they struggled through the narrow canyons and steep flanks of the Kenai Mountains to reach the gold fields. Captain Frank Lowell and his family set up a homestead in 1884 after moving in from Kodiak and found an income feeding the gold seekers using produce from their farm.

The Alaska Railroad

The northern goldfields caused various groups to draw up plans for railroads connecting the fields to the sea. Seattle real estate developer John Ballaine by 1900 had already rejected Ship Creek (modern Anchorage) and the Passage Canal in Prince William Sound (modern Whittier) in searching for a starting point for a rail line. He settled on Resurrection Bay.

Ballaine organized the Alaska Central Railroad sending his brother Frank along with a surveying crew and a few settlers to Resurrection Bay in 1902 to lay out a town and secure as much property as possible for the enterprise.

His construction crews in August 1903 started putting up a terminal, a wharf, and dock facilities. Only eighteen miles of standard gage track had been laid by the end of 1904 though it was through the heart of the rugged Kenai Mountains. But Ballaine seemed to see danger signs. He sold out to a new group in 1905 just as the Fairbanks gold fields hit peak production.

One of the significant signs of events of this early railroad boom for Seward was the construction of St. Peter's Episcopal Church in 1906, the oldest Protestant church on the Kenai Peninsula.

The new owners laid rail for another 29 miles but stopped as the Panic of 1907 hit the nation. The Alaska Central went bankrupt in 1909, but its bondholders reorganized under the name Alaska Northern Railway. Seventy-two miles north of Seward and ten miles from reaching the gold settlement of Girdwood, that railway ran out of funds too.

The railroad had created Seward, but it was old fashion dog teams and not the steam locomotive that was bringing money into Seward. Four Army officers had surveyed the Iditarod Trail in 1907 from Seward to Nome as a means of carrying mail out of the Interior in winter. Then, on Christmas Day 1909, a massive gold find was made at Iditarod setting off the last great Alaskan gold rush. More than 10,000 prospectors landed in Seward making their way on the Iditarod Trail to the newly uncovered gold. By 1912, more than $30 million in gold had been shipped out by way of Seward. Those who had struck it rich were also leaving Alaska by way of Seward. The Iditarod Trail was officially closed by 1924 due to competition with airplanes.

Alaska did not give up on the concept of a rail line from Fairbanks to the sea nor on Seward. Alaskan congressional delegate James Wickersham introduced the Second Organic Act to Congress in August 1912 calling for the creation of the Territory of Alaska. Section 18 of the act gave the President of the United States authority to study and recommend potential railroad routes in the new territory.

A week after passing of the act, President William Howard Taft created the Alaska Railroad Commission. The new commission recommended the Alaska Northern be extended to the coal fields in the Matanuska Valley and then run west into the Iditarod country replacing the Iditarod Trail. Mike Heney's Copper River and Northwestern Railway out of Cordova would be the one extended to Fairbanks.

Fortunately for Seward, Taft's term was coming to an end. He was replaced by Woodrow Wilson, a man who hated the Morgan-Guggenheim syndicate that owned the Copper River and Northwestern Railway. Not only did President Wilson select Seward as the route to Fairbanks but announced in 1915 that the federal government was going to build the railroad rather than rely on private interests.

The first step, Wilson said, was in the U.S. government buying the now defunct Alaska Northern for $1.5 million. The federal government not only took over the line, but its considerable infrastructure in Seward such as the waterfront and docks. Wilson chose Frederick Mears as the man who would ramrod the rails from Seward into Fairbanks. Under Mears, $4.5 million was spent in 1917 just in grade reductions and reinforcing trestles along the Alaska Northern.

Wilson's announcement touched off a real estate boom as men looking for work poured into port. New homes and businesses were built while existing businesses were enlarged.

The completion of the railroad after a total cost of $60 million gave President Warren G. Harding the excuse to indulge in his lifelong dream of visiting Alaska. As President and Mrs. Harding entered Resurrection Bay in July 1923, Gov. Scott Bone named the entrance into Resurrection Bay the Harding Gateway. The huge ice field nearby was also named for President Harding. On July 15, 1923, after leaving Seward in a special car, Harding drove in the spike completing the line and opening the Alaska Railroad for business. Harding fell seriously ill though after leaving Seward for San Francisco and died there on August 2, 1923.

Rockwell Kent

Against the background of the Iditarod Gold Rush and the railroad boom, renowned artist Rockwell Kent brought his nine-year-old son to Seward in 1918. He was able to secure a cabin on Fox Island near the entrance of Resurrection Bay.

For two years, Kent produced dramatic and stark etchings and paintings of the Alaskan landscape. His son at first enjoyed the adventure before complaining about its isolation. When the Kents finally left Seward in 1919, Kent had more than enough paintings for the shows he was scheduled for as well as material for his bestselling book *Wilderness*. Two years later, his son found himself and his father living in a hut on Tierra del Fuego at the very tip of South America where Kent continued his painting career.

Kent had fond memories of Seward, "a tradesmen's town where tradesmen's views prevail—the worst of Seward is itself; the best is the strong men that by chance are there or that pass through from the great Alaska."

Seward also became famous for being the site for the design of Alaska's flag. In 1927 thirteen-year-old Benny Benson won the territorial wide contest conducted by the American Legion for a flag design for Alaska.

Benson's story is heart wrenching. Born in Chignik in 1913, his mother died when he was three years old. Shortly after her death, the family's home burned down. His Swedish fisherman father then sent him and his brother to the Jesse Lee Home in Seward. Taking the thousand-dollar prize for the flag's design, Benson was able to go to vocational school where he learned to be an aircraft mechanic. The skill took Benson out of poverty. He died in Kodiak of a heart attack in 1972 at age 58.

The Methodist Church decided to move the Jesse Lee Home from Unalaska to Seward because of transportation costs in 1924. A hundred acres was donated for the home by Seward residents and the orphanage opened in November 1925 with three teachers and 85 students.

By 1939 Seward had a population of 835, boasting of being the largest town on the Kenai Peninsula. The town had six hotels, numerous cafes, two newspapers, shops, and the Seward General Hospital. More than $9 million worth of goods were going through the port on an annual basis.

World War II

The 1942 Japanese invasion of Alaska forced the U.S. to scramble to protect Seward's ice-free port from potential attack. Quickly Fort Raymond with 3,000 men was constructed alongside Fort McGilvray and Fort Bulkley as harbor defenses. Fort McGilvray held a radar tower, ammunition magazines, and was the firing command for the anti-motor torpedo boat battery at Lowell Point halfway into port. Fort Bulkley also held searchlights, radar, and fire control stations. All three had gun emplacements. Once the Japanese were driven out of Alaska, all three forts were abandoned by March 1944.

Seward was no different than its Southeast Alaskan brethren ports during the war. When naval personnel arrived in port for leave, soiled doves descended. Fairbanks prostitutes routinely flew scheduled Constellation flights when the Navy was due to arrive in Seward. One lady of the evening from Fairbanks named Lillian was overheard yelling at naval personnel in Seward, "If you're not ready, don't stand in line!"

All three forts are well preserved with their concrete structures intact. Fort McGilvray was turned into Caines Head State Recreation Area in 1971.

The war and the Cold War that followed resulted in upgrades to the infrastructure of the Alaska Railroad continuing the labor boom in Seward. By 1950, Seward's population had doubled to 2,000.

The 1950s saw federal and territorial legal pressure for ports to clean up their act in order to achieve statehood. But in Seward local prostitutes were held with the affection shown family loved ones. Learning of a possible federal crackdown on the trade about to take place, Seward's local marshal had all the good time girls arrested and fined one dollar and then released; thus, protecting them from any federal prosecution through the rules of double jeopardy.

The Good Friday Earthquake

The 1964 Good Friday Earthquake reshaped Seward like so many Gulf towns, and like so many Gulf towns, by unique means. In Seward's case, it was through fire.

The oil tanker *Alaska Standard* was connected by hoses to Standard's Oil tank farm when the earthquake struck. The impact set off in an immense fireball. The oil tanker tried steaming out of Resurrection Bay, but not in time. The first of a series of huge tsunami came roaring in carrying the fire eight blocks inland to the Texaco tank farm setting it ablaze. Soon homes, trailers, shops, and the radio station were burning. The fire continued through the night setting the ice-covered mountains around Seward aglow. Now and then, what was left of the town would be rocked by another fuel storage tank being ignited.

The ground dropped anywhere from six to seven feet. The cabin Rockwell Kent had lived in went into the sea along with many of the areas he painted. Seward herself awoke the next morning with most of its structures either charred or swept out to sea. The rail lines north of town were a twisted mess. Once again though she enjoyed a building boom, this time through massive federal aid guided in by President Lyndon Johnson.

The earthquake severely damaged the Jesse Lee Home. Churches across the United States raised $1.6 million to repair the orphanage, but the funds were channeled to other organizations eventually becoming the Alaska Children's Services in 1970. The home was placed on the National Register of Historic Places in 1995.

Beginning in the late 1980s, the tourism boom began hitting Alaska overall as well as Seward. The local economy structured its life around tourism from May to September annually; not only from cruise ships, but from weekend visits by Anchorage residents only ninety miles to the north. Then in the early 2000s, with the completion of the toll road through the railroad tunnel connecting Whittier to the rest of Alaska, the cruise lines pulled out of Seward docking at Whittier instead. Even the Alaska ferry system discontinued service by 2005.

The community's economy has become diverse. Besides the 115,000 square foot renown Alaska SeaLife Center which opened in 1998, the community provides ship repair and services, a coal export facility for the Alaska Railroad Corporation, the Alaska Vocational Technical Center, a state prison (Spring Creek Correctional Center) housing such notorious criminals as Alaskan serial killer Robert Hanson who hunted some 26 strippers with his high powered rifle, and the University of Alaska's Institute of Marine Sciences.

Seward has earned a reputation over the years regarding many special events the community hosts: the Mount Marathon race every Fourth of July which began as a bar bet between two Sourdoughs in

1909, a silver salmon derby in August, and the Polar Bear Jump-Off Festival in January.

Seward is the ninth most lucrative fishing port in the United States. In 2010, $69.2 million worth of seafood passed through Seward.

SELDOVIA

Nestled close to the very southern tip of the Kenai Peninsula, there was a time Seldovia was the largest town on the Kenai, the center of all economic activity on the peninsula.

With a harbor deep enough for ocean going freighters, she was the transportation point for the scattered communities along the Kenai's west coast. It was not until the road system pushed into the Kenai in the late 1940s that Seldovia lost her dominance over the region.

Before World War II, the primary connection between Seldovia and the small villages that clustered around her and the outside world was the monthly visit by the *S.S. Starr*, a converted halibut schooner carrying passengers and freight out of Seward.

Archeologists believe the Little Ice Age (1100-1800 AD) may have driven humans out of the area. Diggings indicate that Seldovia may have been inhabited as far back as 2500 to 500 B.C.

Russia's Dimitrii Bocharov mapped the area in 1784 followed by England's Nathaniel Portlock and George Dixon a few years later. All three reported exposed coal seams. The reports led Alexander Baranov to send men to collect coal for the recasting of iron in the construction of the *Phoenix* at Resurrection Bay in 1793.

Evstratii Ivanovich Delarov of the Shelikov-Golikov Company led hunting parties into the area constructing a trading post in 1788 named

Aleksandrovskaia. Gradually the community growing around the post came to be known as Seldevoy meaning Herring Bay. The first Russian St. Nicholas Orthodox Church was built in 1820 on a hill overlooking the town, rumored over the remains of an older Native village site. The second St. Nicholas The Orthodox Church was built in 1891. It was restored in 1981 through a state grant of $127,000 due to the efforts of Clem Tillian of Halibut Cove and is now a national historic site. The impressive church cemetery was moved away from the church to its present site due to the 1964 Good Friday Earthquake.

Seldovia's Russian trading post competed for commercial dominance of the region with Coal Village four miles outside of Port Graham. Opened as a coal mine by the Russian American Company in 1855, Coal Village held twenty houses, a church, warehouse, sawmill, blacksmith shop, stables, and a small foundry as well as the mine. The dock made of local rock was made by Native labor. The Russians mined coal for their steamers up to the Alaska Purchase by the U.S. in 1867. At one point, the Port Graham-Coal Village community was Russia's third largest settlement in Alaska. Only Kodiak and Sitka were larger.

An American trading post, the Western Trading Company, opened on Seldovia's beach in 1875 and operated it until 1882 when the neighboring American Commercial Company (ACC) bought them out. The rivalry between the two resulted in sea otter pelts going for $112 apiece. But once ACC became the sole trading post, it was purchasing sea otter pelts at a mere $35 apiece.

Natives and non-Natives alike held strong opinions on the man running the post, Adam Bloch. He had kidnapped a married Aleut woman to sleep with while operating the post. But once he formally became married to another woman, he refused to sell alcohol. Still, he was Seldovia's main employer sending out six kayaks to hunt sea otter pelts. At that time, Seldovia had a population of only 74, 38 Creole or mixed blood and 36 Alutiiq. The town itself was a collection of thatch roof homes set back from the two trading posts located on the beach. Overhunting was inevitable. In 1898, only six sea otter pelts were brought in and none by 1898.

A post office was opened in 1898. Two years later the census showed the town having a population of 149, but nineteen soon died from the flu epidemic that same year.

Northern Alaskan Trading Company opened a post in 1906 to compete with ACC for trade with prospectors disembarking on their way to the gold fields to the north. Indeed, traffic to the gold fields grew to the point that a Captain Blodgett started constructing small boats in 1906 calling his operations the Cook Inlet Transportation Company. J.A. Herbert built the first pier for ocean going vessels to dock during the gold rush. Eventually a fleet of some 200 small vessels was based out of Seldovia transporting would be millionaires up Cook Inlet for the McKinley Gold District.

ACC bought the entire fleet in 1909 transferring its operations ten miles away to Port Graham.

The U.S. Marshal for the Cook Inlet region was based out of Seldovia constructing the first jail in October 1910.

Seldovia found itself again competing with Port Graham. In 1907 the coal mines at Port Graham re-opened hiring some from Seldovia as it mined thirty tons of coal. There was coal in Seldovia. Her school children made news in the territory in 1921 by carrying nearly 20 tons of coal back to their school from the beach, saving their school district money.

The first salmon cannery was built in 1910 bringing in thirty new residents made up of Chinese, Germans, and Scandinavians. A second cannery and dock, the Anderson Dock, was built in 1917.

Seldovia saw a boom in cannery construction in 1922 taking advantage of the rich herring, crab, shrimp, and salmon numbers in the area. Food shortages in Europe resulting from World War I caused the boom in herring demand, especially from Scotland. Four years later more than 18 companies were packing herring in Seldovia. Demand for crab meat fell off in 1925 when California banned its importation. The move placed more pressure on the Cook Inlet herring fishery to the point it crashed commercially in 1929.

After World War I, fox farms, mostly silvers, sprung up in Seldovia. The 1920 census showed the town having four trappers, eleven fox farmers, and three fox farms on nearby islands. Rabbits were raised to feed the foxes though many of the kits fell victim to eagles and ravens. A local, Keith McCullough, began selling breeding fox pairs and shipped out seventy pairs in 1923. A mink farm with 100 animals was set up in town in 1931.

Seldovia became the home of the Cook Inlet Blue and Black Fox Farmers Association of Alaska in 1924 with 52 members territorial wide.

The 1920s also had Prohibition with Seldovia being the center of bootlegging operations for the Cook Inlet. Even Russian Orthodox Father Sarikovicoff was caught bootlegging. An Internal Revenue Service boat sailed up and down the coast making small raids here and there. U.S. Marshal Jimmy Hill was killed in Seldovia by bootleggers in 1924. An ad in the newspaper saying "soft drinks for sale" was the tip that a bootlegger had made a delivery in Seldovia.

Growing economic activity in both Seldovia and Port Graham led Lester Busey to start the Seldovia Herald in 1930. It stayed in operation until 1933. A sawmill opened in 1931. The first automobile came to town in 1932.

Aviation came to Seldovia courtesy of the Mad Trapper, Henry Kroll. After only one lesson before his instructor bailed on him for being too wild, Kroll flew roof top level over Seldovia singing while playing a banjo. A windstorm destroyed his plane 500 flying hours later.

A chrome mine opened at Red Mountain in 1942. When it closed two years later, 6,000 tons of chrome had been taken out of Red Mountain after employing 50 people. Mike Seiler opened a second chrome mine on Red Mountain in 1953. Employing twelve men, the ore it extracted was from 70 percent to 90 percent pure chrome. The mine closed in 1957.

Just before the war started in 1940, the Seventh Day Adventists opened a hospital in Seldovia. Eventually the hospital closed unable to compete with Homer's, but a clinic opened in 1980.

1956 was an important date for Seldovia. It was the year the Alaskan road system reached Homer. Homer was a small farm community across Kachemak Bay from Seldovia depended on her for commerce. The new road connection reversed the relationship allowing Homer to pass both Seldovia and Port Graham in growth and importance.

Prior to the 1964 Good Friday Earthquake, Cook Inlet was known for its dramatic tidal changes similar to Canada's Bay of Fundy. Sea levels would rise and fall an impressive 26 feet every six hours during peak tide. The earthquake brought this to an end when the surrounding lands dropped six feet into the sea.

A 1939 snapshot of Seldovia showed it to have a population of 379 with big game outfitting guides, fox farms, three salmon canneries and two herring curing plants. The waterfront boardwalk was busy with coming in and going out to the smaller Cook Inlet communities to the north.

Seldovia's famed boardwalk built prior to the earthquake in 1931was a thick wooden plank and piling system serving as the main street. It was built on the waterfront. Businesses and homes were built on either side of this planking. When the 1964 Earthquake struck, it resulted in high tides reaching 32 feet submerging the boardwalk and flooding the business district. Using fill, the business district was rebuilt on higher ground with a smaller boardwalk system.

The current school with grades one through twelve under the same roof was built in 1972. The Seldovia Native Association sold logging rights at Seldovia Bay amounting to five million board feet of Sitka Spruce in 1975. In 2008 Seldovia took over the Jakolof Bay dock twelve miles away hoping to increase the flow of visitors from Homer.

On the far south side of the bay is the historic *Chilkat*, Alaska's first state ferry dating back to the 1950s.

Now and then cryptologists will descend on Seldovia in their efforts to investigate the strange occurrences that took place in the settlements of Port Chatham and Portlock. Both small Native communities claimed men would disappear while hunting in the Kenai Mountains. The incidents began at the beginning of World War II. Some of the hunters' bodies would be found dismembered along the beach or in a nearby lagoon.

The residents became so spooked they abandoned Port Chatham. Portlock, a cannery town, was also abandoned by 1950.

Seldovia has transformed into a community of summer homes, bed and breakfasts, and unique shops as well as a quality convention center built by the Seldovia Native Corporation and a museum. It holds a tree house like bookstore called the Warehouse with such rare books as the first edition of Rex Beach's *The Spoilers*.

HOMER

Homer residents like to claim their town is "a quaint little drinking village with a fishing problem" while others simply say Homer is the end of the road—literally. The North American road system ends at the tip of the Homer Spit, a 4.5-mile-long narrow gravel bar thrusting out into Kachemak Bay.

The wedge shaped Kachemak Bay drives 40 miles into the Kenai Peninsula teaming with life as currents keep nutrients from escaping into the ocean.

The Homer region had visitors dating to prehistoric times. Archeologists believe Alutiiqs had summer camps in the Homer area for centuries. Pictographs created by Native American Dena'ina date from 3,000 to 1,000 years ago were also uncovered in the area. The Russians were aware of Homer's coal deposits but kept to the ones they had already developed at Port Graham. Explorer William Dall led a U.S. Geological Survey team into the bay in 1880. It was Dall who interpreted the Alutiiq phrase for the bay, "large cliffs by the water" into the name Kachemak. Dall noted in his report both the potentially rich farmlands on the north shore of the bay and the stands of forests along the south shore.

Johann Jacobsen raided Kachemak Bay in 1883 taking some 65 artifacts he had dug up from abandoned Native dwellings around Homer back to his employer, a Berlin Museum.

The promise of quick wealth finally brought people onto the Spit. Gold promoter and con artist 56-year-old Homer Pennock convinced fifty men and women to follow him to Alaska in 1896 in order to pluck gold off the beaches from the Spit up the coast to Ninilchik. He called his new company the Alaska Gold Mining Company.

After constructing bunkhouses for the party to live in, a debate occurred over what to call their community. A woman, Della Banks, suggested naming it after Pennock and the name Homer stuck to the location. A post office for Homer quickly opened, but within a year everyone, including Homer Pennock, had left for the gold fields of Turnagain Arm where there actually was gold.

The Kings County Mining Company from Kings County (Brooklyn) New York landed in 1898 with another 50 men and tried going overland in winter carrying their supplies in wheel barrels. The heavy snow wore them out and they eventually built shelter cabins at Skilak Lake. By next spring, all but three returned obtaining passage back to New York City.

The Cook Inlet Coal Fields Company landed on the Spit in 1899 throwing up a small town with a loading dock. The firm dug horizontal shafts into the coal seams that were exposed on the sandstone bluff. Coal cars were at first pushed by hand down 42-inch narrow gauge rail the entire seven miles to the dock at the end of the Spit.

A small Porter coal burning locomotive was finally brought in to haul the wooden coal cars. Porter locomotives were the workhorse of small railroads that dotted Alaska at the time. The light rail ran along the bluff from today's Saltwater Drive to just beyond Bidarka Creek. Coal cars were winched by cable and diesel fired steam engines to the top of the bluff.

The company ceased operations in 1902 due to the lack of demand. Their market had been the gold rush towns of Hope and Sunrise on the northern end of the Kenai Peninsula. Cook Inlet Coal Fields Company was forced into a bankruptcy sale in 1913 with equipment and railroad purchased by Seattle's Miller Machinery Company.

Other coal mining firms took its place. The Bluff Point Mine operated from 1915 to 1923 and the Homer Coal Corporation operated from 1946 to 1951. Each mining company made improvements until a roundhouse existed by the dock and small locomotives rumbled down from the mines to the Spit. The last coal operation on the Spit was begun by Evan Jones. He had been a pioneer in developing the coal mines at Sutton, north of Anchorage. Jones died in Homer in 1950 with his coal mining firm closing the next year.

Charles Miller staked out the first homestead in 1915 where Kachemak Drive meets East End Road. More homesteaders came during the 1920s fox farm boom and the growth of the herring salteries across the bay at Halibut Cove. From 1911 to 1928, Halibut Cove held 42 herring salteries and had a population of a thousand. Ranches such as the Miller ranch appeared taking advantage of the grasslands on the bench lands and bluffs above Homer.

There were 78 homesteads by 1930 scattering across the Spit and bench lands. Besides fox farms and the commercial fishing industry, farms grew hay and raised bees, cattle, chickens, goats, turkeys, horses, rabbits, and sheep. The attraction for many of these settlers was free coal to heat their homes in winter. It is estimated that the Homer area still has over 400 million tons of coal below ground.

One of these homesteaders was Yule F. Kilcher who came directly from Switzerland. Kilcher was singer and songwriter Jewel's grandfather. While building up his homestead, Kilcher became the first person to walk the length of the massive Harding Icefield. After World War II, he tried to encourage Swiss emigrating to America to come to Homer and be the basis for a Swiss colony there. Kilcher was a delegate to Alaska's constitutional convention in 1958 and served as an Alaskan state senator from 1963 to 1967.

Kilcher and the other homesteaders and ranchers still depended on the Cook Inlet Coal Company dock at the end of the Spit for supplies shipped in from Seldovia. Heavy ice destroyed that dock in 1938 and a new one had to be constructed by the Civilian Conservation Corps.

By the time World War II started, the town had a population of 207 with 150 farms connected by eighteen miles of road. The farmers and Homer residents created a telephone exchange with 35 subscribers. The fact that the Jesse Lee Home of Seward took over a farm near Homer in 1936 as a financial investment and harvested 60 tons of hay as well as potatoes the first year demonstrated that the word was out on Homer's agricultural capabilities.

Ice took out the Spit dock in 1947 after the entire Kachemak Bay froze. This time the need for a new dock and a highway linking Homer with the rest of Alaska had progressed to only a few miles from town, led to the formation of the first local government, a public utility district, with power to tax.

When the unpaved Sterling Highway finally reached Homer, veterans poured in homesteading and setting up businesses. This in turn heated up the tug of war between Homer's two evolving town centers, Bishop Beach and along Pioneer Avenue on the bench land.

The bench land was well drained, level, and blessed with good soil. Bishop Beach though was next to the mouth of Beluga Slough, a small piece of land connecting the Spit to the mainland. Shipping and landing craft were using the slough and Bishop Beach for offloading supplies.

The first post office was on the Spit at the current Salty Dawg Saloon. Then as a community project, a small log cabin was built on Tom Shelford's homestead near the mouth of the slough to serve as a post office in 1927. The Inlet Trading Post opened on Bishop Beach in 1937, also called Berry's after the owners Maybelle and Arthur Berry, with a grocery store on the ground floor and a hotel above. The structure that is today's Driftwood Inn was built in 1931 and was a school, then a cold storage unit, and finally the Inlet Inn Hotel.

Those who staked their future on the bench land would not be outdone. The Homer Cash Store (today's Main Street Mercantile) opened along Pioneer Avenue in 1936 stocked as well as possible with dry goods while the town's dance hall was on the second floor. The Alaska Wild Berry Products opened next door in 1946. The three-story Heady Hotel (today the Heritage Hotel) opened in 1948. The Kanich House, the site of many different businesses, opened in 1944. The Shelford House, built in 1936, was the Sterling Bar and Cafe before becoming today's Kharacters Alaskan Bar.

The Homer library was built on the bench land in 1948 and replaced by a newer structure in 2006.

Another Homer iconic symbol came about in 1957 when Charles Abbot bought the old post office, grocery store, and offices of the Cook Inlet Coal Company located on the Spit. A large water tank came with the purchase. Abbott merged the three structures creating the Salty Dawg Saloon. He refitted the water tank turning it into a lighthouse. Today the Salty's lighthouse tower is an official NOAA marker found on marine charts. Vessels can make the light out from miles out at sea.

As Homer became larger than Seldovia, the need for more infrastructure and schools outstripped the public utility district's power to tax. Residents on the east side of Homer acted first organizing Kachemak City in 1961 but failed to get the rest of Homer to join them.

The formation of a Homer city government came just as the 1964 Good Friday Earthquake struck. The Spit sank from four to six feet with most of the vegetation dying off due to saltwater seepage. It took six years and over $6 million to repair and raise the Spit Road though storms wash away sections from time to time.

Homer's first newspaper, the *Homer News*, began printing in 1964. The *Homer Tribune,* a second newspaper, began in 1991. Though the *News* was bought by Georgia-based Morris Communications in 2000, the two newspapers maintain a healthy rivalry. That a community as small as Homer can financially support two newspapers is a remarkable achievement in itself.

Russian Old Believers, a sect within the Russian Orthodox Church, began arriving in 1968 financed through the Tolstoy Foundation of New York. The first five families settled into 640 acres and lived in tents as they transformed the land into the village of Nikoloevsk. They became naturalized U.S. citizens in a ceremony held at Anchor Point school in 1975.

Their success led to more Old Believers settling in the Homer area. Today three Russian Old Believer villages are to the east of Homer along the north shore of Kachemak Bay, Voznessenka, Razdolna, and Kachemak Selo. But many are moving into Homer proper where several own commercial fishing boats. A number of Alaskan towns boast of their Russian heritage, but only in Homer are found signage both in English and the 33 letter Cyrillic alphabet though Homer did not exist when Russia ruled Alaska.

When the Libertarian party won the 1984 election sending Andre Marrou to the Alaska House, it spoke to the political diversity of the town. One could drive any street and find yard signs supporting all six of Alaska's political parties: Republican, Democratic, Alaska Independence Party, Green, the Republican Moderate Party, Libertarian. Coffee shops are hot with political discussions. In her stores, on the sidewalks, and down on the Spit, ranchers, loggers, fishermen, artists, and Spit Rats (cannery workers living in tents pitched on the beach) mingled with tourists.

When Marrou was elected, Tom Bodett was a construction worker building homes with a part time job for National Public Radio when an advertising executive heard his voice while visiting Homer. He was offered the job of being the pitch man for the Motel 6 chain with the now famous line "We'll leave the light on for you." Since then, Bodett has become a serious author of children books and *As Far As You Can Go Without A Passport* on life in Homer.

Bodett's big break came the same time Atz Kilcher was taking his daughter Jewel into local watering holes singing live and yodeling. Jewel then struck off on her own living out of her van in San Diego before she was discovered in a coffeehouse. Like Bodett, Jewel also wrote a book on her life in Homer that came out in 2000, *Chasing Down The Dawn*.

Shelley Gill, author of children books, calls Homer home as do brothers Andy and John Hillstrand, captains of the *F/V Time Bandit* featured on the television show *The Deadliest Catch*. Besides logging, firefighting, and commercial fishing, Homer resident Geo Beach was the host for *Tougher In Alaska*.

Homer is still a collection of potters, artists, sculptors, actors, and writers as well as fishermen, carpenters, farmers, and workmen. Homes may range anywhere from a million dollars to being a collection of driftwood and flotsam. The town's first streetlight was installed in 2005. A brewery opened in town.

The Center For Alaskan Coastal Studies is a Homer-based nonprofit organization. The village of Halibut Cove and its quaint setting is only a few hours away from the Spit onboard the motor launch *Danny J*. Also, across Kachemak Bay is the 400,000-acre Kachemak Bay State and Wilderness Park, Alaska's first state park. Theater performances are offered year around at the Pier One Theater.

In 2002 the Pioneer dock opened on the Spit to handle cruise ships, U.S. Coast Guard cutters, and state ferries.

The following year in 2003 the Alaska Islands and Visitors Center opened giving people a visual tour of the 4.9-million-acre Alaska Maritime National Wildlife Refuge encompassing the Aleutian Islands and portions of the Alaska Peninsula.

Kodiak and the Aleutians

This world resembles a strand of emeralds set on a steely gray sea as it reaches out for Asia. The Aleutians are crowned by the snowcapped peaks of nearly a hundred volcanic peaks, several active. Here and there can be found the blue domes of small Russian Orthodox churches.

Before World War II, visitors could only travel into this world once a month on an old, converted halibut schooner the *S.S. Starr* as it sailed "to the westwards" as this region was called in Alaska. Today it is the Alaska state ferry *Tustumena* that carries passengers and freight to the westwards, the only link for many of the small ports to the outside world.

The Westwards consist for the most part of what is called the Aleutian Arc. Partially making up part of the mainland in the form of the Alaska Peninsula and in part the Aleutian Islands, the arc is the telltale physical evidence of the subduction of the Pacific tectonic plate beneath the North American plate.

The arc stretches westward from North America for 1,550 miles acting as a buoy separating the arctic waters of the Bering Sea from the waters of the North Pacific warmed by the Japanese current. This arc is inhabited by some 80 volcanoes, many strata-volcanoes. The Aleutian

Islands hold 57 active volcanoes. Pavlov Volcano near Sand Point has erupted 40 times in written history.

The collision of the two tectonic plates has also resulted in historic earthquakes, the most recent being near Little Sitkin Island in June 2014 measuring 7.9 on the Richter scale.

Noted for its violent seas smashing whatever is afloat onto the rocks of the island chain and along the Alaska Peninsula, the Native population developed what is now called the kayak or baidarka to navigate these waters and live.

Two native groups inhabited this world, the Aleuts and the Alutiiq of Kodiak. They warred upon each other until the arrival of the Russians. The Russians in turn warred upon them in brutal fashion in a series of wars until they had subjected the entire region.

Russian Orthodox missionaries began arriving in 1793. Under the dynamic leadership of Father Veniaminov, the Native population became devout Orthodox Christians. Orthodox missionaries led the way in vaccinating the population against a host of diseases. It was a service the U.S. failed to pick up after the American purchase of Alaska.

Through an act of Congress, the region was governed essentially by one man, Captain Mike Healy of the U.S. Revenue Service and his cutter, the *Bear*. Hell Roaring Mike won fame and infamy in stopping seal poaching, bootleggers, and in rescuing stranded seamen and rushing food to starving villagers. His methods were brutal at times but effective.

As the bounty in seafood grew, the region was populated by Scandinavian fishermen who still hold sway in many of the region's communities such as Sand Point.

The region was the only part of North America invaded and occupied during World War II. The Thousand Mile War as it is called saw fierce fighting between Japanese and American and Canadian forces. As World War II drew to a close, the U.S. gave the Soviet Union permission for operating several Russian military bases in the region in preparation for war against the Japanese home islands.

The sea's bounty has led to Kodiak, Unalaska, and Sand Point to be counted among the top fishing ports of the United States.

The region's primal beauty has led to the creation of several significant wildlife refuges and national parks; the Alaska Maritime National Wildlife Refuge, the Kodiak National Wildlife Refuge, the Izembek National Wildlife Refuge, and Katmai National Park. There are also six smaller Alaska state parks around Kodiak Island.

None of these are easy to visit. One must either fly or travel by the less expensive Alaska ferry system.

PORT LIONS

Port Lions is the only town in the United States built by a service organization. With her 256 residents nestled along spruce lined Settler Cove in the northern corner of Kodiak Island, Port Lions was a creation of a service project by Lions Clubs International.

The Lions, along with the Mennonite Disaster Service, rushed aid to the village of Afognak after it was devastated by a tsunami generated by the 1964 Good Friday Earthquake. The earthquake, which measured 9.2 on the Richter scale, struck on March 24th.

It was the strongest earthquake ever recorded in North America.

Afognak was one of ten settlements established by the Russians prior to 1799. Located on the spruce covered Afognak Island, the Alutiiq village was selected as a retirement community for Russians. The town was physically divided into two sections: Russian town close to the beach and Aleut town on higher ground.

Well into the middle of the Twentieth Century, Alutiiq was spoken in Aleut town and Russian was spoken in Russian town.

Though many residents made their living as fishermen, the town had no docks or harbor facilities. Aleut Town was the location of the school while a Russian Orthodox Church with a massive steeple dominated the landscape. The von Scheele family owned the local store and operated the mail boat to the other villages and cannery towns on the island.

In June 1912, Mount Katmai erupted 90 miles to the northwest of the village. The 115 residents of the village of Katmai on the mainland were evacuated by the Coast Guard cutter *Manning*. Along with residents from the village of Cape Douglas onboard, Captain K.W. Perry made for Afognak, the closest village away from the eruption.

Afognak residents had noticed a distinct cloud enveloping the sky. Eighth grader Jessie Petellin recalled how the Alutiiq astronomers in Aleut Town said it was either going to rain or snow. It did neither. For three days there was total darkness as it rained a total of three feet of hot ash.

The Katmai Alutiiq were refugees at Afognak for only a few months. They relocated to the Alaska Peninsula where they named their village Perryville after the Coast Guard captain who saved their lives.

After World War II, Afognak men worked in the island's logging camps or the canneries. Lowell Wakefield closed his father's cannery in Anacortes, Washington, moving the entire operation onto nearby Raspberry Island where he constructed a cannery and company town known as Port Wakefield.

Wakefield became known as the founder of the lucrative Alaska King Crab industry. Not only were Afognak men hired for the modern cannery operation that Wakefield had installed, but so were many women.

Afognak and Port Wakefield eventually fell victim to the massive earthquake which struck on Good Friday in March 1964 with the epicenter along the northern coast of Prince William Sound.

Residents had already learned through radio reports that tsunamis had devastated Seward and the small Native village of Chenega in Prince William Sound.

Suddenly the sea went out. People began scrambling for higher ground.

"Running up the hill, we heard the water coming behind us through the woods," said J.P. (John) Pestrikoff.

The village was hammered by a succession of surges, some reaching up to 25 feet above sea level.

"Waves kept coming in and out thrashing our village," wrote resident David Mullen on his personal account of the disaster.

There were no fatalities among the 220 Afognak residents, but many of the homes were destroyed. Erosion claimed more homes. Residents were evacuated to Kodiak or forced to live in tents. Port Wakefield also suffered damage as Raspberry Island sank six feet into the ocean.

The five village elders decided to move Afognak to Kodiak Island. Lions Club International, hearing of the difficulties Afognak faced, stepped forward with construction supervisors and the money needed. The Mennonite Disaster Service prepared to rush carpenters north to Alaska.

Village elders Oscar Ellison and George Naumoff selected Settler Cove on May 14, 1964. An attempt to homestead the area failed around 1900. A cattle ranch was attempted a few years before the relocation from Afognak but ceased due to losses from Kodiak bears.

There were many reasons for choosing Settler Cove: good water, stable ground, plenty of available lumber.

Wakefield Cannery had selected adjacent Peregrebni Peninsula for a cannery which could be a source of employment for the community. A dozen Afognak families had fished king crab for Wakefield before the Good Friday Earthquake. By placing the town along the same section of Kodiak Island as the town of Kodiak, it ensured the new community would become a stop for the state ferry, the *Tustumena*.

It took a year to prepare the site. Thirty men living in a community hall and in collapsible tents worked transforming raw land into something they could call home.

"I was the paymaster," said Pestrikoff. "At first when we cleared the land, we tried burning all the logs. We couldn't burn all the trees so we tried floating them away. In just a short time, the Coast Guard came after us and told us to stop."

Afognak Natives, Lions Club members, and those from the Mennonite Service worked shoulder to shoulder surveying lots and installing sewage and water systems for 44 homes.

"They dug the trenches by hand for the water and sewer lines," said former Port Lions Mayor Marv Bartleson.

The beginnings of Port Lions consisted of forty-four homes prefabricated in the nearby town of Kodiak. Wakefield had cedar log cabins that had made up his company town barged to the new site as well. A bunkhouse for the men was set up at Settler Cover. Electric power came from the diesel generators installed at the newly built Wakefield cannery.

On December 11th, 1965, the people of the former village of Afognak arrived in private boats or on barges. A drawing was held to see who would have which lot. The churches were allowed to go first. The Russian Orthodox faith had always been a guiding influence for the people of Afognak for more than a century. The Nativity of Theotokos Orthodox Church drew a lot just above the new community.

A timber dam was built on Branchwater Creek creating a 2.5-million-gallon reservoir. The lake fed into a newly installed 125,000-gallon storage tank.

Before leaving, Mennonite workers raised a ten-foot cross dedicating the new village to the hope it would be spared from future tsunamis.

In 1966, when the new village became incorporated as a city, the residents chose the name Port Lions honoring the workers and financial assistance Lions International had made available.

Lowell Wakefield invested $2 million into the king crab processor and a quick freeze plant.

In four years, the town grew from 178 to 400. Enola Mullen opened a general store after operating one in Afognak for fifteen years. Port Lions had a restaurant, a bar, and a small office building.

At first, the school taught only the first eight grades. High school age students either moved to Kodiak to finish high school or to Mount Edgecumbe school in Sitka. The local school had three teachers. By 1986, Port Lions boasted a high school with more than 30 students and two full-time and two part-time instructors.

Then, beginning in the 1970s, Port Lions suffered a series of blows.

The Wakefield cannery burned in March 1975. The following year the local sawmill closed. The local Native village corporation bought the 149-foot *Smokwa*, a floating processor for crab. The processor operated off and on until 1980.

There was some progress in the 1980s. A small boat harbor was built though it had to be restructured in the 1990s due to a storm. The hydroelectric plant at Terror Lake, thirteen miles away, came online in 1984 providing reliable power after years of brownouts.

Then in March 1989, Port Lions felt the effects of the Exxon Valdez Oil Spill. The wrecked supertanker had dumped more than eleven million barrels of oil into the sea. Exxon quickly chartered all the boats available at Port Lions for the cleanup. More than half the town was hired in the effort. Port Lions became a center for the construction of oil retaining booms made from spruce. The oil cleanup effort lasted ten months.

Afterwards, the town's only bar closed, and the community went "damp," a term meaning alcohol could be owned, but not sold. The Squartsoff family took over the town's general store. The store's deli became the place to go for morning coffee and town gossip. But the cancellation of the commercial supply link with Seattle sealed the store's fate.

Port Lions has no doctor, and a senior did not graduate from the high school in 2007, but the town appears to have turned a corner.

Port Lions took over the small boat harbor from the State of Alaska in December 2006 with a planned $2.5 million enlargement of the breakwater. Alaska's Denali Commission has opened a clinic. The 2600-foot gravel airstrip was expanded.

Ironically, the abandoned site of Afognak has given birth to the Russian Old Believers community Aleneva with a population of around 70. The sect holds to ultra-traditional values of the Orthodox Church. Leaving Russia after the Russian Civil War in the 1920s, they first settled in Oregon before coming to Alaska and establishing a number of settlements in the late 1960s and early 1970s, primarily on the Kenai Peninsula.

Port Lions can boast of having Alaska's longest causeway, a half mile wooden foot bridge built to the Peregrebni Peninsula where the dock is located. The structure lessens Kodiak bear encounters that were taking place along the road. Near the peninsula side of the causeway are the remains of a barabara, an Alutiiq traditional earth house.

Port Lions is also the site of a spectacular waterfall known locally as "the swimming hole" as cold pure running water comes shooting out from a rocky gorge as it makes its way to the sea.

Stanford University has maintained a remote radio site in the village since 2006 studying the Earth's ionosphere, lightning, and radio-atmospheric phenomena.

KODIAK

Kodiak was Alaska's first capital, and is the resting place of an Orthodox saint, and the home of one of the largest carnivores on the planet.

When Alexander Baranov was told forests could be found on the north end of Kodiak Island capable of providing lumber for ships and timber for homes, he nearly moved the entire town of Three Saints Bay to a narrow strait between Kodiak and the much smaller Near Island in 1791. He called his new settlement Pavlovskaia or St. Paul Harbor. When the Czar allowed the formation of the Russian American Company in 1799, Baranov was selected as the ruler of Alaska. In turn, he named his St. Paul, later known as Kodiak, the capital of Alaska.

St. Paul being made Alaska's capital was ironic. For most of Kodiak's history, she stands apart from Alaska, a land of her own.

Kodiak Island is the second largest island in the U.S., just slightly smaller than the big island of Hawaii. Running a little over a hundred miles long and from ten to sixty miles wide, with some 3,388 square miles, the Kodiak Archipelago contains 200 islands, several of significant size. The island chain contains some ten communities. Over half of Kodiak Island is grasslands explaining the location of some of the largest cattle ranches in the United States. The Kodiak Fairgrounds hosts one of the largest rodeos in the state.

Residents obtain supplies and goods directly from Seattle. There is no Anchorage connection. While the rest of the state displays shirts and bumper stickers stating, "Alaskan Grown" or " Alaskan made," Kodiak shirts and bumper stickers read "Kodiak grown" or "Kodiak made." The Alaska Aerospace Program, more than fifty miles southeast of the town of Kodiak, launches satellites into space on a regular basis. Kodiak even boasts of its own brewery which has consistently made an annual profit serving the island's 15,000 residents. Besides a small community college, Kodiak is also the home of an Orthodox seminary for the training of Orthodox priests.

The island contains no moose but does have deer—and elk—one of the few places in Alaska. While the rest of Alaska goes salmon crazy during fishing season, Kodiak residents also delight in some of the best fly fishing in the U.S.

The island is known for the gigantic Kodiak Brown Bear with males getting up to 1,500 pounds and five feet tall at the shoulders and ten feet tall when standing on its hind legs. Classified as a unique subspecies of the Brown Bear, they are the largest brown bear subspecies on the planet and are comparable in size with polar bears. DNA tests show they are closely related to Kamchatka Brown Bears and those on the Alaska Peninsula. Numbering around 3,500 on the islands, on average nine are killed annually by people in defense of their lives.

The Alutiiqs

The Yup'ik Eskimos migrated over the Alaska Peninsula to its Pacific coast crossing Shelikof Strait to Kodiak Island sometime between 8,000 to 7,500 years ago. Though in continuous war with the Aleuts, a distinct culture and language evolved until the early Yup'iks became the Alutiiq people with a blending of Yup'ik and Aleut worlds. By the time the Russians arrived, Kodiak, or in Alutiiq Kadiak meaning island, held 9,000 Alutiiqs. Today there are 1,700 Alutiiqs still living on the islands though by 2010 only fifty speak their native tongue.

The Koniag War

Russian explorer Stepan Glotov discovered the island in 1763. Russian trappers hunted the western end of the island for sea otter pelts.

Grigorii Shelikhov was determined to set up a permanent post as far east as possible from Unalaska. He sailed with three vessels and 192 men. He also brought along his wife, Natalya Alexevna, the first European woman to come to Alaska.

With Shelikhov's ship *Three Saints Bay* in the lead, the small flotilla arrived on Kodiak on August 3rd, 1784. Shelikhov began offloading a mile and a half from the Alutiiq village of Nunamiut. Though the Alutiiqs were at first friendly, when they realized the Russians were not leaving, they plotted with other villages on attacking the settlement. Shelikhov learned of this and struck first attacking the nearby village. Thus began the month-long Koniag War.

Hundreds of Alutiiqs were killed in the campaign as they tried fighting with spears against guns. Shelikhov burned villages in punitive raids. Aluttiqs tried taking Three Saints Bay, but Shelikhov had brought cannons with him and held the Natives off. As more Alutiiqs gathered for battle, Shelikhov caught a break. The Sun went into an eclipse. The Russian seized the opportunity informing the Natives he had made the Sun go away. Only if they made peace, would he allow the Sun to return. Thus, the war ended and the Alutiiqs began their long servitude to their Russian conquerors.

Though the Alutiiqs were in essence Yup'ik, they were so similar to Aleuts in hunting and living techniques that the Russians simply believed they were just another variation of Aleuts they had encountered. With subservient Alutiiq hunters and Russians out in virgin hunting grounds, Shekilhov began paying out profits to his investors by 1786. His company was on its way to becoming the largest private firm operating in Alaska.

Shelikhov and his wife then left Kodiak going directly to the court of Catherine the Great to ask for a monopoly on Alaskan trade. He left behind two governors at the small Kodiak colony that turned out to be disasters. Huddled in Three Saints Bay, the Russians no longer went on extended hunts as Alutiiqs again began gathering talking about a final attack. Worse, the company was no longer showing the spectacular profits it had been.

Enter Alexander Baranov

Shelikhov's third selection for a governor of his Kodiak holdings was an odd choice. Unimposing, balding, physically unfit, ravaged by an alcohol addiction, and a financial failure for most of his life, Alexander Baranov could not be described as a leader of men.

At age 33, he had abandoned his wife and child, running off to Siberia with his brother. There for ten years, he managed several businesses that failed for one reason or another. Yet, when Shelikhov first asked him to take the position, he refused. Now in 1790, at age 43, considered old age by the standards of the time, Alexander Baranov agreed to travel to the very end of the Russian world and govern Kodiak.

Baranov relocated the headquarters of the Kodiak colony to his new settlement of St. Paul. Baranov's St. Paul consisted of 24 log cabins, a steam bath, a stockade surrounding the village with watch towers, a warehouse for storing pelts, and outside the stockade special homes for his Alutiiq allies and their families. He also had a vodka distillery and a small shipyard where boats were built to haul pelts back to Siberia. Baranov had the pelt warehouse rebuilt in 1808 and it stands today as the Baranov Museum.

In less than a year, Three Saints Bay was slammed by a tsunami in 1792 washing most of the inhabitants out to sea.

Baranov was given an English shipwright, red-haired James Shields, to assist him in the construction of a merchant fleet. He had requested a priest hoping the presence of a man of God would calm his men down. When his men learned of this, there was grumbling. Sleeping with a Native woman who had been baptized made them uncomfortable. It might be counted as a sin.

Instead of a priest, Shelikhov sent eight monks, four of which were of high order including the Archimandrite Iosaph, to win favor at the

Russian court. Iosaph was angered when Baranov told him they would have to gather their own food and build their own church which they did, the Holy Resurrection Russian Orthodox Church in 1794. The site would see three different churches over the centuries until the final structure with its blue onion domes was built in 1945.

Iosaph constantly wrote to Russian authorities about Baranov's godlessness; he lived with two Native women, one of which was carrying his child, he handed out brutal punishments, and he encouraged his men to sing and drink every night (for morale purposes).

The monks had come with fifty serfs who revolted against Baranov's authority, frightened about living in the Alaskan wilderness. Baranov put the revolt down through hangings and floggings which were also entered into Iosaph's letters. He then sent the serfs off to colonize Yakutat where most of them were massacred by the Tlingits in 1805.

The Three Saints Bay tsunami convinced Baranov to move its agricultural colony closer to St. Paul. The largest cattle herd was relocated outside of St. Paul at Chiniak where wheat and barley fields were cultivated. A cattle herd was set up at Ugak Bay, which now claims to be the first cattle ranch on Kodiak Island along with herds on nearby Spruce and Wood Islands. Pigs and chickens were introduced shortly after and Iosaph opened an agricultural school in St. Paul.

Iosaph died when his shipwrecked returning from Siberia. Baranov sent most of the other monks off on missionary work throughout known Alaska where some met their deaths. Only a young monk named Herman and a second monk remained in St. Paul.

Alaska's first capital

In 1799, St. Paul received word that the Russian-Alaskan Company had been organized after the death of Shelikhov with Baranov as its manager. St. Paul was to be the capital of Alaska save for the Aleutians under the command of Unalaska for the time being.

By 1804, St. Paul was the hub of a small empire with outposts scattered from the Cook Inlet to Prince William Sound to Southeast Alaska where Baranov had just set up the settlement of St. Michael. Unalaska and its holdings by now had been added to Baranov's jurisdiction.

St. Paul changed when word came of the destruction of Saint Michael by the Tlingits. September 1804 found St. Paul's harbor was choked with Aleut, Alutiiq, and Yup'ik warriors in their *baidarkas* and three small sailing ships manned by every Russian Baranov could spare. Baranov was determined to retake St. Michael. After the Battle of Sitka, the capital would be moved from Kodiak to another new city built by Baranov—this one in Southeast Alaska so the Russian governor could be "closer" to his enemies.

Baranov may have gone on to Sitka, but Kodiak never forgot him. The outdoor pageant *Cry of the Wild Ram* on Baranov and the founding of Kodiak ran for 26 years at Fort Abercrombie before its last performance in 1992.

A Russian outpost

Kodiak did not become a backwater the way Unalaska had. The island continued providing beef and grain for Russia America. Many Russians sent to Alaska settled in Kodiak. Kodiak continued as the trade hub for her satellite settlements in Cook Inlet and Prince William Sound. Her shipyards supplied merchant vessels for the colony as quickly as Aleutian storms claimed them. Russians unable to leave their Native families when their tour of duty ended were granted permission in 1835 of either living in St. Paul or the founding of retirement villages such as nearby Ouzinkie, Afognak, and Kasilof on the Kenai Peninsula. With so many staying, the Orthodox church succeeded in lobbying for a ten-bed hospital for St. Paul in the 1840s.

St. Herman

The least in rank of the original Orthodox monks who came to Kodiak in 1794, today the Orthodox Church views Herman as the patron saint of the Americas.

Herman often found himself at odds with the authorities for protecting the rights of the Natives. From 1808 to 1818, Herman lived on Spruce Island where he dug a cave to live in. Today it is his burial site.

Herman nursed epidemic victims after the plague was brought by an American ship. When Kodiak seemed threatened by a tsunami, Herman reportedly placed an icon of the Theotokos on the beach proclaiming the waves would not go beyond it. It worked as far as Kodiak residents were concerned. When a forest fire threatened to consume St. Paul, Herman dug a trench preventing the flames from advancing on the city.

Herman died in 1837. In 1867, Orthodox Bishop Peter of Alaska conducted an investigation of Herman's miracles. His report was published three times before Herman was glorified in 1970 with four feast days set in the Orthodox calendar in his honor. Saint Herman's Orthodox Theological Seminary in Kodiak was named for him in 1972. His burial site on Spruce Island has become a pilgrimage site.

Russia's Kodiak enterprises

As for Russia America, it found itself in difficult financial waters. In spite of the efforts by later governors on management of sea otter hunts, they declined in number. Russia herself could not help due to the debt she accrued in fighting the Crimean War against Britain and France. Other financial avenues were explored. A whaling station was opened on Kodiak Island but mismanaged.

Sensing a market among the newly rich in San Francisco after the California Gold Rush, horses were shipped to Kodiak to assist in the shipping of ice to California in 1852. The Russia American Fur Company won a three-year contract for shipping 1,000 tons of ice to the American Russian Trading Company of San Francisco at $35 a ton. Ice from Lake Tanignak on Wood Island proved better than Sitka ice since it normally was more than ten inches thick.

Impressed, the American firm signed a twenty-year contract with Russia Alaska for not only ice, but lumber, coal, and fish for West Coast and Australian markets.

Two ice houses were erected on Wood Island. A water powered sawmill was set up to provide sawdust for insulating the ice during shipping. From 1852 to 1859, 7,000 tons of ice were shipped not only to California, but to Mexico and South America. Thirteen miles of road were laid, and a twelve-acre oats field was set up for feeding the horses.

It all came crashing down with the invention of an artificial ice making machine in the U.S. Broke, with Alaska becoming an increasing drain on her and fear she would be seized by Britain and added to Canada, Russia sold Alaska to the United States.

Kodiak becomes American

A U.S. Army unit consisting of 114 men and two civilians, Frederick Bischoff with the Smithsonian Institute and a Deputy U.S. Customs agent, did not arrive to take command of Fort Kodiak until the spring of 1868. The name St. Paul was unceremoniously dropped in favor of the name for the entire island. There was already an American in the settlement of 300, a representative of the American firm Hutchinson, Kohl, and Company taking inventory of items within the Russian American trading post.

The new U.S. commander issued an order for civilians to pick up the litter and filth in front of their homes which was ignored. He issued a second order demanding that the locals get their pigs out of the fort. A widow's two pigs were then shot and killed before the order was rescinded. Other than that, duty was peaceful. The residents were still in a state of shock that they had been sold.

When the Army evacuated the fort in 1877 to fight the Nez Perce, they brought back tales of a monster bear.

The Russians never hunted the Kodiak Brown Bear claiming the fur was of poor quality. Americans were also big game hunters and the lure of killing such a mammoth beast drew them north. Kodiak buzzed with activity as Alutiiqs acted as guides. Up to 250 bears were being shot annually, enough to cause both big game hunters and scientists to express concerns about overhunting the island in the 1890s.

Karluk was the location of the first salmon cannery on Kodiak in 1881 followed by a host of others. Overlooked by the Russians, fisheries were drawing people to the island for jobs. Within nine years, Karluk had ten canneries and seemed to be on its way to becoming the center of economic activity for Kodiak Island.

Agriculture still held on. Small cattle herds were still being raised while hay was put up for the winter months. Crops included potatoes and turnips. Dairy cattle were raised on Afognak Island for butter. As Army Lt. Eli Huggins noted in his 1874 book on Kodiak, the island was still too far from markets for cattle to be profitable.

Kodiak Baptist Mission

In 1880, Presbyterian missionary and explorer Sheldon Jackson proposed to the competing Protestant denominations that Alaska was too large for all of them to try to save the Natives' souls and compete with the Orthodox Church. Instead, Jackson proposed dividing Alaska into zones for each denomination. With this understanding, the Baptist Church received Kodiak Island and the Cook Inlet region.

The Women's American Baptist Home Mission Society and Jackson came to an understanding in 1885 that the Baptists were to open a school in Kodiak. The U.S. government made the same conclusion sending Wesley Roscoe to open the first public school on Kodiak. The Baptists decided to open their school on Afognak to be operated by Dr. James Wirth. Roscoe and his wife Ada had a baby girl on Kodiak, Agnes in 1887, possibly the first American born in Alaska.

Roscoe and the Baptists pressed for an orphanage for the island. With the backing of the Women's American Baptist Society, building supplies arrived in 1893. The Baptist society then asked Roscoe to oversee its construction. Roscoe homesteaded 640 acres on Wood Island by Lake Tanignak where the Russians earlier had their ice enterprise. The orphanage took in its first child on the Fourth of July 1893. It also served as a boarding school. The Kodiak Mission soon had both beef and dairy cattle, a barn, and a silo. A boys' dormitory was added later.

The influx of prospectors during Alaska's gold rushes never touched Kodiak. A few ships docked for coal, but most sailed on to Unalaska with its coal station.

W.J. Erskine bought out the Alaska Commercial Company in Kodiak in 1911 transforming part of the holdings into a cannery. The waterfront was dominated by his warehouse and his name painted in bold letters over it. He moved his family into what had been a fur storage warehouse erected by Baranov in 1808.

The Katmai Eruption

The Revenue Cutter *Manning*, under the command of K.W. Perry, was taking on coal near Erskine's on June 6, 1912, when the sky suddenly became black and heavy ash began falling from the sky. Novarupta Volcano, near the Katmai Volcano, had erupted a hundred miles to the north. The eruption flung more than 4.8 cubic *miles* of rock and an additional 3.6 cubic miles of ash into the air.

Ash was coming down on Kodiak to the point of being two feet deep. The town was in total darkness for sixty hours. A photograph from the eruption had a piano sitting in a parlor filled with drifts of white ash. A 20-room log building caught on fire, but people standing a mere 200 yards away saw no flames nor felt any heat due to the thickness of the ash rain.

With streams and wells now buried in ash, Perry rationed drinking water for the town. Above, heat lightning illuminated the sky. A bolt hit the radio tower on Woody Island cutting off communications with the outside world. Ash began triggering landslides and Perry turned his *Manning* into a refuge ship as well as the barge *St. James*. The entire town seemed to come onboard as 500 sought escape.

Misnamed the Katmai eruption because the first investigation believed that volcano had blown its top (It was later determined to have collapsed inwardly), the event was the largest eruption in North America in the 20th Century, ten times bigger than Mount S. Helens in 1980. Worse, geological investigations of the Katmai region after the eruption showed evidence of ten previous eruptions of the same incredible magnitude over a period of 7,000 years.

Panic over the eruption subsided as Kodiak went back to making money from the sea. In 1917 the North Pacific Whaling Company opened a very profitable whaling station at Port Hobron near the whale migratory route through Shelikof Strait. The real money came from salmon. Salmon was seen as such a direct road to instant wealth that federal concerns of overfishing began.

Secretary of Commerce Herbert Hoover proposed to President Warren G. Harding the establishment of the Alaska Peninsula Reserve in 1922 that was quickly expanded to include Kodiak. Fishing in these reserves was to be by permit only. Hoover, who had participated in the Nome Gold Rush in his youth, thought he understood Alaskans. The policy completely backfired. Families needed to fish just to simply live. Things got ugly on Kodiak when President Harding issued permits to the large cannery operators only. Hoover ended up doing a lot of explaining when he arrived in Alaska in 1923.

Just before the outbreak of World War II, Kodiak was a small city of 442 with the Orthodox Church and Erkine's dominating a landscape dotted with white cottages, two hotels and two general stores. Civilians employed by the U.S. military were at the beginning stages in the construction of Fort Abercrombie north of town and a naval base south of town. The fort was to become a secret radar complex in case of war with Japan.

Growing encounters between Kodiak's growing ranches and Kodiak bears led President Franklin Roosevelt to create the Kodiak National Wildlife Refuge by executive order in August 1941. Today the refuge covers two-thirds of the island encompassing 3,110 square miles.

World War II

After Dutch Harbor was bombed by Japanese forces in June 1942, troops and sailors were rushed to Kodiak until they totaled 15,000. A submarine base had already been established, but the naval base itself was not finished until June 1941. It became the rendezvous point for the U.S. North Pacific Fleet preparing to liberate the Aleutians from the Japanese. Three army posts were quickly thrown up: Fort Greely, Fort Abercrombie, Fort Tidall on Long Island, and Fort J. H. Smith at Cape Chiniak.

A sawmill was set up at Chiniak providing the military with 10,000 board feet a day with a final total of 500,000 board feet. Most of the lumber was shipped out to the treeless Aleutians for military base construction. Bell's Dairy at Women's Bay provided milk and its manure went into fertilizer for Army gardens so that troops in the Aleutians could have fresh produce.

The war saw the building of new roads including the first one running south out of Kodiak towards the naval base, Bell's Dairy, and Chiniak. Concrete bunkers soon dotted the coastline around Kodiak town.

After the war, the U.S. Coast Guard began its now famous search and rescue missions from the naval base in 1947. The Navy turned the base over to the Coast Guard in the 1970s.

The Kodiak Bear War

Once the war was over, the federal government encouraged former servicemen to homestead Alaska. On Kodiak Island, the federal government set aside grazing rights to 200,000 acres hoping would be ranchers would take advantage of the offer. The new cattlemen though saw their stock fall victim to hungry Kodiak bears with the federal government seemingly unable to do anything about it.

Thus began the infamous Kodiak Bear War.

Rancher Joe Zentner purchased an airplane in Kansas in 1952 and began flying it without lessons or a pilot's license to spot bears from the air and have them shot. Fellow rancher Dave Henley began doing the same thing, but the ranches continued to lose livestock. The federal government hired self-proclaimed Big Foot hunter Ivan Marks in 1960 with a dozen bloodhounds to track down and destroy Kodiaks menacing the ranches. Marks' hunts proved a dismal failure. The ranchers reacted by mounting semi-automatic rifles onto their planes and gunning the Kodiaks from the sky. Newly elected Governor Bill Egan sent agents of the Alaska Department of Fish and Game to conduct "bear-cattle" studies. ADF&G killed 35 Kodiaks in 1963 and from 1964 to 1968 patrolled Kodiak's ranch lands hunting the bruins down.

Public outcry on Kodiak did not take place until the fall of 1963 when Henley had finished strafing four bears and landed to refuel at the Kodiak airport with the gun visibly mounted. The next day, phone calls protesting the tactics flooded Governor Egan's office and he brought a halt to the bear war. It did make the front cover of *Outdoor Life*'s August 1964 issue which is on display at the Kodiak National Wildlife's visitors center in downtown Kodiak.

The Good Friday Earthquake

Around 5:30 p.m. on March 27, 1964, the second strongest earthquake in recorded history caused the ground in some locations on Kodiak Island to rise 30 feet. The town of Kodiak though sank five feet in elevation.

Unlike other areas of Alaska, it was not the earthquake itself that nearly destroyed Kodiak, but a series of four tsunamis one after another. The fourth wave with a height of thirty-five feet covered downtown Kodiak finally cresting on Mill Bay Road at the base of Pillar Mountain. The 86-foot fishing vessel *Selief* landed nearby with 3,000 live crabs in her hold. When the port operator finally contacted her captain, Bill Cuthbert, asking where he was, Cuthbert responded, "By dead reckoning, in the school yard."

Nearly half of Kodiak's fishing fleet, some 225 vessels, were either sunk or destroyed. A general store was taken out to sea only to be brought back by another wave ending up only a few hundred yards from where it had been originally. Other stores were bashed from fishing vessels hurled inland. Two of Kodiak's three canneries were swept away.

Eight people died, mostly fishermen, trying to save their boats. Roughly 158 homes were destroyed with damage estimates at $11 million.

Kodiak residents would amazingly quip, "Come to Kodiak and see the tide come in and the town go out!"

Remarkably neither the Russian Orthodox Church nor the Baranov-era warehouse were damaged.

A wealth in fish

The answer to the destruction of the fish processing plants was to bring in vessels that were at the end of their lifespan, beach them and turn them into canneries. The World War II Liberty Ship *The Star of Kodiak* was beached near the Baranov Museum and is a Kodiak landmark today.

Kodiak unintentionally won fame as the resting place for the 1930s art deco ferry *Kalakala* brought in from Seattle. Once billed the "World's First Streamlined Motor Ferry," *Kalakala* appeared on roadside billboards across the U.S. in 1934 as the most advance ship afloat. The vessel could carry 2,000 passengers with 500 velvet upholstered easy chairs. Towed into Kodiak in 1967 and transformed into a shrimp processor in 1970, *Kalakala* returned to Seattle in 1998 for an attempted restoration. She was finally demolished in 2015.

Kodiak fishermen and crabbers were able to hold their own against foreign processing factories when the U.S. had a three-mile territorial limit. Kodiak was rank as the largest fishing port in the U.S. in 1968. After the limit was extended 200 miles offshore, pushing foreign competition out of the Bering Sea and other locations, Kodiak boomed. In 1984, a then record $70 million worth of seafood was brought to port.

Then almost exactly on the 25th anniversary of the Good Friday Earthquake, in March 1989, the *Exxon Valdez* oil tanker struck a reef in Prince William Sound and the oil sheen was heading for Kodiak waters.

Exxon quickly hired all the local vessels it could and began stringing out floating booms hoping to contain the spill. The effort lasted ten months, but the damage to the salmon fishery, in particular pink salmon, was done. Kodiak residents found themselves waging a court battle with the oil firm regarding damages lasting into the mid-1990s.

Meanwhile, the old naval base south of town was enlarged into the largest Coast Guard base in the U.S. Besides search and rescue, the Coast Guard maintains a fleet of helicopters and a minimum of three cutters to enforce the integrity of U.S. territorial waters from foreign fishing fleets.

Because of its location, Coast Guard Station Kodiak has become a site for cold weather training for the U.S. Navy's SEALS units.

The Alaska Aerospace Corporation, a State of Alaska entity with no ties to the federal government, selected 27 acres for its Kodiak Launch Facility on a ranch southeast of Kodiak. It launched its first commercial payload in 1998. In 2014, a military satellite on her launch pad exploded damaging the facility.

The ranches on Kodiak Island are shifting from cattle to bison after discovering the buffalo are more resistant to bear attacks. Kodiak is home to the Kodiak Rodeo and the Kodiak Crab Festival held annually in late May.

OUZINKIE

The small village of Ouzinkie is the burial site for Saint Herman, the first Orthodox saint in North America.

The Russian American Company founded several "retirement" villages throughout coastal Alaska. Ouzinkie was the last of these special communities, founded around 1849.

Russian American Company employees essentially signed up for a tour of duty when they came to North America. When the time of their employment came to an end, they found they had a Native wife and children of mixed blood. Czarist Russia would not allow these men to bring Native wives nor mixed blood children back to Russia with them.

The most famous case was Russian Alaskan Governor Alexander Baranov himself. Russians, with their love of children, found the Imperial policy unbearable.

The answer was simply not to return to Russia once one's term of employment ended. Several communities were settled by men who were "retired" from company service with their Native families.

The Kodiak Archipelago had two retirement villages, Ouzinkie and Afognik, on the south end of Afognik Island.

Spruce Island where Ouzinkie was founded already had a shipbuilding yard for Kodiak fourteen miles to the south. A monk from Mount

Athos, Greece, had a home along what is now called Monk's Lagoon from where he tended to the shrine and burial site of Saint Herman.

Ouzinkie itself is a Russian word meaning "narrows" and refers to the narrow strait separating Spruce and Kodiak islands.

In 1889, the Royal Packing Company built a cannery here followed within a year by a second cannery owned by the American Packing Company. Work drew even more settlers and in 1890 the white with green and blue trim Nativity of Our Lord Russian Orthodox Church was constructed. Today the church is a registered national historical landmark.

Cattle herds were introduced in the early 1900s. A post office was established in 1927 and a children's home built in 1938 by the Baptist Home Mission Society. Just before World War II, Ouzinkie consisted of a general store, two docks, an orphanage, and a Territorial school. Only one cannery existed for employment charging workers from a dollar to $1.75 a day for room and board. Seaplanes connected Ouzinkie with Kodiak.

In 1958, the Baptists Mission school became the Christian Center Program with no affiliation with the Baptist church.

A tsunami generated by the 1964 Good Friday Earthquake destroyed the Ouzinkie Packing Company, the community's main employer. Columbia Ward rebuilt the cannery store and the dock, but not the cannery itself. A cannery was finally built in the late 1960s, but burned in 1976.

Ferries of the Alaska Marine Highway System began stopping at Ouzinkie in 2012. The burial site of Saint Herman brings pilgrims to Ouzinkie each year.

OLD HARBOR

Snuggled between the mountains and the sea, it is believed Koniag Alutiiqs settled the area around 5,000 years ago.

Russian entrepreneur Grigorii Shelikhov and his party of 192 including his wife Natalya Alexyevna arrived at Three Saints Bay on August 13, 1784. As head of the Shelikhov-Golikov Company, one of six companies hunting and trading in Alaska, it was his intention to take control of the entire island. He named the bay after his own ship, Three Saints.

He set the small Russian community up on a spit of land a mile and a half south of the Alutiiq village of Nunamiut. At first relations with the Native population were good until the Alutiiq realized what Shelikhov's true intentions were, establishing a permanent settlement.

The Natives planned an attack, but the Russians learned what they were up to and struck first. Alutiiq resistance led to a month-long war across the Kodiak Archipelago.

Researchers only recently discovered the location of Refuge Rock across the straits along the eastern shore of Sitkalidik Island. It was here that Shelikhov slaughtered hundreds of Native men, women, and children as a demonstration of Russian power. The location, now called Awa'ug, meaning to become numb, is considered a sacred place by the Alutiiqs. Anthropologists discovered the exact site in 1991.

When the Alutiiq people finally surrendered, Shelikhov took hostages to ensure the uneasy peace.

Shelikhov left Kodiak in the hands of a series of incompetent, brutal directors. Finally, in 1791, the arrival of Alexander Baranov as the new company director transformed much of Kodiak including Three Saints Bay. Exposed to the ravages of the sea including devastating tsunamis and surrounded by grasslands, Baranov moved the headquarters up the coast to Saint Paul's Harbor (modern Kodiak) in 1793 where towering trees promised the timber he was seeking.

Three Saints Bay dwindled in size from the move but continued as a base of operations. The name changed from Three Saints to Nuniaq in Alutiiq or Starrie Gavan in Russian. Another tsunami laid the village to waste and the residents moved away. The site remained abandoned. When a new village was constructed in 1884, it was not at Three Saints Bay, but up the coast a few miles near Sitkalidak Passage. An American owned whaling stationed was established on the eastern end of Sitkalidik Island from 1920 to 1937 boasting it was the only U.S. owned whaling station in Southwest Alaska. The whaling station at Akutan was Norwegian owned.

A school opened in Old Harbor in 1925 and a post office in 1931.

The 1964 Good Friday Earthquake hurled a tsunami into the village leaving only two homes and the Three Saints Russian Orthodox Church standing. Everything else was swept out to sea as was the nearby village of Kaguyak. The fact that the church was untouched was regarded as a sign of a miracle by residents. Families were relocated to Anchorage for several months while the community was rebuilt.

The Old Harbor Native Corporation was formed in 1973 taking ownership of most of nearby Sitkalidik Island.

The fishing boom of the 1980s saw Old Harbor's population increase to 400 just before the Exxon Valdez Oil Spill of 1989. The man-made disaster resulted in many of the fisheries either closing or decreasing in productivity.

Today Old Harbor has evolved into three divisions: the town center at the original site, Middle Town or Uptown and New Town. A four-mile-long gravel road connects the three sections. It is the home port to the second largest fishing fleet on Kodiak Island.

Old Harbor gained notoriety when Royal Dutch Shell's arctic drilling rig Kulluk ran aground near Ocean Bay on Sitkalidak Island in January 2013.

CHIGNIK

The three Chigniks—Chignik, Chignik Lagoon, and Chignik Lake—may seem like the end of the world to a visitor. Chignik itself is a collection of canneries and houses scattered in tall tundra grass and brush pressed up against the slopes of the Aleutian Mountains.

However bleak Chignik's world may seem, it holds a special place in the hearts of most Alaskans for this is where Benny Benson was born, the child designer of the Alaska State Flag.

Benny Benson

Born in 1913 to parents who were part Russian Aleut and part Swedish, when Benson's mother died three years later, his father found he was unable to care for three-year-old Benny and his brother Carl. He sent the two brothers off to an orphanage in Unalaska, the Jesse Lee Home. The orphanage relocated along with the Benson brothers to Seward in 1925.

In 1927, 13-year-old Benny entered a contest being held by Alaska Territorial Governor George Parks for a design for Alaska's flag while in seventh grade. His design won over some 700 entries. The only part of Benny's design for the flag that was changed was the date "1867" appearing on the flag was dropped.

Benson graduated in 1932 and worked alongside his father on a fox fur farm in the Aleutians for a number of years. He took the $1,000 awarded him for the flag's design and enrolled in a diesel engine repair school in Seattle in 1938. After a divorce, he moved with his two daughters to Kodiak in 1950 where he worked as an aircraft mechanic for Kodiak Airways. His right leg was amputated in 1969 after an injury. He remarried to a former resident of the orphanage and died at age 58 in Kodiak from a heart attack.

Benny's heritage is the story of Chignik.

The Kaniagmuit village of Kalwak was located here when Russian fur traders arrived in the 1700s. The Russians destroyed the village as they rounded the population up and relocated them. The Native population was reduced to serfdom along with the rest of the Aleuts.

The coast became uninhabited from the Russian labor raids. It was not until several decades after the U.S. purchase of Alaska that the town of Mitrofamia came into being briefly 25 miles southwest of current Chignik made up of Russians and Natives from Kodiak.

Both Anchorage Bay and Chignik Lagoon caught the eye of cannery operators in the Pacific Northwest due to strong red salmon runs and its proximity to the Gulf of Alaska fisheries. The Fishermen's Packing Company of Astoria, Oregon, sent out an exploratory expedition to Chignik in 1888 which returned with 2,160 barrels of salted salmon. The next year three firms built canneries at Chignik Lagoon followed by two canneries at Anchorage Bay in 1896 becoming the nucleus of modern Chignik.

The Hume Brothers cannery was built first, employing 20 Whites and 90 Chinese laborers producing 800 cases a day. An example how rich the local streams were can be seen in the salmon taken in the 16 fish traps near the two canneries. From 1900 to 1924, 1.3 million salmon were caught in these traps for processing.

The town that evolved around these canneries was given the name Chignik meaning "big wind" in Alutiiq. The four-mast sailing ship *Star of Alaska* brought in Chinese workers each May to make tin cans for the cannery as well as transporting supplies and other workers from San

Francisco. Japanese workers were then brought in by mid-June of each fishing season for the actual cannery work. Italian cannery workers were also utilized in large numbers.

Some coal mining was done from 1899 to 1915 to offset the cost of importing it. A few gold claims were also staked out inland from the town in the early 1900s.

The two canneries were sold to a single corporation in 1901, the same year a post office was established. From 1910 to 1931, the post office was in the Northwestern Fisheries cannery. Today it is contracted out from a private residence. Chignik had two schools, one government for Natives and the other Territorial. From time to time, a cannery bunkhouse was used as the local school.

In 1910, the Columbia River Packers Association constructed a mammoth seventeen building cannery complex that included what was dubbed the "White House" built in 1912 that acted as the superintendent's quarters. The complex also contained Chinese bunkhouses, a hospital, fishermen's bunkhouses, and foot bridges over Indian Creek becoming the one-lane vehicle bridges of today. A radio shack was built in 1928 for communications with King Salmon, cannery sites and the fishing fleet. Fish traps dotted the landscape until they were outlawed when statehood was obtained. The Oriental camp buildings still existed in 2004. Segregated mess halls came to an end in 1963.

The web house or net house contains graffiti on the walls going back to 1928.

The Alaska Packers Association leased the compound during the Great Depression eventually purchasing the compound outright. A fire swept through the structures in 1975. Workmen using chain saws cut away planking to prevent the loss of the entire dock structure during the blaze. Alaska Packers rebuilt the compound in 1977 and sold it to the Native corporation Sealaska. It eventually was sold to Norquest in 1979 who in turn sold it to Trident Seafoods. Canneries quit canning in 1982, shifting over to process freezing.

The Norquest cannery, maybe the longest continuously operated cannery in Alaska, is one of two historic canneries in Chignik.

However, in the early years of the Great Depression, Chignik's canneries were shuttered from 1931 to 1932. This created an opening for Harry W. Crosby to build an independent cannery at Chignik Lagoon in 1932. He eventually developed a fleet of four fishing vessels and is credited with being the first to introduce shallow draft seine boats to the region.

Asians working at the cannery started developing housing to the south of the canneries. Alaskan Natives coming to work also had their own bunkhouse called Long House. A cluster of homes southwest of the canneries became known as Andersonville with two cemeteries, a collapsed Russian Orthodox Church and a second church.

Chignik became an incorporated town in 1983 and became part of the Lake and Peninsula Borough when it was formed in 1989.

The nearby community of Chignik Lake began in 1903 around the winter residence of a single family. Gradually other Alaskan Native families moved into the area until by the 1950s there were enough people for a school to open. Like the other Chigniks, residents make their living either by fishing or in the processing plants.

In 2002 the majority of local fishermen formed the Chignik Salmon Cooperative. But a minority of salmon fishermen who did not join took the Cooperative to court. In 2006, the Alaska Supreme Court ruled the Cooperative was in violation of the state's limited entry laws.

A timber dam and a 20-acre reservoir were built along Indian Creek in 1948 to supply water for the town. Sewage is collected in community septic tanks while wastewater is discharged into the ocean.

There was some mineral exploration in the 1970s. Two mining firms explored north of Chignik Bay and around Chignik Lagoon in 1975-1976, 1979, and 1981. Deposits of gold, copper, silver, lead, and zinc were found north of the bay. Large veins of galena, some nearly ten feet wide, were found around the lagoon along with pyrite.

A major fire swept through half of the town in July 2008 as the Trident Seafoods cannery went up in flames. Several local firefighters had to be treated for injuries after stopping the flames from reaching nearby ammonia tanks, preventing a major explosion that would have devastated the community. Flames were reported to have been as high as a hundred feet into the air. The 250 cannery workers were housed in the local school.

Chignik Lake became the scene of tragedy in March 2010 when a visiting teacher, 33-year-old Candice Berner was attacked and killed by wolves near the airstrip while jogging.

It was Berner's first year in Alaska having moved from Pennsylvania to be a special education teacher based in Perryville.

SAND POINT

French explorer Alphonse Louis Pinart came to the Shumagin Islands in 1871 in order to research the Aleuts.

Arriving on Unga Island across from modern Sand Point, Pinart hired an elderly Aleut called Lazar to assist him. Lazar took the young Frenchman south to Delarof Harbor where an ancient Aleut village stood called Aknanh.

Lazar became so taken with Pinart's enthusiasm for his people and their history that on the morning of September 30, 1871, Lazar woke him and lead him to a cave. When Pinart entered he was stunned. Before him were three mummies of Aleut men honored with a wide range of ceremonial masks. The mummies, Lazar insisted, had been whaler hunters, heroes to his ancestors and were so honored.

Pinart painstakingly recorded what he found in the cave careful not to disturb the mummies. He gathered up a few of the masks taking them with him to his home in Boulogne-Sur-Mer where they are on exhibit in that city's museum today.

Word of Pinart's find spread throughout the Aleutians. Soon American explorer William Dall entered the cave the same year. He too saw the mummies and he too helped himself to ceremonial Aleut masks which he delivered to the Smithsonian Institute.

The presence of the mummies was never truly explained. Others came to the cavern later only to find them gone.

The story is one typical of the Shumagin Islands, the two largest, 36 square mile Popof island where Sand Point is located, and the larger 171 square mile Unga island, with the ghost town of Unga, on the southern end of the island.

The islands are of volcanic origin with a seismic monitoring station and two substation on the islands. Gold and silver have been found on both Popof and Unga. The legendary Apollo Gold Mine that had operated outside of the town of Unga was the richest in Alaska at one time with private silver mines around it. Gold panners can be seen working the beaches of Popof now and then. The islands are rich in obsidian and slate. A petrified forest of Sequoias lies on the ground in the northeastern corner of Unga Island. The islands also have coal.

Aleut tradition speaks of a massive tsunami striking the islands in 1788. Another came in 1946 resulting in a station manned by the Alaska Tsunami Warning System in Sand Point.

Wild cattle once grazed on the green grasses of Popof and Unga before eradicated by the federal government. They were replaced by bison. The islands are free of bears though one swam over from the Alaska Peninsula terrorizing Sand Point residents in 1993. Another oddity is the fact that most insect species on the islands are wingless.

The Russians arrive

When the Russians reached the Shumagins in the 1760s, only Unga seemed inhabited. Later, after the Russians stabilized the region, four villages grew up on Unga and one on Popof before it was abandoned in 1827. Many died during the 1788 tsunami. Others fell victim to warfare with the Alutiiqs of Kodiak to a degree that the islands became a no man's land between the Aleut and Alutiiq peoples.

In late August 1741, the Russian naval vessel *Sv. Petr* entered the island chain returning from exploring Prince William Sound. A landing party was sent onto Nagai Island for water. The sick were brought ashore as well. One of them, a sailor named Nikita Shumagin, died, and was buried on the island. The Russian explorers gave the entire island chain the man's name.

Of the many companies organized in Russia to exploit the new land called Alaska, the Panov Company was able to dominate trade in the Shumagins. Their captains were from the Popov family who at one time had their own company. For over 20 years, the Panov Company based anywhere from four to five ships in the Shumagins.

When Captain James Cook explored the islands in 1778, he found the Russians had a strong economy going with the Natives who were carrying signed papers proclaiming they were Russian subjects.

Russian Aleut work crews called *artel'* dotted Unga and the other islands. Armed conflicts between Russian Companies on the islands began to take place. Evstrat Delarov, a Greek in Russian employ, wintered on Unga in 1784 giving the harbor his name Delarov Harbor.

Delarov was hired by the Shelikov Company to manage Three Saints Bay on Kodiak Island after the Koniag War in 1787. Sometime during Delarov's reign over Kodiak Island, he founded a small trading settlement in Delarov Harbor named for himself. It was the foundation for the town of Unga and was the first Russian settlement in the Shumagins.

Early Unga had two Russian overseers, eight Aleuts on salary and 44 other Aleuts. Sea otter pelts from the islands and the Alaska Peninsula were stored at Unga along with valuable walrus ivory. In 1826, the sailing ship *Unalaska* was assigned to Unga as its base with regularly scheduled trips to Unalaska and Siberia. Besides a barracks for workers, there were two storage buildings, a cattle yard, a steam bath, vegetable gardens growing potatoes and twelve private homes belonging to Aleut families.

Now called Greko-Delarovske and a major stopping point for shipping between Kodiak and Unalaska, the population was 116 by 1830. The Russians stationed a medical man in Unga to carry out smallpox vaccinations among the Aleuts.

On the north side of Unga Island at Coal Harbor, the Russians mined the coal seams from 1840 until 1865. The mine was expanded, hoping to market the coal in California. Russian-American steamers used Unga coal when they sailed the Aleutian Islands, but the steamers burned through 12 tons of Unga coal in a 24-hour period when the vessels burned only five tons of Vancouver coal for the same amount of time. Twelve Aleut men and eleven Aleut women from Unga worked the seams. In 1865, a steamship became impatient deciding to mine their own coal at the site. Slabs tumbled down killing a sailor and the Chief Manager of Russia America ordered coal mining on Unga to stop.

Unga's importance is seen by the opening of an Orthodox chapel, the Church of the Virgin Mother of Vladimir in 1843. New chapels were constructed in 1861, 1863 and again in 1874.

Smaller Russian settlements in the Shumigans sprang up such as on Korovin Island in the 1840s. By 1855, the settlement was large enough for an Orthodox chapel. The Orthodox church maintained a school on Korovin from 1898 to 1899. Salmon runs were strong enough for a fish trap to be installed on the island in 1920. The settlement had 35 residents in 1879 made up of four extended families. The people were known for their horse herds. But by the 1930s, they and their horses abandoned Korovin for Sand Point.

Wosnesenski Island also had a small settlement in 1846 with a chapel. By 1920 only the Osterback family remained on the island. They too moved to Sand Point where Alvin Osterback became a member of the Alaska State Legislature in the 1970s.

The Russians set up a small settlement on Popof in 1861 though it did not last and there was a small cluster of sea otter hunters on the other side of the island at Pirate Cove.

The American Purchase

After the 1867 American purchase, the U.S. passed a law stating only Aleuts or those married into Aleut families could hunt sea otters. The number of interracial marriages skyrocketed. By 1880, there were fifteen white men living in Unga with Aleut wives. Most of these men were Scandinavian.

Missionary and explorer Sheldon Jackson set up the first Methodist mission and school in Alaska in 1886 at Unga. Mr. and Mrs. John Carr were sent to operate the school, which in 1886 had 74 students, where they taught until 1917. After the death of Mrs. Carr in 1917, the mission went inactive until the establishment of a Methodist church in Unga in the 1930s.

The Russians and Aleuts were by now calling the settlement Ougnagok. A year after opening a cod fishing station at Sand Point, the firm Lynde and Hough opened one at Unga in 1888 calling the town Ounga. It was shortened to Unga five years later.

U.S. authorities were interested in Unga's coal deposits for a while. The *USS Humboldt* mined coal from the old Russian workings at Coal Harbor in 1872. From 1882 to 1884, twenty men were employed at Coal Harbor for the small steamers used in the seal hunting trade. Tidewater Consolidated Company transported the works in 1884 installing bunkers and a steel conveyor belt. The firm shipped 700 tons of coal to San Francisco in 1882. It is not clear when Tidewater closed operations. The Apollo Gold Mine tried using local coal to heat their bunk houses and other structures in Unga but found the grade inferior and eventually shipped coal in from outside sources.

The Apollo Gold Mine

Gold was discovered on Unga in 1886 by George King. Three mining operations soon opened. The Apollo and Sitka mines were opened within five miles of the town of Unga while a third mine opened at the head of Baralof Bay or Squaw Harbor. Reports of other gold findings were said to be two miles south of Coal Harbor.

The Alaska Commercial Company quickly organized the Apollo Consolidated Mining Company led by the ACC agent in Unga, Captain Otto Carlson. Gustav Niebaum, a Finn who had worked for the Russian American Company since 1846, was selected as the president of the Apollo venture.

By 1890, the Apollo mine had 48 Whites and more than a hundred

Russian creoles working the mine. The mine itself was a five-stamp mill with four amalgamators and a Frue concentrator, all driven by a seventy-horsepower engine.

Within six years, the Apollo was operating 358 days a year with 150 men. It was producing $400,000 in gold and $40,000 in silver. A small lake was created for a water source and a tramway was added.

In 1897, the Apollo built a small narrow-gauge railroad from Unga wharf to the mine using a 0-6-OT Baldwin locomotive. This line became the westernmost railroad in North America. The Apollo mines extended the rail beyond the mine up the valley from Unga before the mine was closed.

With Apollo's expansion and the fact there were smaller gold and silver mines employing people, the town of Unga transformed into a modern community from the days it had been a fur trading post. The town now had a school, a courthouse and two churches. A newspaper, *The Alaska Pen*, began in 1934 and for years was the only periodical published west of Kodiak.

Unga obtained mail service in 1891 and the Apollo Consolidated Mining firm opened a hospital with a resident physician in 1895. The mining firm also set up Unga's telephone service.

The town's growth was so stunning that in 1897 the U.S. Custom House was moved from Sand Point to Unga, and a U.S. Marshal stationed in Unga with jurisdiction over the Shumagins and the Alaska Peninsula. A Scotch-Irishman named McCallum served as marshal from 1918 to 1922, his descendants live today in Sand Point. In the harbor, floating on the tide was a small fleet of cod dories.

A new cannery was opened just to the north at Squaw Harbor in 1920 with a resident doctor as well.

Eventually a total of $2.1 million in gold was taken out of the Apollo mine along with silver. The mine was closed in 1904, re-opened in 1908 at a lower rate of production. George Cushing announced he had found the main vein to the Apollo in 1916, and though the news made headlines, nothing came of it.

Sand Point saw benefits from the gold find. It was also a staging and outfitting center for would be prospectors bound for the Nome Gold Fields. In 1904, gold was found on Popof with prospectors setting up sluice boxes on the beaches around Sand Point.

Pirate Cove was where Thomas W. McCollam and Company set up the first shore station in the Shumagins as a cod saltery in 1874.

Seeing the growing fishing activity, San Francisco based Lynde and Hough built a shore service and trade station on the spit that would become Sand Point in 1887. By then Unga was already a thriving community with an Alaska Commercial Company trading post and the opening of the Apollo mine.

Sand Point founded

Lynde and Hugh appointed Civil War veteran James O'Brien as the Sand Point manager. O'Brien filed for Popof land as his war allotment. His firm also began filling the surrounding waters with cod schooners manned by rough and tumble men who often jumped ship settling on the many isles of the Shumagins. Drunken quarrels, revenge, and murder became the order of the day. In 1889, the U.S. Revenue Steamer *Richard Rush* was sent to jail and ship to San Francisco, Louis Sharp after he wounded O'Brien and murdered W.H. Dingley.

Three years earlier, three very interesting men landed separately in Sand Point making it their home, "Pistol" Pete Anderson, Pete Larsen, and Andrew Grosvold. The owner of a sailing yacht, the *Alice*, Larsen gained fame for his bear hunting exploits. Anderson's fame rested on his skills as a sea otter hunter and trapper. He became a power to reckon with in the Shumigans.

As for Grosvold, he was the "Pooba of Sand Point" as locals liked to joke. He pioneered commercial fox farming in the Shumigans, brought in the first cattle herds, traded in chickens, and raised horses for business and pleasure. He married one widow, outlived her, and married another.

In 1900 he went off to the Nome Gold Rush returning with over $30,000. With his gold finds, he bought the old Lynde and Hough trading post as well as Sand Point's other store. He developed a fleet of ships, some built in Unga, for fishing and freight. Grosvold was able to secure the mail contract for the islands delivering mail with his *Blue Fox* to all the many communities and freeholds that dotted the Shumagins. The postmaster position in Sand Point itself was held by O'Brien when a post office opened in 1891, but Grosvold was able to be appointed in 1905 holding the position until 1927.

Meanwhile he opened the town's only saloon and a processing plant.

Grosvold took pride in his American citizenship. He made sure he was in charge of all Fourth of July activities for Sand Point and played Santa Claus during Christmas.

Sand Point became the rendezvous site for the fur sealing fleet bound for the Pribilof Islands. Here in the Shumagins, vessels from many nations, especially the Japanese, anchored sharing information, food, and tall tales. Due to this, the U.S. opened a customs house in Sand Point in 1889.

St. Nicholas Orthodox Church was established in Sand Point in 1907, the same year an Orthodox church was opened at Pirate Cove. The original Sand Point church was replaced with a newer building and a parish house in 1936 and was placed on the National Register of Historical Places.

Tom Devine kept Pirate Cove going as a town. In 1920, it had a larger population than Sand Point, 98 residents as compared with Sand Point's 60. However, the local post office closed in 1919 making Sand Point the only post office on the island with its two stores, saloon, and processing plant. By 1930, Pirate Cove had only seven residents, the bulk moving to Sand Point across the island.

A territorial school was established in Sand Point in 1923 through 1939 when jurisdiction was transferred to the Bureau of Indian Affairs. It returned as a territorial school in 1944 until 1976 when it was given to local control.

Up to 1962 only an eighth-grade education was offered. Those seeking a high school education had to move to Sitka's Mt. Edgecumbe School. Eventually a new school was eventually built allowing students to finish their high school education in Sand Point.

Though the 1990 census showed 410 of Sand Point's 878 residents were Aleuts, the town's growth came from other towns folding up and moving to Sand Point. There is a small section of town called "Little Sanak" where migrants from Sanak Island's two villages settled. There is "Russian Town' where Russians settled.

This migration to Sand Point was hurried during World War II when the military had people living in outlying areas moved into Sand Point in case of invasion. Just prior to the war, Unga had a population of 150 while Sand Point had 69 residents. Catalina patrol planes used Sand Point as a stopover during their patrols. Naval vessels made shore leave calls from time to time as they did at Unga.

Mail service to Unga was suspended during the war. Administrative officers were relocated to Sand Point after the war. Finally, Unga's territorial school closed in 1959. Parents relocated to Sand Point. By 1969, there were only seven people living in Unga and they moved that year to Sand Point. An interest by two mining groups in opening the Apollo mine occurred in 1981, but no activity took place.

Sand Point's main industry was cod until that market bottomed out in the 1920s. The first salmon cannery in the Shumagins was built at Squaw Harbor in 1920 north of Unga. Sand Point's first salmon cannery was built in 1933 and a hand pack cannery was built over the site of the old cod station in 1935. A king crab industry started in 1947 with Sand Point becoming the center for crab processing for the eastern Aleutians. King Cove crabbers brought their catch to Sand Point until 1958 when their own local cannery began crab processing. King crab was no longer commercially fished after 1983. The tanner crab fishery ended in 1989.

The New England Fish Company (NEFCO) purchased the first cannery in the 1960s converting it into a fish buying station. A fire in 1980 burned part of the plant. NEFCO sold what was left to Ocean Beauty Seafoods. They in turn sold the site to a local group.

Aleutian Cold Storage took over Andrew Grosvold's processing plant in 1947 and used it for halibut. Wakefield Fisheries leased part of the plant taking complete ownership in 1966. Wakefield operated the plant during the crab boom, and then when it died down, sold the plant back to Aleutian Cold Storage in 1981. Trident Seafoods purchased the plant in 1986. Peter Pan opened a packing and shipping site near the Sand Point airport after it closed its plant at Squaw Harbor.

John Nelson brought to Popof some cattle from Unga after World War II. Harold Nickles shipped in 70 Herefords in 1955, but the bulk of his herd perished the first winter when they were unable to find food or went over the cliffs into the sea.

The U.S. Fish and Wildlife Service using helicopters and marksmen began eradicating the herds in 1987 to protect marine bird habitat. This evoked outrage among Sand Point residents. Beef is an expensive import to the island community.

Harold Nickles also brought in four buffalo from Oregon in 1955 landing them at Red Cove. The bison adapted to Popof's climate and prospered into a herd of around 120 head.

U.S. Fish and Wildlife asked the State of Alaska to manage the herd rather than slaughtering them the way they had the cattle herds. The State of Alaska soon found themselves in a dispute with the Shumagin Native Corporation over the herd's ownership. The dispute was settled with the herd being thinned out from time to time by lottery drawings. Two female bison were brought in from the Alaska Wildlife Conservation Center at Portage in 2009 to diversity the gene pool.

Today some 150 fishing vessels call Sand Point home. The town has a hotel, several restaurants, a bar, a taxicab firm, repair shops, and an Alaska Commercial Company store along with the Trident processing plant.

A Baptist church was established in the 1960s and has outpaced the Orthodox church in membership. The church has become a focal point in society, especially in hosting potluck dinners for visiting fishing vessels arriving for the salmon season.

Sand Point, also called Qagun Tayagungin in Aleut, is the headquarters for three local native corporations.

Sand Point residents made headlines in August 2013 when they refused to allow a suspected local drug dealer to disembark from an airliner. The individual was given a "blue ticket" or one-way ticket out of the community.

"Blue ticket" is an Alaskan term for being banished or exiled from a community without formal charges files. It is a tradition that dates to the Gold Rush Era.

KING COVE

ONE OF THE ELEMENTS FOR LIFE NOT BEING EASY at King Cove is the large number of massive brown bears roaming the area. In the mid-1990s, a ten-year-old boy was killed by a brown bear in the street. The Peter Pan cannery, one of the largest in Alaska, posts a bear advisory daily concerning the bruins. The town radio station tracks bear movements and children live with a "bear" curfew forcing them indoors to play.

The huge bear population has led the town to be the home for legendary Alaskan big game hunters and trappers such as "Danish Pete" Larsen for whom Larsen Bay on Kodiak Island is named, Mike Utticht, Axel Samuelson, Edwin Bendixen, and Tommy Dobson—all of whom were subject of big game articles and who sold their furs as far away as St. Louis, Missouri.

Even though King Cove's port is ice free, and winters are relatively mild, avalanches are a danger. Though the average snowfall is around four inches, snowfall can be heavy, especially along the mountain slopes. Storms coming off the sea trigger avalanches. A five-member family was killed when a snow slide crushed their home.

King Cove gets its name from Robert King. He and his brother George, arrived from England in 1880, as fur buyers settling in nearby Belkofski. The town had been settled in 1823 by Aleuts sent there by the Russian

American Company to hunt sea otters and walrus ivory. The town was built on a bluff to avoid tsunamis and thus had no harbor. Surprisingly, the town site was selected without any salmon streams nearby.

By the time the Kings arrived, Belkofski had three stores. The Russian Orthodox Church had made Belkofski its administrative center for the eastern Aleutians and the western portion of the Alaska Peninsula. It maintained a school with a student enrollment of 50.

Instead of buying pelts, the Kings set up a fish processing plant. Brother George left for San Francisco to buy lumber for the new plant and then traveled on to England where he got married. When George and his new wife returned to Belkofski, they discovered Robert had married a local woman and moved to a cove twelve miles away. There he had built a two-room sod house called a *barabara* near fields of wild strawberries.

Robert was lost at sea in 1883. George and his wife left on board the U.S. Revenue steamer *Bear* in 1884. Sailors began referring to the area as King's Cove. In 1910 the Pacific American Fisheries conducted a commercial survey of King Cove finding it highly promising for salmon traps.

The steam schooner *A.G. Lindsay* arrived on April 28, 1911. Her crew quickly set about building a cannery in less than three months under the guidance of cannery superintendent Harry Smith. He was the nephew of the President of the Pacific American Fisheries.

Smith directed his men in a nine-day unloading of supplies including two hundred tons of coal first rafted in and then hauled by wheel barrels over single board planks onto the sand and gravel spit they were building. The first structure erected was called China House, a bunkhouse for Chinese workers. Jap House was next for Japanese workers. Both groups arrived in June 1911. The cannery also had a small group of Whites and Aleuts in the work force.

Communications with the outside world came by way of company steamer arriving once every six weeks. Salmon were obtained from roughly 50 fish traps placed around King Cove. By the end of the first season, more than forty-five thousand cases of salmon had been canned.

Most of the workers felt Smith had overstepped his authority when he issued an order that the men must take one bath each week and those coming in from fishing duty had to wash immediately. When the men tried to ignore Smith, he had those disobeying seized and scrubbed down with a hose.

The cannery resembled a farm with pigs and chickens roaming the grounds providing food for the Chinese workers who cooked over three enormous outdoor kettles. A small Chinese cemetery was located up the valley without markers.

Smith found he had to use guns for maintaining order between the Chinese and Japanese employees. When a Japanese worker stabbed to death one of his countrymen during the first season, a U.S. Marshal had to be sent from far off Unga. When the accused and witnesses arrived in Unga for trial, they were treated to dances and celebrations before the official hanging.

By 1916, Asian workers were no longer hired for King Cove as a cost saving measure even though canning capacity had grown to 75,000 cases a season. Management tried not hiring Aleuts believing them to be undependable. Instead, they experimented in shipping in Inupiat Eskimos from Nome. Yup'ik and Alutiiqs also moved into King Cove for work. There was never enough, and management ended up hiring Aleuts from nearby Belkofski.

The cannery insisted that all workers live in framed homes as a means of ensuring they would finish out the season. By 1914, the beaches of King Cove were lined with white cottages with gingerbread trim of red, yellow, or blue.

Traditionally a seasonal town boarded up during the off season, eight families settled in King Cove permanently in the 1920s. Half of the families had a Scandinavian father and an Aleut mother. Barney Simmons, famed bootlegger known for out running revenue cutters, was one of the first settlers. Australian Thomas Dobson moved in from Sanak to open the local trading post.

As time went by Belkofski residents began moving to King Cove for work. The 1940 census showed King Cove with 135 residents while

Belkofski had 140. Ten years later King Cove had 162 people while Belkofski had 119. The 1960s began with King Cove at 290 residents and Belkofski with 57. Belkofski's school closed in 1976, and by the 1980 census, the community was down to ten residents while King Cove had 467. Most of the former Belkofski residents set up homes at the Rams Creek subdivision, later annexed by King Cove.

One reason for the death of Belkofski was conveniences. As King Cove grew, residents were obtaining satellite television, telephones, water, and sewage. Belkofski was still using gas and kerosene for heating and cooking, using outhouses, and hauling water from streams. The lack of a harbor and the fact that there are no salmon streams nearby also led to Belkofski's demise.

King Cove found herself as a supply staging area during World War II for Cold Bay. The military took over the cannery as well as the Frog Pond Theatre, the local movie house. King Cove was placed under martial law, but not evacuated into internment camps. Guns were set up in the hills while scout planes used King Cove as a base looking for Japanese activity. Soviet ships used King Cove as a loading point for lend-lease supplies before escorted in convoy by the U.S. Navy.

After the war, a power struggle over control of the village occurred between the school teacher at the Bureau of Indian Affairs school and local chiefs in 1948.

King Cove had its first school in 1929, a territorial school before it was turned over to the BIA in 1940. The power struggle between traditional chiefs and the BIA teacher led to King Cove incorporating as a second-class city in 1949. The school was placed under the jurisdiction of a city school district in 1952 to prevent any issues of authority arising again.

Meanwhile, pressured by the machinist union, King Cove and the cannery pooled resources to hire a full-time nurse, Janet Allan, and provided her with a small clinic inside the cannery. The clinic also served as Allan's housing.

In her first year as a nurse, she delivered two babies, pronounced two people dead, treated injuries from bar fights, and lacerations at midnight.

Her sofa served as the waiting room. The local healer, Mattie Samuelsen, obtained formal medical training, becoming Allan's assistant.

In 1982 a clinic was constructed, and a physicians' assistant was hired. King Cove also hired a police chief and officers. King Cove was listed with 450 residents in the 1990 census. The town then annexed housing additions that were built on the mainland away from the sand spit. The result was King Cove nearly doubling its population to 720.

The city found itself in a confrontation with the cannery in 1984 over taxation. The city at first passed a one-percent tax on all sales including the sale of fish for processing in 1981. Three years later the city increased the tax to two percent. The cannery refused to pay, declaring the tax unfair. The cannery quit giving residents credit at the company store, cashing checks for free, and giving a discount on commercial fishing gear. It also raised store and stockroom prices seven percent.

The King Cove Village Corporation, a native corporation, built a business complex leasing space out for a small hotel, a video arcade, and a large bar. The drinking establishment contains a 97-foot-long horseshoe shape bar, boasted as the longest in Alaska. An apartment complex was raised as a joint venture between the Native corporation and the cannery.

King Cove fishermen harvested and sold king crab to the Sand Point cannery since the local cannery would not buy their crab until 1958. When the State of Alaska banned fish traps in 1959, the cannery financed locals purchasing fishing boats if their catch went to the cannery and not to other buyers.

A fire in 1976 partially destroyed the cannery, the first time it was closed since 1911. The damage was quickly repaired.

Though most King Cove residents are Orthodox, the town did not have a church until the 1980s. Prior to the church's construction, King Cove was part of the Belkofski parish. The Belkofski priest visited King Cove twice a year. As Belkofski faded away, King Cove resident Semeon Dushkin designed an Orthodox church for King Cove so that the iconostas of the former Belkofski church would fit into the new structure.

Hundred mile per hour winds caused the Belkofski Orthodox Church to collapse during a blizzard in November 1992. It was listed as a National Historical Landmark.

A Protestant church, King Cove Bible Chapel, was built in 1958 by the Slavic Gospel Church of Wheaton, Illinois.

The cannery, owned by Peter Pan, is one of the largest cannery operations under one roof in Alaska. Over 500 seasonal workers are brought into King Cove every summer for fish processing. The North Harbor provides moorage for 90 fishing vessels.

King Cove has pushed for the construction of a 27-mile gravel road through the Izembek National Wildlife Refuge to the airport at Cold Bay. Residents believe the $14 million proposed roadway would save lives during emergencies. Fierce crosswinds make King Cove's own 3,360-foot gravel runway undependable. Environmental interests have successfully blocked such a road link.

King Cove is connected to Cold Bay by way of a hovercraft, but the vessel has been in a constant state of disrepair.

The need for the road link was demonstrated in February 2011 when three separate medevacs occurred rushing residents from King Cove to medical facilities in Anchorage. When an 80-year-old woman reported severe chest pains, the U.S. Coast Guard flew in a helicopter from St. Paul Island 300 miles to the north only to be forced down by bad weather at Cold Bay for a day before the woman could be picked up in King Cove.

COLD BAY

Cold Bay is a government community existing simply because of its huge runways of 10,000 feet and 5,000 feet (fifth largest in Alaska) and their strategic location to Asia and North America.

Almost always windy, almost always overcast, and usually always shrouded in fog, Cold Bay experiences 12 clear days a year while averaging 200 days of rain annually. Her legendary winds are underscored by the fact that the Grant Point Kiosk is held in place by cables after the first two blew away.

Russian Count Feodor Kutke mapped the region in 1827 naming Izembeck lagoon for the surgeon onboard his sloop *Moller*, Karl Izembeck.

Cold Bay's strategic location caught the notice of the Harrison Administration. By Executive Order in 1890, the region became a naval reserve. Then the U.S. Navy's influence over the District of Alaska gave way to the U.S. Army and the Reserve stayed inactive until World War I. Military surveys of Alaska in 1923 identified Cold Bay as having the potential of being an advance staging area.

With World War II underway in Europe and hostilities with Japan likely at any time, Army General Simon Bolivar Buckner ordered the construction of an advance army air corps base called Fort Randall at Cold Bay in 1940. So not to tip off Japanese military intelligence on fishing trawlers operating in the Bering Sea, supplies were marked for cannery operations involving a made-up firm, Saxton & Company, and landed at nearby King Cove and then freighted to the site.

There was one problem. Fred Meishinin, the sole trapper on the Reserve and a Navy pensioner, had his driftwood cabin right where the runway was to be constructed and he refused to move. The Civil Aeronautics Administration (CAA), forerunner to the Federal Aviation Administration, intervened, building Meishinin a new cabin at the CAA's expense just off the airfield.

Once Pearl Harbor was bombed, the U.S. Army stationed a handful of P-40 fighters at the new military installation.

On the morning of June 3, 1942, Japanese carriers launched a surprise attack on Dutch Harbor. Within four minutes Cold Bay launched her fighters. They traveled the 180 miles to Dutch Harbor tangling with Japanese aircraft still overhead at the port.

Cold Bay eventually became the staging point for the assault on Japanese occupied Alaska with more than 20,000 troops, combat aircraft, and naval ships gathering there for the counterattack. A road was constructed from the runway to Grant Point on the Bering Seaside, for coastal artillery. Once the assault was made, Cold Bay became a support station.

When the invasion of Attu, or Operation Landcrab as Buckner called it, was launched some thirty-four ships steamed out of Cold Bay including the battleships *Idaho, Pennsylvania,* and *Nevada.*

As the Thousand Mile War against Japanese forces was slugged out to the west in the Aleutians, Cold Bay was also designated a lend lease port under the code name Hula Two. Ships were brought to Cold Bay where Russian crews waited to man them for voyages to the Soviet Union. The landmark Volcano Club, a Soviet officers' club, still stands and is on the National Register of Historic Places.

Cold Bay, in 1945, became the sight for secret military training of Soviet troops for their possible help in a proposed invasion of Japan, a nation the Soviet Union had a neutrality treaty. Some 12,400 Russian soldiers received training here for amphibious landings before being sent back to Russia onboard battleships flying the Soviet flag.

Remarkably, with the fighting close by and lend-lease with the Soviets active at Cold Bay, Bob Reeve was able to secure regular passenger service for civilian contract workers with his Reeve Aleutian Airways. The airline was quartered in an abandoned Quonset hut manned by a married couple.

The U.S. Air Force took over the military facilities in Cold Bay on January 1, 1947, renaming Fort Randall Thornbrough Air Force Base a year later. The U.S. Fish and Wildlife Department opened a one-man post in 1948 increasing the civilian population to three.

Cold Bay's military importance after the Korean War was as a Distant Early Warning Station. When the Air Force completed construction of the early warning site in 1958, the runway facilities at Cold Bay were turned over to the Federal Aviation Administration while the weather station was turned over to the National Weather Service.

Though Reeve Aleutian still had most flights, they had to share the runway with Canadian Pacific and Northwest Orient airlines. Cold Bay was becoming civilian though it still had, and has, a military look to it. A post office was established in 1954.

Northwest Orient even built a combination restaurant and bar called "The Weathered Inn" to service airline passengers weathered in and unable to leave Cold Bay.

Alaskan statehood in 1959 resulted in federal jurisdiction transferred to the state including the runways. The federal government, however, continued to have a significant presence when the 415,000-acre Izembek National Wildlife Refuge was created in 1960. So many government workers and their families living in town resulted in the need for schooling. The first school, established to instruct grades one through nine, opened in 1961. Cold Bay's runways saw heavy traffic through the 1960s and early 1970s due to the Vietnam War.

During this time, the legendary Flying Tigers flew freight out of Cold Bay at the rate of 30 flights per month. The Flying Tigers held a near exclusive contract to operate a hotel, restaurant, bar, store, movie theater and bowling alley. Any other firm would have to file an intent eighteen months in advance for services not being offered by the Flying Tigers. The Tigers even took over and renovated The Weathered Inn.

As the Vietnam War ended, the Tigers began using 747s for transporting cattle from Washington State to Japan with refueling at Cold Bay. By 1985, the Tigers pulled out selling their interest to Reeve Aleutian who had expanded its Aleutian Islands operations.

There was a brief oil exploration boom in 1979 causing the State of Alaska to put 143 acres on the east side of town up for bid after subdividing the land into 46 parcels. The appraised value of each unimproved tundra plot was $13,500. One man paid $3 million for ten acres. The 13th Regional Native Corporation bought the largest tract of land hoping to set up a fish processing plant. It failed as did the search for oil.

Meanwhile, from 1984 to 1995, the federal government made an extensive attempt to clean up contaminated waste from leaking fuel tanks and corroded pipelines from Cold Bay's days as a military base.

The Aleutian East Borough put in a large multi-purpose dock hoping the Aleutian marine fleet would offload fish to be flown out from Cold Bay's runways with mixed results.

Today The Weathered Inn has become the eight room Bearfoot Inn along with the Bearfoot Inn Bar. The Bearfoot also acts as the local grocery store and supply point. The Cold Bay Lodge has the only restaurant. The school has one teacher instructing seven students.

A hovercraft which began operations in 2007 links Cold Bay with King Cove. A road link between the two communities has been planned with the federal government acting as a roadblock to its construction due to the wildlife refuge. Vehicles would have to drive across seven miles of the refuge. King Cove residents want the road to reach Cold Bay's airfield during medical emergencies. Since 1979, eleven King Cove residents have died trying to reach Cold Bay for medical help.

A Delta Airliner with passengers had to make an emergency landing at Cold Bay in October 2013, an example of the town's airport strategic location for Pacific flights.

The latest census at the Izembek National Wildlife Refuge showed 130,000 Pacific Black Brant, 62,000 Emperor Geese, 50,000 Taverner's Canada Geese, 300,000 ducks, and 80,000 shorebirds.

Izembek is the smallest national wildlife refuge in Alaska.

FALSE PASS

THE SMALL COMMUNITY OBTAINED ITS NAME from an optical illusion of sorts. Isanotski Strait between Unimak Island and the Alaska Peninsula seems to offer a short cut for vessels trying to go from the North Pacific into the Bering Sea. Shallows and swift tides on the Bering side prevent this from being a reality.

The small fishing community sits at the very eastern edge of massive Unimak Island where the Aleutian Islands begin, and the Alaska mainland ends—the sudden contrast in flora and fauna can be stark at times. Uminak is the largest island in the Aleutian chain and the ninth largest in the U.S. covering 1,571 square miles. It is home to Mount Shishaldin, one of the ten most active volcanoes in the world and to the Fisher Caldera with its many small lakes and vents within its crater.

On the far western end of the island was the location for the Cape Scotch Lighthouse established in 1903. On April 1, 1946, shortly after the 8.1 Aleutian Earthquake of 1946, the lighthouse was struck by a 130-foot massive tsunami at 2:18 a.m. that literally collapsed the structure into the sea killing the five U.S. Coast Guard personnel stationed there.

Research shows that Unimak Island supported a large population before the arrival of the Russians with at least twelve villages, primarily on the Bering side of the island with its accessible beaches and drift whales as a food source. Unimak Aleuts were known as fierce warriors battling Russian fur traders even before the Russians reached the island in 1761.

When the Russians did arrive, warfare was bloody on both sides with no mercy shown. The atrocities conducted against the Aleuts on Unimak by the crew of the *Gavriil* were so brutal in 1762 that the crew was put on trial when the ship returned to Siberia.

The Unimak Aleuts killed the entire crew of the *Nikolai* in 1763 after it wintered near present False Pass, but not before the crew massacred a Unimak village.

The Unimak War finally cooled in 1769 due to heavy losses taken by the Unimak Aleuts. This was noticed by Russian Orthodox priests coming to Unimak in 1796 to perform baptisms. They noted the island now had only three villages. According to the 1821 Russian census, the entire island had only 125 people. By then, Unimak had been pacified and made part of the Unalaska District. The island had only two villages in 1825. Epidemics were seen as the cause for this later decline.

Isanotski Strait between the Bering and Pacific became a rendezvous point for Russian ships. Nine ships alone wintered there in 1784.

The 1867 Purchase witnessed the emptying of Unimak as first nearby Morzhovoe and later Ikatan had canneries open offering employment. These canneries were owned by P.E. Harris who amassed a fortune in the Nome Gold Fields.

False Pass had its humble start when trapper John Gardener constructed a cabin on the shore in the early 1900s. The advantages of straddling two bodies of ocean were not wasted on Harris. He bought the homestead relocating his Morzhovoe cannery there in 1920. Harris had buildings from Morzhovoe towed in by tenders. Natives looking for work from the villages of Morzhovoi, Sanak Island, and Ikatan settled at the new site.

A division of labor took place with local Aleuts and Sanak immigrants becoming the fishermen for the cannery while Aleuts from Morzhovoi worked in the cannery. What was astonishing about this division of labor was the fact that canneries nearby tried not using Aleut workers at all. Filipinos usually worked inside the canneries while the fishermen were usually Scandinavians.

The cannery maintained a medical staff and a company store open to the public. A small hospital facility was even opened by the cannery and later donated to the community for a school.

Harris died in 1951 and the cannery eventually came under the ownership of Peter Pan Seafoods.

Alaska opened a territorial school at False Pass in 1929 operating it until 1937 when student population dropped. From 1962 to 1976, a state school operated in False Pass. Until destroyed by fire in March 1981, the cannery remained open continuously with the exception of 1973 to 1976 when unusually hard winters depleted the fish resources.

False Pass incorporated in 1990. The sale of alcohol is restricted to the package store. The community is more than half Aleut. The school has eleven students.

Though primarily a commercial fishing town, False Pass is an important refueling stop for fishing fleets operating in the Bering Sea even though it has no boat harbor, just dock facilities.

Recently False Pass residents and the State of Alaska have found themselves battling the U.S. Fish and Game Department on the issue of wolves. Unimak Island is the home for the nation's only naturally occurring insular caribou herd. In 2002 this herd numbered 1260 but was down to 300 by 2011 with only 20 bulls. The decrease has been blamed on the island's wolf packs. Unimak wolves differ from mainland wolves in coloration and sometimes size. Historically, Unimak wolves are larger with a light coat and a dark stripe running down the spine of the animal.

The wolf population today has been reported to be in poor health. Two wolves were shot and killed by the mayor's sons when they entered False Pass in 2010 looking for dogs as a food source.

In 2011, False Pass complained to the U.S. Fish and Game that the wolves had grown bolder frequently coming into town and showing no fear of man, but the federal department took no action. Indeed, they took the State of Alaska to court in March 2011 successfully blocking a planned state hunt on the wolves.

The island's fox population was wiped out by a rabies epidemic in 1992.

However, the brown bear population is large. The bruins often can be seen on the beach by passengers onboard the ferry *Tustumena* as it comes into False Pass.

AKUTAN

As the Alaska state ferry *Tustumena* approached the Akutan dock at five in the morning, glowing embers filled the air. The side of the mountain by the village was burning from the shoreline to the summit. Crew members were telling the few passengers who were awake that the volcano must have erupted. But, when dawn came on that June day 2007, light showed it had been a mere grass fire set off by a tossed cigarette. However, it illustrated just how intertwined Akutan is to the 4,100-foot volcano that hovers over it.

This was demonstrated mid-March 1996 when Akutan volcano jarred Akutan with a series of tremors. More than 800 minor quakes during the day of March 13th and again March 14th brought an army of scientists to set up seismometers as half the community boarded seaplanes for nearby Unalaska. The volcano, though, did not erupt.

Akutan is Aleut for "I made a mistake." It has the distinction of having been both the only whaling station in the Aleutian Islands and a secret Soviet base on American soil.

When the Russians arrived at Akutan in the 1760s, the island was divided by five villages: Chaxigada being the largest with a hundred inhabitants. They were known for their tradition of chasing down and killing whales that entered Akutan Bay.

Several Akutan warriors joined in the Unalaska War against the

Russians in 1764. Under Ivan Solov'ev "the Destroyer," as Aleuts called him, Russian traders launched a massive retaliation raid that took in Akutan. All totaled, the Russians killed anywhere from 200 to 300 Aleut warriors for the killings of Russians on Unalaska.

Solov'ev, who later founded the town of Unalaska, was so successful that when the Russian Navy began exploring Akutan in 1768, men of fighting age hid up on the slopes of the volcano. For the most part, the Unalaska War was not Akutan's war and before long Akutan villagers acted as interpreters and guides for the Russians as they moved onto the Alaska Peninsula and the Kodiak Islands.

Several *toions* or Akutan chiefs were taken prisoner by the Alutiiqs and tortured to death in spite efforts by the Russians to free them by force. Warfare against and with the Russians took its toll on Akutan. Within twenty years, Akutan villages went from five to three. By 1821, the island had only one village.

The Russians developed a fondness for Akutan in the 1830s appointing a caretaker for maintaining a rest and recreation facility at one of the many hot springs on the island. What drew the attention of visiting Russians from Unalaska was the fact that the hot springs spouted next to a cold-water spring. Both were believed by the Russians to have curative powers.

The Akutans by now not only spoke Russian but had visited Russian towns in Siberia. One *toion*, Semeon Pan'kov, assisted Bishop Ioann Veniaminov in translating the Gospel of St. Mathew into Eastern Aleut. On nearby Akun Island lived the Aleut prophet and seer Smirennikov during the same time.

Akutan and the other villages of the Krenitzin Islands felt the devastating effects of a smallpox epidemic in 1838. Pan'kov rallied his people and Akutan became a model regarding prosperity and order for other Aleut villages.

However, the pull for employment offered in other villages eventually led to the Aleuts abandoning Akutan by 1867.

Current Akutan

The modern village of Akutan began in 1878 as a trading post for the Western Fur and Trading Company. The first Aleut family to move back to Akutan was Epoti and Esi Petikoff. The couple slapped together a mud house where the southwest corner of the future town would be. By the end of the first year, when the post was in operation, Akutan had 63 residents. They constructed a new Russian Orthodox Church with a part time school dedicated to Saint Alexander Nevskii. It was replaced by a new chapel in 1918.

The next year the Alaska Commercial Company bought the trading post sending in its first and only manager, Hugh McGlashan. From Scotland, McGlashan ran away from home for the sea at age 16. He had already worked in the South Pacific, Australia, and Hawaii before coming to Alaska where he hunted sea otters for six years. The Western Fur and Trading Company hired him to manage their post in Unalaska. After Western Fur sold out to Alaska Commercial (ACC), McGlashan was sent back to Akutan to operate the former Western Fur store. He moved with his wife Feckla and their family, unusual for that era. Successful at managing the post and treating Akutan as a home rather than as an assignment, he bought the post from the ACC in the 1890s.

The entire community was economically threatened in 1911 when the U.S. entered into an international agreement under President William Howard Taft banning the hunting of sea otters.

A whaling station

However, the Pacific Whaling Company constructed a land based whaling station at Akutan in 1912 on the other side of the bay. Akutan was the only whaling station in the Aleutian Islands operating until 1939. A company post office was set up in the village in 1914 and a U.S. post office in 1920. A local stream was dammed in 1927 for a source of drinking water for the village.

The Alaska Whaling Company was a front for Norwegian whaling interests wanting to hunt whales in U.S. territorial waters. Norwegian whaling firms were infamous for devastating whale populations wherever they operated from around the world. The Canadian government ordered them out of their waters in the early 1900s. One firm, operating out of Sandefjord, Norway, decided to try operations in Alaskan waters by forming a business partnership with Norwegian-Americans living in Minnesota. Akutan was selected because of its proximity to Dutch Harbor and to Unimak Pass which was a migratory whale passage.

The firm built both a land based whaling station across from Akutan and anchored the *Admiralen*, a floating processor, in the bay. In the first complete year of operations in 1912, the station slaughtered and processed 162 fin whales and 148 humpbacks. The high cost of bringing in supplies from Norway (there was no Panama Canal at this time) caused the firm to re-organize as the North Pacific Sea Products Company with an entirely Minnesotan board of directors. Knut Birkeland, a Lutheran pastor, was selected to manage the whaling station though he had no prior experience. He was also one of the investors.

Birkeland segregated the workers into three separate housing units: one for Whites, one for Asians and one for Aleuts from Akutan. He organized the work schedule into a six-day work week which conflicted with the religious requirements of the Orthodox Church. Birkeland came to an arrangement with the local priest concerning holidays and church services that kept Aleut workers happy.

When President Taft set the Aleutians aside as a refuge in 1913, the firm's political influence won a stay of execution from the Taft Administration with whaling resuming in 1914. President Woodrow Wilson amended Taft's refuge order in 1913 to allow for the operations of the whaling station.

Operations grew to the point that besides the land station, six whaling vessels were operating out of Akutan by 1925. The following year the firm renamed itself the American Pacific Whaling Company. By the Great Depression, the facilities were sold to Toronto-based Victoria Whaling Company.

The whaling station had an immediate impact on Akutan starting with diet. Instead of eating whale only intermediately, the village had all the whale meat and blubber they wanted. The meat itself was dried into strips while the fat was put up for the winter. The company allowed the Aleuts to have all the meat they wanted, and the community grew healthier as a result.

The other change was the material wealth individuals and Akutan were experiencing. The U.S. customs records in Sitka show that in 1911 only $440 worth of goods was shipped to the general store in Akutan just prior to the opening of the whaling station. Years later more than $331,000 worth of goods were shipped to the Akutan general store.

Also, the racial makeup of Akutan was being transformed as reflected in the station's payroll accounts. Out of 718 receiving a payroll check, only 138 were Aleuts. The remainder were White and Asian.

Work was exhausting and dangerous. The whaling vessels shot the whales with exploding harpoons. They were then "floated" with air and towed to the station where a steam powered winch dragged them over a ramp into a flensing area. There butcher crews with 18-inch-long knives cut the blubber off the carcass and then sliced up the blubber, meat, and bones of the giants into small pieces.

Boiling the blubber took place inside the station. Meat and blubber were transferred to the company's fertilizer factory.

McGlashan and his son, Hugh, were also hiring locals to mine sulfur from the volcano. In 1915 the McGlashans built a dock and a processing shed for cod, operating it until the late 1930s.

Most of the Aleuts took a staggering economic blow when President Taft in 1913 set aside all the Aleutians as a preserve for native birds, the propagation of reindeer and fur bearing animals, and the development of area fisheries.

From traditional egg gathering to selling pelts, Aleuts found themselves as law breakers if they even tried subsistence living in their homeland. Of all the villages save Unalaska, Akutan offered an economic refuge through its whaling station and cod industry. Aleuts, including those in Akutan, were also dying from another smallpox epidemic in the first decades of the 1900s. Anti-American feelings ran high since the U.S. made no attempt to immunize Natives unlike the Russians who routinely vaccinated the Natives against smallpox.

This epidemic was soon followed by the 1919 Spanish Flu epidemic that took the life of Feckla McGlashan.

With the backing of the whaling firm, a public school opened in 1921, but was closed off and on for the decade until 1930 when student enrollment finally reached 19 students with two teachers. From 1930 until Akutan's evacuation during World War II, the school managed to continually stay open.

Akutan residents in 1938 supported the construction of a hydroelectric plant providing DC power to the town until the early 1980s. The facility was operated and maintained for most of its life span by Luke Shelikoff.

Visitors to Akutan in the late 1930s complained of the smell from the whale station miles out to sea before reaching the village of now 71.

The next year the whaling station ceased operations hiring George McGlashan, Hugh's grandson, as caretaker.

Secret Soviet base

When Japanese forces attacked Dutch Harbor in 1942, the U.S. military moved Akutan residents to an internment camp just outside of Ketchikan. When Akutan Aleuts learned they were going to be evacuated, they grabbed most of the historical valuable icons that were in their Russian Orthodox Church and buried them in a sandy beach across the bay. Military authorities told them they could take the icons with them, so they were dug back up, placed in barrels, and transported to Ketchikan where they waited out the war.

It was a good thing the residents did. The United States turned Akutan over to Soviet authorities during the war. The Soviet base was used as a refueling station for Soviet warships and in ferrying lend lease planes from the U.S. to the Soviet Union. While living in the now abandoned homes, Soviet naval personnel did extensive vandalism throughout Akutan. The U.S. government reimbursed the community for structural damage with a mere $27,000 and for the loss of personal property of only $306.

For Akutan residents, life was also not easy in Ketchikan. The death rate among Akutan Aleuts was the highest of all the internment camps at 17.8 percent of the internment population; in part due to venereal diseases and bad alcohol provided by Ketchikan residents as well as improper medical care.

Akutan became the location for the turning point in the aviation war in the Pacific theater. A Japanese A6M Zero fighter piloted by Tadayoshi Koga crashed on Akutan Island in June 1942. The United States Army Air Corp recovered the fighter the next month. Known as the Akutan Zero, it became the template for U.S. tacticians developing dog fighting techniques against Japanese air power. American superiority in fighting tactics over the Zero was one of the turning points of World War II. Akutan was resettled in 1944 though many Aleuts did not return to the village.

Returning Akutan residents found their town overrun by villagers from Kashega, Makushin, and Biorka after the federal government discouraged them from returning to their own communities. The whaling station was dismantled, the wood used for new housing.

In 1968, Wakefield Seafood Processors sent in a vessel to catch and process king crab. Wakefield constructed a new dock facility on land leased from the Orthodox Church, stationing the *M/V Akutan* there. Seawest bought the facilities from Wakefield in 1979 just as the king crab boom began. By 1981 Akutan Bay was home to thirteen floating processors employing over a thousand workers.

The 1971 Alaska Native Claims Settlement Act gave Akutan enough funds to build Bay View Plaza housing the civic government, a laundry, the post office, and a four-room hotel along with two private apartments.

Akutan became an incorporated community in 1979. Trident Seafoods maintains a large plant on the west side of the village in order to process cod, crab, pollock and fish meal. The plant handles its own sewage, water, and electricity.

Things began unraveling for Akutan in 1983 when king crab stocks in the area crashed. Seawest pulled out while the Trident plant experienced a devastating fire destroying the main processing plant, cold storage, and the freezing and handling sections. The fire cost an estimated $12 million in damages. Within a few months though, Trident was back in operation.

Feeling the need for a stronger form of representation on the state level, Akutan joined in organizing the Aleutians East Borough in 1987.

A major fire swept through the community again in 2002 destroying a 30,000 square foot gear storage facility. Firefighting units from Unalaska were brought in to help Akutan firemen put out the blaze.

There were eighteen students in the Akutan school in 2010. The town does not have a landing strip. Connections with Unalaska are maintained by both the state ferry system and seaplanes such as a Grumman Goose, all affected by high waves determining if docking and landings are possible—especially in winter.

The city of Akutan owns a landing craft, *M/V Akutan*, which brings in supplies from Unalaska.

Surprisingly only sixteen percent of the population is Aleut. Though 24 percent are White, Asians account for the majority of the population at 39 percent followed by a Hispanic population of 20 percent; all present to work at the Trident plant.

Akutan's only bar, The Roadhouse, is operated by Tommy McGlashen, an ancestor of Hugh McGlashan who came to Akutan in 1879.

With nearly 800 residents, Akutan has wooden boardwalks connecting the various well-kept homes and the Orthodox Church. The town boasts of having an internet connected library, a quality museum on Akutan's whaling days, a grocery store, two churches (Orthodox and Catholic), a gym, a restaurant, and a small hotel. Small wooden ramps line the waterfront near the dock allowing individuals to launch their own boats from the beach.

Still, when the state ferry arrives, residents come to the dock to order hamburgers and fries from the ferry's kitchen.

UNALASKA and DUTCH HARBOR

Explorer Aleksei Druzhinin tried to understand what the Aleuts were telling him without much success. He had anchored his ship the *Zakharii I Elisaveta* off Hog Island in 1763 believing he was only the second white man to have visited Unalaska Harbor. Stepan Glotov had been there first in 1759.

The Aleuts were describing a masted sailing ship of a quite different design from what the Russians used. The only nation with such a ship design were the Dutch as far as Druzhinin knew. What was a Dutch ship doing in this far corner of the world? Still, he marked it down on his sea chart, Gollandskaia gavan' or Dutch Harbor.

When Glotov arrived in 1759, Unalaska had 24 villages scattered throughout the island. Unalaska was divided into Native alliances east and west with the 6,680-foot Makushin Volcano as the boundary line. Ounalashka itself means "near the peninsula." The Russians corrupted the word becoming today's Unalaska.

The Russians took the chief or toion's children as hostages while their hunters, called promyshlenniki, fanned out among the islands collecting pelts for the trip home.

Druzhinin beached his boat at Captain's Bay south of the bridge now connecting Dutch Harbor with Unalaska. Relations between Druzhinin's men and the Aleuts were growing tense when the Natives learned that the Russians had whipped the son of a toion, an unheard-of thing. The Aleuts now sought retribution. They brought to the post furs for trade when one of the Russians saw a spear hidden amongst the pelts. The Russians drew their weapons as the Aleuts attacked. All the Russians were killed and Aleuts from other villages tracked down and killed the Russian hunting parties save the one at Beaver Inlet.

Those survivors made their way across the island to Makushin Bay where another Russian ship anchored. Thus began the bloody Unalaska War.

The Unalaska War

The survivors were picked up by Glotov then arriving on a third voyage. At Kashega Bay on Unalaska was Ivan Solov'ev with his trading vessel. He rallied the remaining Russians in the region for a brutal counterattack lasting a year ranging from Unalaska up to the Alaska Peninsula. Solov'ev earned the name The Destroyer from the Aleuts after killing 300 Natives, burning their villages, destroying their boats, and smashing their hunting and fishing equipment.

Solov'ev the Destroyer founded the first permanent settlement in North America for Russia. Sometime around 1772 Solov'ev settled Iliuluk on Unalaska just south of Dutch Harbor. The name came from the Aleut word meaning "dwelling together, harmonious." The Russians experimented with several names of their own for the small settlement, Dobrogo Soglasiia meaning harbor of good accord, and Gavanskoe selenie simply meaning village on the bay.

The Russian captains needed a permanent base of operations with a sheltering harbor. They were finding the world they had stumbled upon immense and the voyage back to Siberia long and difficult.

The Aleutians are the meeting place between the warm Japan current and the cold frigid waters of the Bering Sea. The results are storms with hurricane force winds. The Aleutians had begun earning their reputation as the "cradle of the storms" it is known for today. Indeed, the lowest sea level pressure ever recorded took place here in 1977 at 27.31 millibars.

The Unalaska War continued with Glotov and roughly 69 Russians dying on Unimak Island. By the end of the war, Unalaska was reduced to only 16 villages and a thousand Aleuts. Word of the atrocities committed under Solov'ev reached Catherine the Great. Solov'ev was recalled to Siberia, tried, and died in poverty.

England's Captain James Cook spent 23 days in Unalaska in October 1778. He noted just how integrated into Russian culture the Aleuts had become, even conducting Orthodox religious rites. This was underscored when Orthodox monk Macarius baptized most of the Aleuts on Unalaska Island into the Orthodox faith in 1795. The Spanish under Estevan Martinez arrived in 1788 claiming the island for Spain naming it Puerto de Dona Marie Luisa Teresa.

Grigorii Shelikhov, who had set up a colony on Kodiak, set up a base on Unalaska in 1791. A year before he had hired a merchant named Alexander Baranov to manage his company's interests in Alaska. Baranov ended up shipwrecked on Unalaska for a year before he was able to continue to Kodiak as the new manager for that outpost. Shelikhov died in Russia in 1795. His company's shareholders retained Baranov as manager of the firm's holding from Kodiak eastward, but in 1797 they sent Emelian Larionov to be the manager of the company's Unalaska post and all holdings west of Kodiak.

Russia's Emperor Paul in 1799 decreed that the Shelikhov Company would have a monopoly on trade in Alaska and the firm quickly reorganized as the new Russian American Company. Baranov was appointed the new Chief Manager, in essence the governor of Alaska, but Larionov would continue overseeing what was now becoming the Unalaska District. Baranov's authority was finally extended to Unalaska and all points west in 1802, but Larionov was still allowed to govern the Unalaska District where Aleuts claimed he was like a father to them.

With the support of Larionov, Fedor Burenin built the first chapel in Unalaska in 1808. Orthodox priests had been ministering Unalaska from Kodiak as early as 1795. In 1821, after the re-chartering of the company, Orthodox missionaries were directed to train Natives in becoming clergy.

Ioann Veniaminov

A milestone for Aleuts and their relationship with the Orthodox Church took place in 1824 with the arrival of Father Ioann Veniaminov with his wife and son. A giant of a man, later called Paul Bunyan in a cassock, he championed the causes of the Aleuts, learned their language, and with the assistance of Chief Ivan Pan'kov of Akun and Stephan Kriukov of Nikolski, developed the Aleut alphabet.

He literally paddled thousands of miles in a kayak visiting scattered villages throughout the Aleutians and the Alaska Peninsula. He shocked church goers when he gave a sermon in strictly Aleut and wrote in Aleut a pamphlet concerning the essence of Christianity that went through forty editions.

A man who built clocks and furniture with his own hands, Veniaminov trained Aleut men in carpentry arts, locksmithing, blacksmith, brick, and stone masonry while at the same time opening an elementary school for Aleut children in Unalaska in 1825. He rebuilt the chapel in 1825. The current chapel which stands at the head of the town of Unalaska, was constructed in 1858 by Father Innokenty Shayashnikov retaining some of Veniaminov's original chapel, Church of the Holy Ascension of Christ. It is a registered National Historic Landmark. The Bishop's House was built for the church by the Alaska Commercial Company in 1882.

Besides the chapel, by 1834, Unalaska consisted of 27 sod houses, five wooden houses, three stores, the elementary school, a small hospital, and an orphanage housing twelve girls. Scattered throughout the settlement were pigs, chickens, domesticated ducks, and a cattle pen.

There were rats brought in unintentionally on the *Finliandiia* in 1828.

The entire Aleut population by Veniaminov's day numbered only 1,474 living in ten villages on Unalaska. Veniaminov was transferred to Sitka in 1833 and eventually became Bishop of Alaska. Later he would be selected as the Metropolitan of Moscow, the head of the Russian Orthodox Church.

The U.S. Purchase of Alaska

Unalaska was suffering from neglect as a small distant outpost of both the Russian Empire and Russia Alaska when the U.S. Revenue Cutter *Lincoln* docked in 1867 with news Alaska had been sold to the United States. The cutter then proceeded north to the Pribilof Islands to begin her patrols against seal poachers. Behind her, came representatives of the firm Hutchinson, Kohl, and Company out of San Francisco taking over the trading post that had belonged to the Russian American Company.

Hutchinson Kohl sold out to the Alaska Commercial Company (ACC) in 1868. In 1870 ACC won a federal contract for the harvesting of 100,000 fur seals annually in the Pribilofs for the next twenty years. Unalaska's ACC facilities were to be the forefront of this operation. The ACC built six two story high warehouses and a major wharf. A store as built along the bay, connected to the warehouses by rail for the transfer of goods from storage to retail. ACC general manager Alfred Greenbaum had a three-story structure erected to serve as ACC's headquarters as well as his living quarters. Special quarters were built for the best of ACC's Aleut hunters to live in as a reward for service.

Unalaska in 1881 had a population of 400 that now included a U.S. Customs House when Naturalist John Muir visited the port.

International whaling fleets began calling on Unalaska for repairs using the ACC facilities. Mail boats and freighters dropped off supplies to be dispersed throughout Western Alaska. A coal station was set up for international shipping.

Hell Roaring Mike and the Bear

ACC soon discovered it had a problem in the form of poachers primarily from Japan and Canada raiding the Pribilofs.

In response, the U.S. sent a series of revenue cutters to patrol the waters of Western Alaska based out of Unalaska. These revenue cutters were required to do more than track down international poachers. They were to rescue stranded whalers, stop bootlegging, provide medical treatment for the Native population, conduct the U.S. census, record geological and astronomical information, explore the Alaskan Interior, and act as a floating courthouse trying cases as they cruised some 20,000 miles of isolated Alaskan coastline.

Two legendary revenue cutters were the *Thomas Corwin* and the cutter/ice breaker, the *Bear*. In command of first the *Corwin,* and later the *Bear*, was Hell-Roaring Mike Healy, an alcoholic with a violent temper. His nickname was earned in many a bar brawls in the dives of San Francisco.

The U.S. Treasury Department gave Healy *carte blanche* in arresting anyone he suspected of violating the law or posed a danger to others as well as seizing their property. This power was later confirmed by an act of Congress. To try curbing his notorious temper, the U.S. Revenue Service allowed Healy to be the only captain to have along his wife Mary.

"People don't have faith in God," said Alaskan missionary Ellen Lopp in the 1890s. "Instead, they place their faith in Captain Healy's power to kill people and blow their town up with guns!"

With the *Bear*'s reinforced hull, Healy braved icepacks and howling gales rescuing sailors and stranded gold seekers, put down mutinies and track down seal poachers, rum runners, and gun smugglers. His exploits were front page news for West Coast papers.

Healy was the law along the West Alaska coast for more than a decade. He had requested the assignment, not because it was where the action was, but so he could hide. Healy had a terrible secret. He was black in an age when no black could be a captain. His light skin and having a white wife allowed him to get away with the masquerade.

There is evidence that the higher ups in the Revenue Service knew but turned a blind eye. Healy was effective. The Revenue Service believed it could not function in Alaska without him in spite of serious charges that he had hung and whipped sailors of other vessels he caught breaking U.S. sovereignty while intoxicated in 1889.

Alcohol finally brought him down. Healy rendezvoused with four other Revenue cutters at Unalaska preparing for the voyage back to San

Francisco. Invited onboard a British warship as a guest, Healy became uncontrollably drunk shouting obscenities at the British naval officers. Two days later, still intoxicated; Healy fell off the ACC wharf in front of his men. Healy was found guilty in a court martial in 1895 and stripped of his command.

By then Unalaska had become the newly designated headquarters for the Revenue Service's Bering Sea Patrol with U.S. naval warships assisting. Captured poachers were brought and jailed directly to Unalaska where punishment was administered.

Meanwhile Healy's close friend, Presbyterian missionary Sheldon Jackson, arranged the construction of the Jesse Lee Memorial Home and Industrial School at Unalaska in 1887. John Tuck was sent as its first headmaster taking in its first orphans in 1890. Accusations of misconduct and not cooperating with the local Orthodox Church resulted in Jackson dismissing Tuck in 1896. He was replaced by Dr. Albert and Agnes Newhall who brought the orphanage into high regard by both Aleuts and whites alike in the Aleutians.

The Jesse Lee Home grew into a campus of several buildings including a boys and girls dormitories housing 67 children by 1922. It was moved to Seward in 1925.

Dutch Harbor is born

The ACC lost its seal harvest contract in 1890 to the North American Commercial Company. The ACC remained in Unalaska, but the new firm decided to build its dock and warehouses at Dutch Harbor, the first development of the port. Both Dutch Harbor and Unalaska soon had warehouses, hotels, residential homes, and saloons, a surprise since Alaska still legally had prohibition and the number of federal offices were located in Unalaska.

The center of social life in the growing community was both the three-story ACC building that held dances and the gingerbread home of the wife of the new North American Commercial agent, Molly Brown. Though she entertained U.S. Naval officers and officers of visiting navies as well as locals, it was never forgotten that she was the daughter of the assassinated President James A. Garfield.

Two Americans arriving during this era helped develop Unalaska. Samuel Applegate came in 1881 as a weather observer for the U.S. Signal Service, quit working briefly at the ACC post before becoming a sea otter hunter. He eventually got his own vessel earning money transporting hunters throughout the Bering Sea. When otters began to dwindle in number, he turned to ACC manager Rudolph Neumann, a Bavarian, who had worked the ACC post at Saint Michael, proposing a partnership.

The two men established fox farms at Unalaska and the surrounding islands for a number of years. Applegate obtained permission from the Russian government to trade with Siberia. The two men opened a sulfur mine on the slopes of Makushin Volcano in 1906, but their real fortunes came with the Klondike and Nome gold rushes.

Mining the miners

Unalaska boomed during the gold rushes as locals mined would be miners. Both the Yukon River route to the Klondike Gold Fields, called the Rich Man's Route, and the Nome Gold Fields, required prospectors to come through Unalaska.

The docks and beaches of Unalaska from 1897 until 1900 were jammed by anything and everything that could float from sidewheelers to barges to converted whaling ships to salmon fishers. Prefabricated vessels built in the Lower 48 were unboxed and assembled in Unalaska. One reason for the ship traffic was the coaling station the North American Commercial Company maintained at Dutch Harbor.

For those who came late and found themselves blocked by Bering Sea pack ice, Unalaska became their home for the winter with local merchants like Neumann enriching themselves even more.

By 1900, when the last gold fields around Nome no longer offered easy pickings, it was like a light had gone out in Unalaska. The Roosevelt administration tried transforming nearby Dutch Harbor into a naval base after Theodore Roosevelt set aside 23 acres for a Navy coaling station in 1902. The Navy's conversion to fuel oil killed the plan.

Applegate was not going to let the economic depression get the best of him. He loaded his schooner with nine kayaks or native *baidarkas* and sailed out for one last major hunt of sea otters. Their pelts were bringing $2,000 a piece on London markets, and he promised $300 a pelt to his Aleut hunters. His entire hunt for the summer only brought in nine pelts.

It had become obvious sea otters in the Aleutians needed protection for their numbers to return. The federal government issued such protection in 1910.

Herring and cod processing took up some of the employment slack. Unalaska took an economic blow when President William Howard Taft signed an international agreement in 1911 banning the hunting of sea otters in the Aleutians.

The Great Corpse Race

Unalaska left its mark on the Golden Age of the Alaska Bush pilots in the 1930s.

A fisherman in Dutch Harbor died in 1938 leaving $1.4 million to his niece living in Seattle. The niece now wanted to give her favorite uncle a fitting burial in that city. She offered $12,000 to anyone who would bring his body from Unalaska to Seward where it would be shipped to Seattle.

All the legendary Alaskan Bush pilots of the age took a shot at the prize, but it would be Alex Holden who would win.

He had the body dug up after obtaining an exhumation order from an Anchorage judge over his radio while in flight. He then island hopped from Seward to Unalaska struggling to keep his plane from crashing into the sides of mountains and volcanoes as he fought through fog and high winds that would have grounded another pilot.

Arriving, Holden had the body painted with shellac to slow its decay. To his horror, he could not get the corpse to bend in order to fit it into his plane. He ended up tying the corpse down over the wing before repeating the island-hopping flight back to Seward where he collected the $12,000.

Otherwise, Unalaska seemed quiet during the 1930s. Kathryn Seller, an Aleut who taught in Unalaska for 29 years, took the high school band for visits to outlying villages entertaining people living in isolation.

Japanese spies

The arrests of two Japanese spies in 1935 should have perked some interest that things were just not right in the Aleutians. The man had been jailed before for selling illegal alcohol while his girlfriend had prior charges of being a prostitute. Visiting sailors offered to pay her bail since she was the only prostitute in Unalaska.

There had been a long history of Japanese interaction with Alaska. In 1806, Baranov had shipwrecked Japanese fishermen that had washed ashore at Sitka, returned to their homeland. Japanese workers were used in the early days of the cannery boom throughout coastal Alaska. A Japanese whaling fleet operated in the Bering Sea and the U.S. dealt with Japanese poachers around the Pribilofs.

Thus, no suspicions were raised shortly after the arrest of the two alleged spies when Japan requested she be allowed to conduct a nautical survey of the Aleutians in the 1930s. Each year in the 1930s, more and more Japanese scientists arrived to study geology and fauna in the Aleutians and West Alaska.

After the Japanese bombers damaged the U.S. Naval gunboat *Panay* in 1937, Congress authorized funding for Pacific defenses. When Russia and Nazi Germany signed their non-aggression pact in 1939, the U.S. began expanding its military presence in Alaska.

There were only four Aleut villages left on Unalaska when the Navy bought the North American Commercial Co.'s holdings at Dutch Harbor in 1940. Seeing the military in their future, Unalaska incorporated in 1941to increase their property values.

Supplies and equipment marked misleadingly for Blair Packing Company were offloaded at Chermofski Harbor and ferried to

Umnak Island where an airfield was being built in secret. Seventy miles west of Dutch Harbor, Fort Glenn was the answer for air cover. Unalaska was soon flooded with 5,000 civilian workers. The Marines barracks was completed in 1940. By 1942, the civilians were replaced with Navy Seabees.

Fort Meiers was built closer to the town of Unalaska with an infantry garrison and coastal battery setups. These were turned over to the Navy in 1942 as the Army units moved to Unalaska Ridge guarding the approaches to the bay. By October 1942, the U.S. Army had 9,976 soldiers at Unalaska which then consisted of 300 residents and five women working a local house of prostitution. The house, self-dubbed Pleasure Island, was closed by the U.S. Marshal in September 1941.

After the attack on Pearl Harbor, a submarine base was set up at Margaret Bay on Dutch Harbor in January 1942 housing old World War I submarines called "sewer pipes" by their crews.

U.S. code breakers by May 1942 knew a Japanese attack on both the Aleutians and Midway Island was coming. A small North Pacific Fleet was sent to assist Alaska and was stationed in Kodiak rather than Dutch Harbor. A patrol net was thrown around the Aleutians consisting of one gunboat, five Coast Guard cutters, and 14 fishing boats hoping to detect the incoming Japanese fleet. The Navy stationed nine destroyers at Makushin Bay away from Dutch Harbor.

The Japanese invade Alaska

Japanese aircraft carriers hid within a storm front avoiding discovery as they approached Unalaska. At 5:45 a.m., June 3rd, the Japanese launched their air strike against Dutch Harbor. Fort Glenn's weak radio system failed to alert the planes stationed there of the attack, but Cold Bay was able to launch a counterattack. The initial attack killed 25 U.S. soldiers and blew up harbor facilities.

The two Japanese carriers were now less than 180 miles southwest of Unalaska. They launched another air strike the following morning damaging a wing of the Native hospital in Unalaska.

This time U.S. forces were ready. As Japanese bombers and fighters left the Dutch Harbor port in flames, they tangled with fighters coming in from Fort Glenn. The sky was soon dotted with dogfights. The U.S. lost eight planes while the Japanese lost nine. The Dutch Harbor attack totaled 76 U.S. dead over the two-day attack and 28 wounded. Japanese bombers had been successful in setting the old freighter *Northwestern* on fire. The ship was an Alaskan legend. She had survived sixteen groundings in her career. Now beached and being used as barracks, she survived this attack as well.

Japanese forces seized Attu and Kiska to the west of Unalaska. Dutch Harbor quickly transformed into a base of operations to repel the invader from American soil. The Naval station had a 250-ton marine railroad, seven docks, two floating dry docks, ship repair shops, 17 office buildings, a 200-bed hospital, and housing and recreation facilities for more than 5,000 men.

Dutch Harbor and Unalaska were liberally peppered with concrete pill boxes that are present today.

Enlisted men spent their time at Blackie's Cocktail Lounge, the only bar in Unalaska with the bar itself the length of one of the walls. There were no furnishings. "They splintered too easily in a fight," the owner said. There were two small cafes and a 180-seat movie theater showing out of date films. USO shows were often, and troops were entertained by Errol Flynn who came up to Alaska to be with the servicemen. For three days in December 1943, the USO World Series played in Dutch Harbor. Unalaska already had 32 teams in four leagues by this time. In his after-hours with nothing to do, sailor Gore Vidal wrote his first novel at Dutch Harbor, *Williwaw*.

Aleut internment

When word came that the Japanese had captured the Aleut village on Attu and had taken its people to Japan, a decision was made to evacuate as many Natives as possible from Unalaska. On July 5, 1942, Aleuts from outlying Unalaska villages were evacuated. Those living in town were evacuated onboard the *SS Alaska* July 19th. A week later they arrived at Wrangell in Southeast Alaska and housed at first in an abandoned cannery.

After living in Wrangell for over two years, they returned home in the spring of 1945. They found their houses vandalized. The federal government gave the entire Aleut community $28,837 for supplies such as coal for the coming winter. The U.S. Army moved 35 of its 16 by 20-foot cabanas into the village for additional housing for the returning Aleut families.

Finally, in 1989, Congress awarded $27 million in reparation payments for the Aleut community.

Dutch Harbor was demilitarized almost as fast as the military presence had been built up. For Meiers was put on housekeeping status in August 1944 with most of its troops moved out. Beginning in 1944, the Naval facility began monitoring Soviet ships rather than search for Japanese until the based was decommissioned in 1947.

In 1952, the US Corps of Engineers put on the market the 232 buildings owned by the U.S. Army along with 447 acres of land. In 1985 both the Dutch Harbor Naval Operating Base and Fort Meiers Army Base were designated as national historic landmarks.

The 200-mile limit

Unalaska and Dutch Harbor were sleepy little hamlets until 1977 when Congress passed the Magnuson Fishery Conservation and Management Act. The historic three-mile limit was now extended to 200 miles placing most of the Bering Sea in U.S. control and forcing the foreign factory ships out.

Shortly after the law was passed, two significant events shaped Unalaska's economy. Japan feared she might lose her traditional source of surimi, a protein rich fish paste that has been a staple of Japanese diets for nine hundred years. To secure sources of surimi, Japan invested heavily in Unalaska and Dutch Harbor's fish processing plants.

The second event was the demand for king crab coming out of the Bering Sea exploded.

Large American trawlers were soon based out of Dutch's deep harbor as loads of crab made ship captains millionaires in one season. The waterfront became crowded with cranes and workers as infrastructure was laid down for new docks, dry docks, and more processing plants. A 13-million-gallon fuel farm opened in 1986 to handle fleet traffic.

A bridge was built in 1981 connecting Dutch Harbor with Unalaska for an initial 150 vehicles a day. By 1990, 9,000 vehicles—mostly trucks—used the bridge on a daily basis.

Unalaska soon had 13 taxicab companies, more than a dozen docks handling 575 vessels, and a $9 million sewer system in 1991 replacing one that was using wooden pipes. Construction and instant wealth on crab boats caused the 3,000 resident community to swell to 20,000 in the summer months. There was soon a housing shortage. People were sleeping in the pill boxes while drawing wages that would be envied in the Lower 48.

The local Native Corporation, Ounalashka, went into the construction of apartment complexes. Business malls near the connecting bridge went up. Crabbers just paid with dollar bills coming out of their pockets became renown for wild drunken exploits at the Elbow Room, declared by *Playboy* to have been one of the rowdiest bars in the U.S. and drawing such entertainers as Jimmy Buffett in 1991.

Where the old submarine base was during World War II, UniSea erected the three-story tall red roof Grand Aleutian Hotel in 1993, a five-star hotel. Its seafood, all you can eat buffets, became legendary across Alaska.

The influx of money was reflected in the city's schools. The Unalaska City School District placed in the top 100 districts in the U.S. by Forbes Publications.

Unalaska became the number one port in the U.S. for seafood for the first time in 1989 when close to a half billion dollars' worth of fish was unloaded at her docks.

The fisheries around Unalaska have changed over time. The fisheries supporting the mammoth king crab harvests crashed in 1982 and the mid-1980s saw the transition to bottom fishing. Still Dutch Harbor has been the largest fisheries port in the United States in terms of volume of seafood caught every year since 1981. It was the top U.S. port in terms of dollar value for its catch until 2000 when it was passed by New Bedford, Massachusetts.

Dangerous seas

To harvest so many fish in such violent seas is not without a price. The Bering Sea openings have been known to claim a fishing trawler each season. During one season, a deck hand was claimed by the sea every week. This was highlighted when the *Arctic Rose* went down during the 2001 fishing season taking all fifteen crewmen with her.

The port facility lies on the great circle route between Asia and North America. Following the curvature of the Earth, San Francisco is a thousand miles closer to Tokyo than Hawaii is. Due to this, a huge volume of shipping comes close to the Aleutians and her violent seas. Not all the freighters pass by unharmed. Freighters tangled on the rocks of an island or having a hole punched into a hull has resulted in undersea salvage and repair being big business in Unalaska.

One of the more famous cases occurred in 2006, when the 14 deck *Cougar Ace* nearly rolled completely over with more than 4,703 new Mazdas worth $103 million. The Titan Salvage crew had to scale over upside down vehicles most of the 14 levels to right the freighter resulting in the death of one of its team members.

TV audiences saw a glimpse of this lifestyle in 2005 when the Discovery Channel's *Deadliest Catch* began airing. The program has drawn would be crabbers to Unalaska unaware of the limited number of positions in the crabbing fleet. Even the fisherman's hangout they saw on television, the Elbow Room, is now closed.

Born in Western Oklahoma and a graduate of Phillips University, Mike Coppock came to Alaska in 1985. He worked in canneries and general stores before becoming a flight specialist for the FAA, a state parks site manager for the Alaska Natural History Association, editor of The Valdez newspaper, history teacher at the Yup'ik village of Tuluksak, and human resources assistant director at Glacier Bay Lodge, Glacier Bay National Park and Preserve.

His articles on Alaska have appeared on *USA Today*, the *Los Angeles Times*, *The History Channel Magazine*, *American History*, *True West* and others.

www.ingramcontent.com/pod-product-compliance
Lightning Source LLC
Chambersburg PA
CBHW011549070526
44585CB00023B/2515